MW00653933

Claimed by the Sea
Long Island Shipwrecks

To KEN —
ENJOY THIS DIVE
INTO HISTORY!

By
Adam M. Grohman

Also by Adam M. Grohman

Non-Fiction

Non Liquet
The Bayville Submarine Mystery

Runner Aground
A History of the Schooner William T. Bell

Ugly Duckling
Liberty Ship - *S.S. C.W. Post*

Mask, Fins & Knife
A History of the U.S. Navy UDT & SEAL
Diving Equipment from World War II to Present

Beneath the Blue &Grey Waves
Sub-Marine Warfare of the American Civil War

Non–Fiction with Andrew Campbell

Dive GTMO
Scuba Diving in Guantanamo Bay, Cuba

Fiction

A Bright Shining Light

Surfer Girl – A Love Story

Claimed by the Sea
Long Island Shipwrecks

Underwater Historical Research Society
By Adam M. Grohman, UHRS Chief Diver & Researcher

Copyright 2008

ISBN 978-0-578-00807-3

No part of this book may be reproduced or duplicated
without written permission from the author.
Cover Design – Andy Campbell
Cover artwork "Going to the rescue" and author photograph – Author's Collection.
For more information – www.uhrs.org
Author's website – www.adamgrohman.com

This book is dedicated to the passengers,
crews and vessels that were *claimed by the sea.*

Table of Contents

Disclaimer - The following book describes several shipwrecks which have occurred in the waters surrounding Long Island, New York. It is imperative that those wishing to venture into the depths to explore these wrecks first hand utilize this text as a guide only. Prudence, proper training and preparation are vital to successful and safe diving on these and any other shipwreck. It is the sole responsibility for those wishing to become SCUBA certified to contact a training facility to begin their underwater adventures. The printed information is based on research and the author recommends those wishing to explore deeper to review the books and websites listed on the *Getting Involved* page for more information.

In addition, if you feel that any of the information contained within this text is inaccurate or requires revision; please contact the author at Adam M. Grohman, P.O. Box 78, Locust Valley, NY 11560.

Remember, there are bold divers and old divers, but no old bold divers.

Acknowledgments

I would like to give special thanks to the following people that made this book and research possible; my wife Kendall who continues to listen to various stories about ships and shipwrecks; my sons Aidan Jack and Liam Patrick who are growing up much too quickly; my parents, Dennis and Joyce, my brother Michael, his wife Mari-len, their children Madison and Michael Jr., aka "Curly" and to my in-laws Robert & Charlene Vessichelli for all of their continued support in regards to my various projects. A special thanks to all of the following persons and/or organizations that assisted by providing information during the course of the research and writing of this book: George Nammack for writing the introduction; Tony Bliss for reviewing advance versions of the text; Larry, Sue, Michelle and the entire crew of Seascapes Dive Shop in Syosset, NY; the librarians and staff at the Locust Valley, Oyster Bay, Glen Cove, Easthampton and Bayville Libraries; Long Island University C.W. Post and Brooklyn Campus librarians for their assistance in locating various publications upon my requests; Marci Vail for her assistance with the *S.S. Savannah* log book information; Sara Reres, Director of the Sea Cliff Village Museum; Adam Altman, President of Wrecksploration; Bill Pfeiffer, President of Long Island Divers Association; Divers and early reviewers of specific chapters – Bob Auteri, Mark Silverstein, Capt. John Bricker, Doug Acker, Harold Acker, Tony Bliss and the rest of the diving community who assisted in locating artifacts and providing information; Ms. Laura Poll, Monmouth County Historical Association; Mr. Wallace Broege, Director of the Suffolk County Historical Society; Ms. Caroline Locke, Suffolk County Library; Stephanie Gress, Director of Curatorial Affairs, Suffolk County Vanderbilt Museum, Centerport, New York; Long Island Maritime Museum; Ms. Marie Gilberti, Communications Manager, The Ward Melville Heritage Organization; Ms. Caitlin Cole for her assistance with the nautical and diving terminology appendix; Mr. Joseph Kearney for his assistance and permission to utilize photographs of his *Andrea Doria* replica; and to Robert B. MacKay,

Ph.D., Director, and Nicole J. Bubolo, Exhibit Coordinator/Associate Registrar for the Society for the Preservation of Long Island Antiquities, S.P.L.I.A. for contacting, advising, assisting and for producing a museum exhibition highlighting various Long Island shipwrecks for which I have been honored to write this companion. Lastly, thank you to the members of the Underwater Historical Research Society, friends of the family, and supporters of the project since its inception. I could not have completed this research and book without those listed above. If I have forgotten anyone or any organization, I apologize in advance.

Introduction

Without getting very far into this impressive book, readers examining the author's credentials, varied interests, operational style and other published work would collectively, perhaps unanimously agree that he possesses the energies of at least a dozen people.

When Adam M. Grohman assigns himself to a project, it is initially illuminated in the high beams of his demanding mind, then dissected carefully and with characteristic thoroughness, so the smallest meaningful details may be observed and preserved for integration, analysis and eventual presentation. He is an enthusiastic maritime historian, who, in writing *Claimed by the Sea, Long Island Shipwrecks,* has placed in our hands, and within our libraries and schools, a fascinating, exciting labor of love.

Fellow Long Islander Grohman has readers hovering above (not aboard, thankfully) all eleven vessels he features in the book, stricken vessels doomed to spend their remaining time rolling and rotting deep beneath the surfaces of Long Island Sound and the Atlantic Ocean. The intriguing voyages of these unfortunates provide vicarious thrills to we, the finless, who frequent, in the main, terra firma, despite some of us being lifelong boaters and anglers.

Mr. Grohman explains his inclusion of footnotes and a listing of recommended books for those who want to delve the deeps more, to learn about the valuable history that rests below the waves around Long Island and, significantly, "...to illustrate to the reader the importance of reviewing multiple sources when investigating historical events." This is encouraging advice for young writers from an established pro.

The book is liberally enriched with an abundance of photographs, charts and illustrations, many from the author's collection, others from elsewhere and, where at all possible, sourced. The eleven vessels whose tragically attenuated lives are covered include the *S.S. Savannah, Lexington, Circassian, Seawanhaka.*

U.S.S. Ohio, Oregon, Louis V. Place, General Slocum, U.S.S. San Diego, Andrea Doria, and the *Gwendoline Steers.* The author makes clear that *Claimed by the Sea* "is more than just a story of shipwrecks in the waters surrounding Long Island, New York. It is not just the story of old wooden or steel vessels that were constructed by man to ply the waters of the world for military, commercial or recreational use. It is more importantly the story of extreme bravery in the face of absolute cowardice. It is the story of complete thoughtfulness in the midst of complete selfishness. It is the story of stubbornness in the fog of carelessness...the story, in essence, of man's attempt to control the uncontrollable, unflinching and unknown nature of the sea."

It has been my good fortune to meet and work with Adam Grohman, whose popular column "In Our Waters" appears monthly in *Long Island Boating World*, a publication I have served as Editor for more than a decade.

George S. Nammack

Author's Note

Maritime history surrounds us like the great oceans, seas, lakes and rivers on which those vessels of that history once traveled. To understand and appreciate the vessels, their crews, their missions, and their voyages, we have to study the history of these vessels so we can begin to understand what drives man to sail from the safe haven of harbor into the unknown of the future. The waters that surround Long Island, New York have long been the nautical gateway to North American settlements. Whether entry was gained via the Long Island Sound or from the southern approaches from the Atlantic Ocean, the dense maritime traffic provided for a booming trade. The waters, once plied by thousands of vessels on a yearly basis, under the power of sail, steam and eventually diesel engines are still busy to present day.

But not all the vessels bound to or from New York waters have completed their intended voyages. Whether by storm, equipment failure, collision, fire, military action, or accident, many have slipped below the waves never to be seen again. *Claimed by the Sea, Long Island Shipwrecks* is an introductory look at eleven vessels that ended their nautical careers in either the Long Island Sound or in the Atlantic Ocean. I have provided only the tip of the proverbial iceberg in regards to the vessels researched.[1] My goal is to introduce to the reader a sampling of the almost engrossing maritime history that abounds beneath the surface of our local waters.

I have provided for the reader an intimate, introductory look at eleven vessels including the *S.S. Savannah, Lexington, Circassian, Seawanhaka, U.S.S. Ohio, Oregon, Louis V. Place, General Slocum, U.S.S. San Diego, Andrea Doria* and the *Gwendoline Steers*. *Claimed by the Sea, Long Island Shipwrecks*, is by no means an all encompassing or definitive history of these eleven vessels or the

---

[1] I hope that my readers will excuse the pun and reference to the most infamous shipwreck of all time, the *R.M.S. Titanic*, but I could not resist.

9

thousands of others that litter the waters that surround Long Island, New York.[2] At the conclusion of my research I have provided a listing of recommended books, research publications and sources that I would recommend for those who have been quickly immersed and found themselves wanting to learn more, to read and explore. Throughout this text, I have included footnotes to clarify, extrapolate, provide additional insights, and outline discrepancies. The differences that are provided are not included as an insult or to disrespect the author or authors of previously written texts. They have been included to illustrate to the reader the importance of reviewing multiple sources when investigating historical events. In addition, it ironically provides the reader with a stark example of the sometimes hazy image that pervades historical research. It is the reported or recorded differences that make the voyage into the history of a ship, in the case of this text, as an example of the need to proceed at a rather cautionary speed. Looking back upon history is, when looking at the true foundation of the research, nothing more than attempting to look into the fog of the unknown.

In my most humble of opinions, when looking at the shipwrecks, it is important to understand why they now rest on the bottom of the sea or under the shifting sands of the beach. Some were lost unceremoniously at the hands of salvagers while others fought the bitter sea in climatic struggles that pitted man versus nature. Others were ravaged by the disastrous efficiency of shipboard fire and others simply from gross human error. Some of the vessels slowly slipped beneath the waves with no loss of life. Others however dragged some unfortunate souls into the bowels of the dark waters for an untimely death.

Claimed by the Sea is more than just a story of shipwrecks in the waters surrounding Long Island, New York. It is not just the story of old wooden or

---

[2] Though the *Andrea Doria* is not a Long Island shipwreck, I would have been remiss to not include it in this important overview of the maritime disasters and shipwrecks in our "local" waters. The *Andrea Doria* referred to by many as the "Mount Everest" of the diving world, is an important aspect of the northeast diving community and maritime history.

steel vessels that were constructed by man to ply the waters of the world for military, commercial or recreational use. It is more importantly the story of extreme bravery in the face of absolute cowardice. It is the story of complete thoughtfulness in the midst of complete selfishness. It is the story of stubbornness in the fog of carelessness. It is the story, in essence, of man's attempt to control the uncontrollable, unflinching and unknown of nature and of the sea.

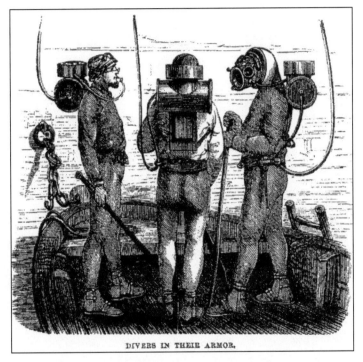

DIVERS IN THEIR ARMOR.

Early illustration of underwater explorers. Author's collection.

These eleven wrecks went to the bottom. Some of their final resting places are known to man, while others remain a mystery. It is as if the shifting sands of the hourglass and nature have joined to erase the evidence of the scattered remains for all time. Scuba divers have visited those that are known and have returned to the surface with information and artifacts that allow for others to learn more about the history of the wreck. Divers will still hunt the unknown bottom anomaly and attempt to determine "Is that it?" Researchers, historians and divers will continue to explore, conduct research and find evidence that will provide for others and future generations, a porthole into the past.

Exploring the history of a shipwreck is diving into the past. It is a journey back to when the vessel sailed or steamed the local waters for trade, pleasure or military purpose. They are underwater museums that provide a scuba diver the ability to look upon a time capsule. Interestingly though, they also provide the diver a look upon the future. As the vessels slowly become embedded into the marine environment, they slowly become symbiotic partners with the animals and plant life of the sea. As time moves forward and the effects of the elements and marine life take their toll on the remains, there will be less and less of these shipwrecks to be studied. All that will eventually remain will be the last vestiges of the skeletons and they too, eventually will break down and disappear. Ultimately, it will be the history and the artifacts collected from the wrecks that will survive and continue to tell the stories. *Claimed by the Sea* therefore marks not only the history of eleven ships that met their end in our waters, but more importantly, it provides a porthole into the past for future generations to gaze, dream, learn and remember.

Adam M. Grohman
Chief Diver and Researcher
Underwater Historical Research Society

While sailing from her namesake port of origin, the *S.S. Savannah* grounded in the rough surf in the waters off Fire Island, New York. It was in the early morning hours of November 5, 1821. The captain of the vessel, Mr. Holdridge, had been navigating through a series of storms and as the *S.S. Savannah* continued to be battered by the stormy surf, he launched a small boat to go ashore. After meeting up with some locals, who had probably been alerted to the vessel's duress when the captain had ordered the cannon "fired as a distress signal," the passengers, crew and cargo of cotton were unloaded to shore. (Field, 98) The battered packet ship remained in the surf line and by November "12th the ship had worked further ashore and a week of pounding had split her hull open."(Field, 98) As efforts continued to remove her cargo the struggling vessel sank deeper and deeper in the sand to a "depth of nine or ten feet." (Field, 98) In the end, the *S.S. Savannah* broke apart, sank into the sand and disappeared from maritime world. The shipwreck of the *S.S. Savannah* was more than just another ship that grounded and broke up in the surf. The vessel that ended her days on the New York barrier island during those early hours in November had a short-lived but important life on the seas. Approximately two years earlier, the *S.S. Savannah* had made history by being the first vessel to utilize steam power for propulsion during a transatlantic voyage. [3]

The *S.S. Savannah's* roots began as the idea of Captain Moses Rogers. He had a "daring record of firsts in the history of steamboating and had been associated with Robert Fulton and Colonel John Stevens." (Cavanaugh, Hoskins & Pingeon) Captain Rogers had met Stephen Vail, an engineer and businessman from Savannah, Georgia while on board a steamboat traveling to Charleston,

---

[3] Confusion occurs frequently as a "second" *Savannah* wrecked in the same area on October 22, 1822. All 11 men, including Captain John Coles of Glen Cove, New York perished in the storm. Several sources list the details of this shipwreck with the *S.S. Savannah* which causes much confusion. It clearly illustrates the difficulty of historical research.

South Carolina. The two men struck up a friendship and developed the initial plans to revolutionize transatlantic travel using steam engines. Upon his return to Savannah, Captain Rogers convinced a group of wealthy businessmen on the concept. On May 7, 1818 the Savannah Steamship Company was formed. Utilizing an existing vessel, in this case a packet ship, Captain Rogers was already on his way of achieving his goal.[4] He purchased a vessel that was "already under construction at Fickett and Crockett shipyard at Corlears Hook, New York." (Cavanaugh, Hoskins & Pingeon)[5] The vessel, upon completion was one hundred feet long with a twenty-five foot, ten inch beam and was "well designed for Atlantic storms." (Cavanaugh, Hoskins & Pingeon)[6] The plan to place a steam engine was completed, but so too was the standard sailing rigs of the era. The steam engine would serve as an auxiliary propulsion unit that would allow the vessel to make way when sailing conditions were unavailable or poorly suited.

The concept was novel and so too was the design. "For use under steam, she had a 17-foot bent smokestack that could be swiveled in any direction to the wind." (Cavanaugh, Hoskins & Pingeon) This allowed the crew to send the sparks and cinders from the stack away from the wooden decks and sails of the vessel and off into the water. The engine turned a set of paddle wheels which were placed amidships. The wooden paddles of each wheel were linked using iron chains and when the vessel was using her sails, each of the paddle wheels could be "compressed like a fan and the side wheels secured on the deck."

---

[4] The packet ship design was the precursor of the clipper ship.

[5] No known drawing exists of the *S.S. Savannah*. Models have been built however based on available information. One model was presented by the "Newcomen Society in North America to the Science Museum in London," and another model of the historic vessel is in the permanent collection at the Mariner's Museum in Newport News, Virginia. The model at the Mariner's Museum was utilized "as the basis for the United States Post Office Department's commemorative three cent stamp first issued on National Maritime Day, 22 May, 1944." (Williams, 110)

[6] Rattray listed the *S.S. Savannah* as 120 feet long with a 29 foot beam in *Ship Ashore!* It is important to note that this confusion may be the result of confusion with the second *Savannah* wreck as outlined in the first footnote of this chapter. In addition, the length of the *S.S. Savannah* ranges according to the source. Peter Freuchen lists her as 98 ½ feet in length and Edgar Bloomster lists her as 100 feet long with a 26 foot beam.

Building the engine and necessary components proved to be a testing experience that required the skilled craftsmanship of many men. The Speedwell Iron Works located in Morristown, New Jersey were integral in the completion of the engine and its placement on board the vessel. Though Captain Rogers "had hoped to see the *Savannah* completed before winter," she would not be ready for test runs until the beginning of February 1819. (Cavanaugh, Hoskins & Pingeon)

The *S.S. Savannah* with her steam paddle wheels. Author's collection.

Glowing reports were made exclaiming the technical prowess of the *S.S. Savannah*. On March 28th, 1819, the *S.S. Savannah* sailed south and arrived in the port of her name on April 26 where she became the "immediate object of curiosity and approval," by the local community. While in Savannah, President James Monroe and Secretary of War John C. Calhoun "boarded her to make an inspection cruise of the city's forts and defenses along the Savannah River." Though it had been suggested by the President that the government should purchase the *S.S. Savannah* to aid in the ridding of pirates plaguing the coast of Florida, the true nature of the vessel was yet to be undertaken. The reason for the delayed departure to fulfill the mission of transatlantic commerce under steam propulsion was because many believed that the vessel was nothing more than a steam coffin.[7]

Finally, upon its arrival in New London, Connecticut, Captain Rogers and first officer Stevens Rogers were able to complement the vessel with a crew. On May 22, 1819, a little less than three months after her successful completion, the *S.S. Savannah* embarked on her voyage to Europe. Utilizing her sails for the majority of the trip and after encountering stormy conditions at sea, the *S.S. Savannah* reached Liverpool, England. The entire transatlantic voyage took twenty-nine days and four hours which was a "good, but not exceptional time." (Cavanaugh, Hoskins & Pingeon)[8] While steaming towards the coast of England a spotter along the shoreline believed he saw a vessel on fire. With no sails upon her rigging and the tell-tale signs of smoke emanating from her decks, the man alerted the authorities who dispatched a vessel to rescue the "burning" ship. After several hours of chasing the *S.S. Savannah*, the *Kite* finally reached her and realized the reason for the smoke. The newspapers of the era enjoyed the story, but the entire episode was not fully known until many years later when it was learned that the "only way the *Kite* could stop the *Savannah* was by firing several warning shots." (Cavanaugh, Hoskins & Pingeon)

Captain Rogers had succeeded in making a grand entrance to England. The story of the technological achievement spread throughout Europe. The stir of excitement however was mixed with a certain amount of jealousy displayed by the British Admiralty as it was illustrated that the Americans had trumped the British Navy. The admiralty was also concerned about the rumors that were circulating at the time. They were concerned "that the steamship was to be a gift

---

[7] The concept of a steam coffin would reappear during the early years of the submarine service when the dangerous conditions of the new crafts were realized by the crews. The truth behind the superstitious sailors claim that they were "iron coffins" soon became a terrible reality for many submariners during both war and peace time operations.

[8] The travel time to Europe varies according to sources. Peter Freuchen states that she reached Liverpool in twenty-six days; Capt. Alan Villiers lists her Atlantic crossing taking twenty-seven days. In addition, the number of hours fluctuates from less than eighty hours to "mostly under steam." (Langer, 770)

from the United States to the Russian Czar or Jerome Bonaparte had hired the *Savannah* to free his exiled brother from St. Helena."

A page from the *S.S. Savannah's* log book. Author's collection.

Rumors aside, the *S.S. Savannah*, her Captain and crew were warmly received by the English. According to Duncan Haws' research the arrival of the *S.S. Savannah* ruffled a few members of the British Navy.

> The S.S. Savannah *"steamed into Liverpool Bay flying a large 'Stars and Stripes'. At the Liverpool Bar, the officer on duty on the guardship addressed his opposite number through the loud hailer.*
> *'Why,' demanded the English officer, 'are you flying that pennant, Sir?'*
> *'Because my country allows me to,' came the reply.*
> *'My commander thinks it is done to insult him.'*
> *'It is done as a courtesy, Sir. This is an American vessel.'*(Haws, 116)

After some time in England, the *S.S. Savannah* traveled to Sweden where she was visited by Crown Prince Oscar, the American Ambassador Christopher Hughes, King Charles XVI and an enthusiastic public.[9] From Sweden, the *S.S. Savannah* sailed and steamed to St. Petersburg, Russia in five days, utilizing steam for twenty-five out of the eighty-six hours. The level of enthusiasm generated by the vessel continued while in Russia. Czar Alexander Pavlovich was so impressed by the vessel that he offered Captain Rogers the "exclusive

---

[9] King Charles XVI offered Capt. Rogers $100,000 worth of hemp and iron for the *S.S. Savannah*. Capt. Rogers did not accept the offer. (Cavanaugh, Hoskins & Pingeon)

17

steamboating rights over all Russian waters," but he declined. The *S.S. Savannah* began her voyage back to America and while in route made brief port of calls in Copenhagen and Arendal, Norway. By November 1819, the *S.S. Savannah* returned to her namesake port.

Though the transatlantic voyage utilizing steam power as an auxiliary propulsion system was a success, the *S.S. Savannah* became a financial burden. After multiple attempts to garner contracts to transport cargo and passengers across the Atlantic on board the revolutionary steamer, the Savannah Steam Ship Company realized that it had to do something with the vessel which had become an anchor in their financial portfolios. Though President Monroe had provided a favorable view of the vessel previously, their attempt to sell the *S.S. Savannah* to the government also fell on deaf ears. "Beset by creditors and depression in 1820, the owners pathetically advertised their steamship for sale," the entire venture, with the exception of the history achieved, a dismal financial failure. (Baughman, 109-109) The successful use of steam propulsion for an entire transatlantic voyage would not be completed until 1838.[10]

The steam engine and equipment were removed and the *S.S. Savannah* began her second career as a cargo vessel. It would be a short lived venture that untimely ended on the beach of Fire Island, New York. As its grounding and subsequent breaking up in the surf occurred prior to the establishment of the Fire Island United States Lifesaving Service stations in the area, little information was left as to the exact location of the wreck.[11]

Frank O. Braynard while the public relations manager of the Moran Towing and Transportation Company of New York, not only wrote a history of

---

[10] The conquering of the Atlantic under steam for the entire voyage was completed by the *Sirius*. Leaving Cork, Ireland, she reached New York in 18 days and ten hours. The crew "burnt up all her coal and when she made landfall had also consumed the cabin furniture, doors and one mast." (Ellis, Illustration caption, #152) Interestingly, the *Sirius* would face a similar fate as the *S.S. Savannah*, wrecking in 1847. (Williams, 111)

[11] The Bellport U.S.L.S.S. Station was not established until 1849. Though the exact location of the wreck is clouded in speculation, the other stations in the area, Blue Point to the west and Smith's Point, Forge River and Moriches to the east were not established until 1855, 1855, 1871 and 1849 respectively.

the *S.S. Savannah*, but also attempted to locate her remains in 1958.[12] In a press release published in *The Long Island Forum* in September 1957, Braynard indicated that "through the help of the Navy's Hydrographic Office, a latitude and longitude for the wreck," had been found.[13] (*The Long Island Forum*, 176) On November 14, 1958, Braynard met with members of the Patchogue U.S. Power Squadron to discuss information including maps, surveys and other documents that he had compiled with the assistance of the "Navy, Coast Guard, Army Corps of Engineers, Telephonics, Inc." (Smith, 28-29) In May of 1959 Braynard worked with members of the Empire State Underwater Council working in the waters off of Fire Island. The goal of the group was to utilize a hydraulic probe which was able to "dig its way through the sand and locate solid objects as far as 40 feet below the ocean floor." (*The Patchogue Advance*, 21MAY1959) In an interview during the same time frame, Braynard explained to Mr. Harry L. Ober a reporter for the *New York Mirror* that his hope was to locate the figurehead of the vessel. "What would be really grand would be the figurehead - a male type it was," as it, as stated by Braynard would greatly assist in the positive identification of the wreckage. (*New York Mirror*, 24MAY1959) When asked by the same reporter why another team of divers the previous summer [1958] had not located the wreckage, Braynard explained that "they were 300 yards off the beam," of maps he had recently found and researched. (*New York Mirror*, 24MAY1959)

 Utilizing "naval blimps using magnetometers," Braynard believed that the remains of the *S.S. Savannah* were located "a hundred yards out from the 1821 beach line somewhere between the old Bellport life

---

[12] Mr. Frank Braynard, in a September 1957 press release included his title as Director, Bureau of Information, Merchant Marine Institute, Inc. (*The Long Island Forum*, Sept. 1957)

[13] This information would prove to be inaccurate as the remains of the *S.S. Savannah* have never been found.

saving station and the Smith's point station." (NUMA) Braynard was unsuccessful in his attempts at finding the remains of the *S.S. Savannah*. Scuba diver Lee Prettyman from Gillman's Club from Hartford, Connecticut, which according to Braynard, "located an ancient wreck with a copper-lined hull in 20 feet of water, just off the beach. He hacked off a piece of copper and brought it up." (*Fire Island News*, 20 26JUN1997) Subsequent attempts by both Prettyman and other divers however, failed to relocate the wreckage.[14]

Braynard was not the only one looking for the *S.S. Savannah* in the late 1950's and early 1960's. In July 1960, Jackson Jenks and a team of six divers onboard a "specially outfitted research boat," named the *Dorothy W. II*, began its search for the elusive *S.S. Savannah*. Jenks' plan was to place any and all artifacts he and his team found in his "New England Archeological Museum," located in Newport, Rhode Island. (*The Patchogue Advance*, 19JUL1960) Jenks had located thirty-five wrecks previous to the *S.S. Savannah* expedition and had estimated that the search would require a financial obligation of "approximately $5,000." (*The Patchogue Advance*, 19JUL1960) The search continued for quite sometime, but Jenks' crew of divers was not successful in finding the vessel.[15]

In 1982, the National Underwater and Marine Agency, more commonly referred to as NUMA, under the direction of famous author and shipwreck hunter Clive Cussler, conducted a search for the *S.S. Savannah*. Though the wreck was not located, the group found several promising "hits" using a gradiometer.[16] Based on the search results, it is believed that the wreckage is very close to the

---

[14] Braynard stated that Prettyman's discovery and recovery of the piece of copper from the unidentified wreck was "probably the closet we would ever come to really locating the SAVANNAH." (*Fire Island News*, 20-26JUN1997) In this same article, Braynard indicated that he was still after the remains of the *S.S. Savannah*, almost forty years after he had started in earnest in his attempts.

[15] *The Patchogue Advance*, August 11, 1960 issue identified five of the divers of the crew. Ed Torkelson, Lyman Bullar, James Tarasenko and Chester Osborne.

[16] Clive Cussler recounts a comical incident that occurred on the beaches of Fire Island during his search for the vessel in *The Sea Hunters*, pages 27-28. In addition, according to *The Sea Hunters*, the search for the vessel took place in April of 1983, not 1982.

shoreline.[17] Whether the skeleton of the *S.S. Savannah* remains under the shifting sands of sea or if she is finally located, the true legacy of the *S.S. Savannah* will always hold a significant marker in the history books. Her "10,280-mile voyage-from Savannah to Liverpool, Helsingor, Stockholm, Kronstadt, St. Petersburg, Copenhagen, Arendal, and return," marked a defining moment in both transatlantic travel and maritime design. (Baughman, 108) Though the vessel was a financial bust, instead of boom, her showcase of technological advances was a silver lining on her overall career at sea. Upon her return to America, "few people realized that almost by accident she [the *S.S. Savannah*] marked an epoch." (Villiers, 255) Her historic design and voyage will remain in the books as her final resting place continues to be a mystery to this day.

---

[17] According to the National Park Service's Submerged Resources Center, two other projects have been launched in the waters. In May 1998, World Geoscience "conducted an airborne mag survey searching for the *Savannah*" in conjunction with NUMA and in September 1987, a "SRC reconnaissance team headed by Larry Murphy conducted a diving and instrument assessment of several historic wreck sites in the park."

Bound for Stonington, Connecticut from New York, the passenger steamer *Lexington* had made the voyage many times previously. With over one hundred and fifteen souls on board, the steamship would never complete the twelve hour trip.[18] As the wind blew harshly from the north, the temperature was close to zero degrees. A varied lot of passengers remained inside the main cabin, having enjoyed their evening repast and some light entertainment. Among the passengers were several steamboat captains, other men, women, and children. One of the passengers, Adolphus Harnden, who worked as "a superintendent of an express company operating between New York and Boston," was transiting with "some sixty or seventy thousand dollars" in silver coins and bank notes. (Rattray, 81)[19] The crew manned their normal underway stations. At the helm was Captain George Child and by his side acting as the pilot was Captain Stephen Manchester. As the *Lexington* steamed at full speed through the frigid, ice floe-filled Long Island Sound, a small ember of fire floated from the smokestack casing onto a bale of cotton. First spotted on the aft deck, the small glimmer of fire would soon spell disaster. The captain, crew and passengers were about to have the wrath of hell unleashed. It was seven-thirty at night on January 13, 1840. Only four men would survive to tell the tale.[20]

The *Lexington* had been constructed by Bishop & Simonson in New York. She was 220 feet long had a 26 foot beam and a total tonnage of 488.[21] She was constructed under the personal supervision of Cornelius Vanderbilt. She was

---

[18] Reports as to the total number of passengers and crew differ. Rattray lists between 118-161, Gentile, 126-165, and the article on Long Island Genealogy, 115 passengers. A closer look at the Nathaniel Currier print states that there were 87 passengers and 40 crew who perished and four who survived, thus putting the total loss of life at 123.

[19] According to an article on the Long Island Genealogy website, the monies were $20,000 in silver coins and $50,000 in bank notes.

[20] Rattray states that five persons survived including Captain Stephen Manchester, Captain Chester Hilliard, fireman Charles B. Smith, second mate David Crowley and an unidentified man who made "his way to a tavern in Southold." (Rattray, 85) Most histories however only identify four survivors.

[21] There are several variations on the length and beam of the *Lexington*. Length varies from 120 to 220 feet and the beam from 21-26 feet.

built with the very best of available materials including white and yellow pine, chestnut, locust and cedar. Vanderbilt even remarked that the *Lexington* was so finely constructed that she was the only boat that, "during four years of navigating the Sound, never lost a trip." (Gentile, 130) The vessel underwent alterations including the construction of cabins and berths so that she could accommodate passengers for evening voyages. These changes provided the *Lexington* with more commercial versatility.

Vanderbilt sold the *Lexington* to the New Jersey Steam Navigation Company who then further altered the vessel. The original boilers were converted to burn coal instead of wood. This transition provided a higher level of steam "for the vertical beam engine, and made it run faster, thus increasing the rotational speed of the paddlewheels and consequently, the speed of the vessel through the water. (Gentile, 130) The cost of conversion, $60,000 for the alterations from wood to coal burning boilers and $12,000 for the interior spaces, paled in comparison with the ability for the steam ship company to provide first class and expedited passage for cargo and passengers. (Long Island Genealogy)

These alterations would matter little as the *Lexington* churned further east on the Long Island Sound on January 13, 1840. Embers from the smokestack casing had ignited a bale of cotton that was being transported as cargo on the disastrous voyage. "One hundred and fifty bales of cotton" had been placed aft of the smokestack casings, thus setting the stage for a hellish last act for the *Lexington*, her crew and passengers. Captain Child immediately began turning the helm and steamed for the north shore of Long Island. The flicker of fire however had begun to spread. The crew attempted to engage the fire fighting equipment and the "crew members in the engine room were forced out by the flames before the engines could be shut down." (Long Island Genealogy) Flames began to engulf the vessel and the *Lexington* continued to steam at full speed, the north wind and forward movement fanning the flames, through the icy waters as if she was the devil's chariot of death.

(Previous page) An illustration of the disaster printed by Nathaniel Currier.[22]

---

[22] Currier would eventually become a "senior partner in the famous firm of print-makers, Currier and Ives." (Rattray, 84) The illustration was drawn by W. K. Hewitt and printed by "N. Currier, Lith. & Pub. 2 Spruce St. N.Y." The print was a huge success and overnight "N. Currier became a national institution." "It revealed the tremendous sales potentialities of newsworthy pictures at a time when the various processes now in common use for the swift and accurate reproduction of drawings and photographs were mostly unknown." The prints sold at wholesale for six cents a piece and averaged fifteen to twenty-five cents." (Peters, 1-2)

The fire was soon noticed along the shores of Connecticut and Long Island. As the *Lexington* continued to succumb to the ravages of the fire, heading southeast towards shore, suddenly the captain lost control of the helm. Instead of steaming towards land and possible safety for her passengers, she began to head east. The tiller rope which allowed for the ship's wheel to adjust the rudder had parted due to the fire. The *Lexington*, with only three life boats capable of carrying only "seventy people or less than half of the number of passengers and crew" would have to provide a mean's of escape. The *Lexington* continued her erratic trip at full speed, the fire continuing to spell doom for the passengers and crew.

As the flames grew, witnesses on shore began attempts to aid the vessel. The weather, low tide and ice however hindered the ability for vessels to get underway. Captain Meeker, in Southport, New York had seen the vessel on fire and had attempted to provide assistance with his sloop *Merchant*. While attempting to traverse the harbor, his vessel ran aground. He would not be able to free from her position until the morning hours.[23] Others attempted to launch small boats to provide assistance but were unable to get through the rough waters. The would-be rescuers watched helplessly from shore as the vessel continued to burn and drift further eastward. No vessels underway that evening rendered assistance. One vessel underway on the Long Island Sound that night, the *Improvement*, did not realize the terrible situation that had overcome the steamboat. From between "ten or twelve miles downwind" Captain William Terrell of the *Improvement*, would not have been able to assist even if he had known. (Gentile, 137)

With all hope lost, Captain Child ordered the launching of the life boats. But launching the boats proved difficult with the vessel steaming at full speed through the rough conditions. Captain Manchester lost sight of Captain Child. Manchester headed forward to assist in the launching of the boats. When he

---

[23] Captain Meeker of the *Merchant* would eventually find three of the four survivors.

arrived at the first boat he found several men already hard at work in prepping the boat for launching over the side. Though he had told the men to put a line on the lifeboat, they did not and when put over the side into the water, the lifeboat disappeared from sight. The two other lifeboats were also launched full of passengers, crew and water. They never served their purpose, swamped by a combination of panic and icy water. Panic gripped the passengers and crew alike. Men continued to throw water on the fire using anything that would hold water. The silver coins being transported by Mr. Harnden were dumped onto the deck so that the wooden box could be used in an attempt to fight the fire. (Long Island Genealogy) No amount of money could have provided anyone onboard the *Lexington* a ticket clear from the danger. From the lowliest passenger to prominent businessmen, none were able to avoid the inevitable.

While attempts of a bucket brigade to fight the fire continued, other passengers continued to throw baggage, parts of the ship and anything that would float, into the water. Passengers began to jump into the water in an attempt to save themselves from the heat of the flames. Some drowned quickly in the freezing waters, others attempted to grab onto the flotsam that now littered the water. The engine at this point had finally succumbed to the ravages and destruction of the fire but the damage was already done. According to Captain Manchester, "there were then only eight or ten persons astern on the steamboat, and about thirty on the forecastle. They were asking me what they should do, and I told them I saw no chance for any of us." (Gentile, 132)[24] The choice was painfully obvious. Stay onboard the burning funeral pyre or jump into the icy waters of the Long Island Sound and pray that they would survive the ordeal.

Only four souls lived to recount the disastrous final moments of the *Lexington.* They told amazing stories of how they grabbed onto bales of cotton or flotsam, freezing, suffering hypothermia and watching the death toll mount from the terrible ordeal. One survivor, David Crowley, the second mate on the vessel,

---

[24] Captain Manchester, while in command of the *Rhode Island*, a packet ship, would also face a shipwreck on November 1, 1846. (Rattray, 85)

drifted over fifty miles on the top of a bale of cotton for two days and two nights.[25] The bodies of men, women, children and small babies floated amongst the remnants of the vessel. Some of the debris and the dead were pulled from the waters or from the beaches of the north shore, over the next few days. The lifeboats, already short in supply, never provided any vestige of safety for any of the passengers and crew[26] The *Lexington* continued to burn and began to slowly lower into the water. She drifted through the icy waters, her path of destruction littering the water in her wake. Some passengers and crew remained on the vessel until she finally disappeared to the depths below. By three o'clock in the morning, the vessel was slowly heading to the murky bottom of the Long Island Sound.

The *Lexington* disaster created a huge public outcry. "The coroner's jury returned a verdict of malfeasance," with the largest issue being that the crew fell short of the jury's expectation to efficiently fight the fire. (Gentile, 139) In addition, the jury felt that the main reason that more members of the passengers and crew did not survive was due to the fact that examples of self-preservation outnumbered the attempts by members of the crew to complete one's duty. The lack of leadership coupled with the willingness to carry cotton in large quantities aboard vessels carrying passengers was unconscionable. The *Lexington* disaster though, as terrible as it was, would not be enough of a catalyst for the much needed regulations onboard passenger vessels. As pointed out eloquently by Gary Gentile, "it took more than a few such catastrophes to inaugurate an era of concern for human safety." (Gentile, 141)

The remains of the *Lexington* had sunk beneath the waves. A few years after her tragic end the vessel would again be found mentioned in the news. In

---

[25] Crowley "kept the bale of cotton in his Providence, Rhode Island home for many years until he sold it for the Civil War effort." (Long Island Genealogy)

[26] As pointed out by Gary Gentile, the lack of lifeboats for the passengers and crew was a "haunting premonition of future catastrophes such as the sinking of the *Titanic*. (Gentile, 140-141)

the August 12, 1842 issue of *The Long Islander*, the following report was printed:

> "The *Lexington* – The divers have found the remains of the ill fated steamer, and have thoroughly examined the after part of the hold. The centre was covered by a part of the bow, which had broken off near the engine and fallen over upon it. The men say that there is no sand in the ship and nothing to prevent her being raised, though she lines in a hundred and twenty feet water. It will be recollected that the iron chest on board the *Lexington* contained a large sum of money in specie and bank notes. So far, no (illegible) have been discovered, and it is not probable that any remained on board when she went down. Arrangements are now making to raise her immediately."(*The Long Islander*, 3)

In the same paper a month and a half later, a brief paragraph stated that the vessel had been raised to the surface on September 20, 1842, only to have one of the chains break, sending her once again to the bottom. (Gentile, 141)[27] Allegedly, "a thirty pound melted mass of silver was recovered from inside the hull" before she plunged to her final resting place. (Long Island Genealogy) A year later, a brief paragraph, again in *The Long Islander*, listed a more successful recovery effort. As reported in the Friday, June 2, 1843 issue of the newspaper, "A part of the hull of the ill fated steamer *Lexington*, has been discovered, and recovered by Mark W. Davis, of Newark, with a diving bell. On the 22nd [referring to the previous month] he succeeded in raising a piece about six tons, which is in the possession of George A. Wells of the city of New York." (The

---

[27] Rattray interestingly makes no mention of the 1842 article, but instead states that the *Lexington* was raised in August, 1850. (Rattray, 80) Gentile believes that the 1850 reference is related to one of two vessels of the same name that may have been raised in the waters of Lake Michigan. (Gentile, 141) A review of *The Encyclopedia of American Shipwrecks by* Bruce D. Berman lists three vessels named *Lexington* in the waters of the Great Lakes; a schooner lost on June 11, 1846 off Point Moullie with a cargo valued at $100,000; a steam side wheeler stranded on June 15, 1850 off Port Washington, Wisconsin; and a steam side wheeler that exploded at Rome, Indiana killing thirty persons on June 30, 1855. (Berman, 252)

Long Islander, 2) The *Lexington* would not be found again for over one hundred and forty years. Her condition on the bottom when relocated however would shed some interesting insight into the reports of her temporary time on the surface in 1842.

A colorized version of the *Lexington* disaster was also sold to the public.

The final resting place of the *Lexington* was mired in mystery for many years. Many believed that the vessel couldn't be found at all in Long Island Sound waters because she had allegedly been successfully raised and towed away. Not completely satisfied with the various versions of the vessel's fate, Clive Cussler and members of NUMA set out to get to the bottom and find the remains of the vessel in 1983. Utilizing sonar equipment, the group's second attempt to locate the remains proved successful. Diving to a depth of approximately 140 feet, the divers found themselves in a dark world that Cussler described as "if you're groping through a haunted house in the dead of night glimpsing its ghosts from the corner of one eye." (Cussler, 31) The divers were able to retrieve some wreckage and burnt wood from the remains of the *Lexington* which appeared to be "broken into three sections." (Cussler, 30) One of the pieces of wood recovered from the wreckage later was identified as yellow pine, one of the materials utilized in the building of the *Lexington*.[28] An additional clue the divers found was a kind of green wire which appeared to be wrapped around the wreckage. Upon further investigation, it appeared that the wires found on the wreckage were the last vestiges of the iron cables that had been attached to the *Lexington* during the initially fruitful, yet ultimately unsuccessful raising of the vessel in 1842.

The *Lexington* remains in the deep and dark waters of the Long Island Sound off of Eaton's Neck. Though Loran numbers differ slightly depending on the source utilized, the depth of the wreckage is within an attainable reach by divers, with the "paddle wheel in 78 feet of water" and "the bow in 140." (Gentile, 142)[29] The vessel's wreckage is a silent reminder of the dangers of sea travel, the lack of foresight in the preparation, training and successfulness of fighting fire at sea, and the apparent dangers of self-preservation when others are counting on one to get the job done right.

---

[28] Three fragments of the charred remains of the *Lexington* were donated to the Suffolk County Vanderbilt Museum. Though part of the collection, they are not currently on display according to Stephanie Gress, Director of Curatorial Affairs.

[29] Though attainable by the standards of recreational diving limits, diving the *Lexington* wreckage should only be attempted by those qualified and trained to work in a near-zero visibility with strong currents. Additionally, the wreck is located in a highly transited maritime area, so dangers lurk above and below for divers.

Captain Smith stood at the helm, stressed and unaware of what the future held for his men and his vessel, the *Heath Park*. Bound for London with a cargo of slate, he and his twelve crewmen had left Perth Amboy, New Jersey, just two days prior. The rough weather had intensified and as a result his vessel had sprung a serious leak. His men vigorously manned the bilge pumps to keep the incoming flood at bay, but it was only time before the waters of the Atlantic inundated the hold and took the vessel to the bottom. The *Heath Park*, a bark of one hundred and twenty-four feet, five inches in length and of three hundred and nineteen tons, began to languish under the strain of the water in her hold.[30] To give his vessel and his men a chance, part of the slate cargo was jettisoned overboard. The *Heath Park* slowly turned toward land, but "little progress was made." (*NYT*, 15DEC1876)

For two full days the crew fought the incoming surge of water and attempted to repair the leak that could eventually spell doom for the vessel and the men. If forced into a small launch, or worse, into the winter sea, the frigid waters of the Atlantic would quickly remove any chance of survival. Captain Smith and the remainder of his crew not manning the pumps kept a sharp look out for a vessel on the horizon that might be able to render assistance. On the sixth day, one of the men spotted a ship. The order was immediately given to send up a flag of distress. Slowly the distant ship began to turn and the men on board the *Heath Park* realized that their savior was making way toward them. They might, they thought, survive the sinking ship after all.

---

[30] The *Heath Park* was 124 feet, 5 inches in length, had a beam of 25 feet, 6 inches, had a 15 feet, 6 inch hold and a draft of 14 feet. She was owned by J. Thain of Dundee Scotland and had been originally built in 1855. A bark or barque is "a three-masted vessel, having her fore and main masts rigged like a ship's, and her mizzen mast like the main mast of a schooner, with no sail upon it but a spanker, and gaff topsail." (Chapman, 440x) This type of vessel and her rigs "were effected[sp] mainly for ease in handling and economical reasons, the fore-and-aft rig requiring less crew than the square." (Bloomster, 6)

Once the rescue vessel was within distance, Captain Smith gave the order to abandon ship. He had done all that he could to save his vessel but the attempts were an exercise in futility. Preparations were made to launch the vessel's small boats and soon after, the Captain and his crew were rowing to the vessel which had come to their rescue. The men were soon on board the decks of the *Circassian* and watched their ship, the *Heath Park* in her final moments. With "the water no longer fought by the pumps, rapidly filled her hold, and, finally, carried her down." (*NYT*, 15DEC1876) As Captain Smith and his men met their rescuers, the stiff wind began to increase. The *Circassian*, having completed her successful rescue of their maritime brethren, returned to her original course bound for New York. Soon however, all aboard would find their lives in the balance once again, thanks to the wicked hand of Mother Nature.

The *Circassian* was originally built in 1856 in Belfast, Ireland for J.S. DeWolf and Company of Liverpool, England.[31] Built as an iron steam vessel she was two hundred and forty-two and a half feet in length, with a beam of thirty-nine feet and had a draft of twenty-two feet at her hold.[32] "At the time of her construction the *Circassian* was the largest vessel ever built in Ireland, at slightly more than one hundred tons larger than her predecessor and close approximation in build, the *Kheronese*." (Gentile, 38)

News of the *Circassian* reached the United States in 1857. The new steamer would be part of the Liverpool and Portland Line of Steamers. In the fourth heading under the *Marine Items* section of the *New York Times* in February 3, 1857 edition, it was reported via the *State of Maine* newspaper that the line would be "touching at St. Johns, N.F., and Halifax." (*NYT*, 3FEB1857)

---

[31] Various spellings of the owner's name exist. Variations include J.S. DeWolf, S.S. DeWolf, and T.A. de Wolf. (*NYT*, 31DEC1876, NYT, 31DEC1876, and Gentile, 38 respectively)

[32] As is normal with historical research, the specifications vary depending on source. Tonnage varies from 1558 tons burden (original) to 1,900 tons burden altered. (*NYT*, 15 and 31DEC1876) Gentile, Rattray and Field also differ between 1742 gross tons and 1741 tons respectively. Regarding length the shortest length listed is 242.5 (*NYT*, 31DEC1876) to 254 (Gentile) to Rattray and Field's 280 feet. Draft of the vessel also varies from 19 ¾ (Rattray), 20 (Field), 22.4 of the hold (*NYT*, 31DEC1876) to 30 feet (Gentile). (Various sources as indicated.)

According to the article, "plans have been matured and arrangements made for the maintenance of the line, commencing on March 7, with the *Circassian*, a screw propeller of 2,300 tons, having engines of 359 horsepower," (*NYT*, 3FEB1857) Mention was also made of her sister ship the *Khersonese* and that the voyages of the steamers would be monthly.

On March 22, 1857, Halifax reported that the *Circassian*, "which was appointed to leave Liverpool for this port via St. John's N.F. on the 7 inst.," had not been heard from or sighted. (*NYT*, 23MAR1857) The weather report was grim with a "thick snowstorm" with a "prevailing easterly wind." (*NYT*, 23MAR1857) Though the snowstorm abated, the *Circassian* "now 17 days out from Liverpool" remained out at sea. (*NYT*, 24MAR1857) Eventually, the *Circassian* reached Halifax and by April 10, 1857, she had completed her first transatlantic trip, making Portland, Maine. (*NYT*, 11APR1857) The vessel remained in the port for seven days and then began her return voyage from North America leaving Portland, Maine at six p.m. on April 17th heading to Liverpool, via Halifax and St. Johns, N.F. She arrived in Halifax a day and a half later and then remained until four in the afternoon when she then steamed for her last stop at St. Johns. As she headed out of Halifax, her sister ship *Khersonese* was inbound, the two steamers on opposite crossings. (*NYT*, 22APR1857)

Until the early 1860's the *Circassian* sailed under the British flag in normal trade activities. With the beginning of the American Civil War however and the subsequent Union blockade of southern ports, the *Circassian* and other foreign flagged vessels which were deemed suspicious, ran the risk of capture by Union Naval forces.[33] The *Circassian*, engaged in alleged blockade running activities in late May of 1862 was soon sighted by the commander of the *U.S.S.*

---

[33] By early June of 1862, the blockading squadron had successfully captured the following steamers: "The Circassian (British), Bermuda (British), Swan, Labuan (British, since restored), Magnolia, Florida, Ella Warley, Stettin (British), Calhoun, Lewis, Wallace, Fox, and the rebel gunboat Planter…the aggregate value of these vessels is over $5,000,000." (*HW*, 14JUN1862) During the American Civil War "Union records show that over 1,400 ships and craft were captured or destroyed while engaged in blockade running, 295 of them steamers." (Anderson, 221)

Somerset, Lieutenant Earl English.[34] Approximately "twenty miles east of Havana," the *Circassian* found herself being pursued by a determined Union naval vessel. (*HW*, 7JUN1862)[35]

The *Circassian* (far right) in New York after her capture in 1862.[36]

The *Circassian*, its "English ensign flying from her mast was ordered to heave to." (Gentile, 39) But the ship did not show any signs of wavering to the demands of the Union officer. When the Union naval officer hailed the vessel, the vessel "answered the hail of the American evasively, and declined to stop."

---

[34] Several newspaper reports of the capture list the officer in charge of the *U.S.S. Somerset* as "Captain Eagleson." (*NYT*, 23MAY1862) The *Dictionary of American Naval Fighting Ships* however lists Lieutenant Earl English as the officer-in-charge. The *U.S.S. Somerset* was a "wooden-hulled, side wheel ferryboat built at Brooklyn in 1862," and had been purchased on March 4, 1862 by the Union Navy. She had been commissioned on April 3, 1862, a few weeks before her capture of the *Circassian*. The *U.S.S. Somerset* would continue her wartime duties until sold at public auction in poor condition in July of 1865. She was repaired and served as a ferryboat in New York until 1914. (DANFS)
[35] Though the *Circassian* is not specifically listed in Bern Anderson's book, *By Sea and by River – The Naval History of the Civil War*, he does indicate that Havana, Cuba was "the principal depot for the Gulf ports," for foreign goods bound for the blockaded Confederate ports. (Anderson, 218)
[36] According to the corresponding article in the *Harper's Weekly* of October 18, 1862, the *Circassian*, shown with other war prizes was "formally one of the Galway line of steamers. She is about 2300 tons, and is a very fast and stanch vessel. She was captured in the Gulf, with an assorted cargo on board, bound for rebeldom[sp]. She is at present at the Navy-yard, where she will be put in order for the purpose, it is said, of carrying out the first colored emigrants to Chiriquí."

(*NYT*, 23MAY1862) The lieutenant "then ordered a blank shot fired, which they paid no regard for, keeping under full speed." (*NYT*, 23MAY1862) Orders rang out aboard the *U.S.S. Somerset* and the gun captains then launched another shot across the bow and another to her stern, yet the unknown vessel continued to ignore the shots. Lieutenant English realized that if a more direct type of approach was not made, the faster and more powerful ship might escape. He then ordered his gun crews to "hit her, which they did carrying away their main rigging on one side." (*NYT*, 23MAY1862) The *Circassian*, now clearly aware of the devastating power and accuracy of the Union guns, hove to the naval vessel. Her days of blockade running were over.

The boarding party of the *U.S.S. Somerset* quickly boarded the *Circassian* and found the ship's papers to be "irregular" and that they reflected a large and valuable cargo shipped from Bordeaux, but "consigned nowhere." (*NYT*, 23MAY1862) It addition, it was ascertained that another set of ship's papers had been burned by the skipper of the *Circassian* prior to the boarding party's arrival. The irregular information obtained in the still surviving ship's papers coupled with the vessel's attempt to outrun the *U.S.S. Somerset*, indicated to the Union boarding party that the vessel was engaged in an attempt to run the Union blockade. The vessel was immediately put under custodial control by Lieutenant English and taken in tow as a war prize under Admiralty law. The *Circassian* was reported to have been an "old vessel, very sparingly fitted out and in bad order." (*NYT*, 23MAY1862) The *U.S.S. Somerset* and her war prize reached Key West Florida on May 7, 1862. Upon her arrival at port it was reported that she was "heavily laden, and although the exact contents of her cargo" had not yet been determined by press time at the *Harper's Weekly*, there was little doubt that she carried "arms and provisions for the rebels." (*HW*, 7JUN1862) Eventually, her cargo would be determined by inspectors.

The taking of the *Circassian* as a war prize was reported widely and drew fire from Europe. First to vindicate statements and reports that the vessel was engaged in running the blockade was Zachariah C. Pearson, who sent a letter to the London Times. Mr. Pearson, who was later identified as the former Mayor of Hull and owner of the vessel, had lodged complaint that the information of the *Circassian's* intentions was "to say most distinctly that such a statement is essentially and extremely false." (*NYT*, 24JUN1862) Mr. Pearson's statements however were met with a return volley in the form of a letter from Judge Marvin of the Admiralty Court from Key West, Florida. Judge Marvin believed that there was evidence to show "that the vessel was sailing with an agreement, signed by Pearson himself, that the vessel should go to Havana, Nassau or Bermuda, and thence go to a port of America, and to run the blockade and that the freighter had agreed that the goods should not be disembarked but at the port of New Orleans, and to this effect he engages to run the blockade." (*NYT*, 24JUN1862)

Mr. Pearson was unaware that the skipper of the *Circassian* at the time of the boarding had only burned one set of the ship's papers. Thus, Mr. Pearson must have been "thinking that the evidence of his untruth would not be forthcoming." (*NYT*, 24JUN1862) The very burning of any papers, whilst a boarding party made its way aboard the suspect vessel, plus her failure to heave to the Union vessel warranted the "condemnation of the steamer and her cargo as lawful prize." (*NYT*, 24JUN1862)

The day before the article was published denouncing Mr. Pearson's statements regarding the taking of the *Circassian* as unlawful, the vessel was ordered, with its full cargo, to New York via Port Royal. At Port Royal, the *Circassian* landed General Bannan and his staff, and then steamed north toward New York. She arrived in port on the 31st of June.[37] On August 5th, under the order of "James C. Clapp, United States Marshal for the Southern District of Florida," a portion of the cargo of the *Circassian* was sold at auction at the

---

[37] General Bannan and staff, as well as the following passengers were aboard when the *Circassian* left Key West, Florida: Mrs. MacGregor and son, Mrs. Lieut. J.S. Gibbs, Mrs. Dr. Bailey and daughter, Mrs. Brightman and son, Mr. D. O'Grady, Mr. Jackson, Theodore Clapp and Capt. Hunter of the *Circassian*. (*NYT*, 1JUL1862)

"Union stores of Ward & Goves, Brooklyn, near the Hamilton-avenue ferry." (*NYT*, 6AUG1862) Only about half of the cargo "being confined to the articles less easily preserved in good condition," was auctioned. In addition to a large portion of the cargo purchased by those in attendance at the sale, a large assortment, not listed in the article, was "purchased by the Marshal on Government account." (*NYT*, 6APR1862) The total amount raised by the first auction was approximately $125,000. (*NYT*, 24OCT1862)

On October 23, 1862, another portion of the cargo was placed at auction at "No. 18 Murray Street by Mr. Jones." (*NYT*, 24OCT1862) A "spirited" event followed due in large part at the large attendance of bidders and "that the articles offered were in the main, of a superior description." (*NYT*, 24OCT1862) Items of all types were sold at the auction including porcelain "embracing vases, fruit dishes, wine coolers, and mantle ornaments…two dozen boxwood rulers, half dozen Kent hammers….miscellaneous articles of French manufacture, glass tubes, leather spectacle cases and fancy articles in general." (*NYT*, 24OCT1862) In total, 107 lots were offered ranging in price from twenty-five to twelve-hundred dollars. The proceeds of the second auction amounted to approximately one hundred thousand dollars. A few days later, another part of the *Circassian's* cargo was sold, again totaling in approximately one hundred thousand dollars of revenue for Mr. Hewlett Scudder at his store at Park-place. This time no porcelain objects or fancy objects were sold. Instead Mr. Scudder decided to sell one product and one product only – brandy.

After the auctions had taken place, the *Circassian* was sold to the United States Navy on November 8, 1862. She was then "re-rigged as a bark" and was outfitted at the New York Navy Yard with armament including four nine inch smooth bores, one one-hundred pounder, and one twelve pounder. After her outfitting as an armed Union naval vessel, she was commissioned on December 12, 1862 and placed in the command of "Acting Volunteer Lieutenant W.B. Eaton." (DANFS)

During her wartime duties, the *Circassian* served "as a supply ship for the East and West Blockading squadrons" and between December 17, 1862 and April 11, 1865, "she completed nine cruises from New York or Boston delivery supplies to ships and stations along the Atlantic coast and in the Gulf of Mexico, as far west as Galveston, Tex., and up the Mississippi River to New Orleans, La." (DANFS) Having delivered her cargo of supplies upon arrival at southern ports, the empty vessel was utilized in returning "men to be discharged, invalids, prisoners of war, cotton and provisions" on her northbound voyages. (DANFS) In July of 1864 the *Circassian*, now a seasoned wartime vessel also "captured two prizes and participated in the search for the Confederate Steamer *Florida*." (DANFS)[38]

Her days under the Union ensign were drawing near but prior to her return to commercial use the determination of Judge Marvin in May 1862 was once again under scrutiny in the legal system. The concept and legality of war prizes had "given rise to so much discussion, oftentimes acrimonious, in England and France, about the principle of prize law and the rights of neutrals." (*NYT*, 3FEB1865) The *Circassian* case, which was one of many, reached the Supreme Court where Chief Justice Chase determined that Judge Marvin had been justified in his initial ruling that the *Circassian* be considered a war prize due to the incredulous evidence found aboard her in both written documentation and her cargo holdings. Specifically, the bills of lading that consigned "the goods directly to merchants at New-Orleans, to whom also there were letters directed, and no bill of lading called for their delivery anywhere else." (*NYT*, 3FEB1865) The

---

[38] The *C.S.S. Florida* was one of the most successful Confederate raiders of the American Civil War. As outlined in the *Harper's Weekly*, August 8, 1864 issue, "have now a peculiar interest from the fact that these vessels [referring to the rebel privateers *Florida* and *Rappahannock*] are, now that the *Alabama* is sunk, the only cruisers of any importance left to the Confederacy." The *U.S.S. Wachusett* would eventually capture the *C.S.S. Florida* on October 6, 1864 in Bahia, Brazil. She was towed to Hampton Roads and during a political debate as to the circumstances of her capture (a whole other story) the Union government capitulated and the vessel was to be returned to Brazilian authorities. Before that could take place however, the captured vessel was "rammed and sunk by an Army transport in Hampton Roads. Whether this was an accident or deliberate scuttling was never established." (Anderson, 203-204)

decision stood and the *Circassian* remained a Union naval vessel for a few more weeks.

The *Circassian* was de-commissioned on April 26, 1865 and sold less than two months later on June 22 to Mr. Arthur Leary. He paid "$70,000 for the vessel (minus the armament), and converted her back to a full rigged ship." (Gentile, 40) Her impressed service during the Civil War completed, the *Circassian* once again began plying the seas as a commercial vessel.

On October 20, 1865, with Captain Cavendy in command, the *Circassian* was inbound to New York via Halifax when she began to take on water. Captain Cavendy determined that his only option was to run the vessel aground intentionally to save her. With six hundred and fifty passengers and four hundred and fifty tons of cargo, he put the *Circassian* on a sandy beach at Rocky Bay, near Arichat, Cape Breton. The American Consul in New York "arranged through Messrs. Cunard, to have *Delta*, now on the passage from St. John's to Sydney, to render assistance." (*NYT*, 21OCT1865) In addition, *H.M.S. Royalist* was also dispatched to assist. By the 24th, steamer *Delta* arrived at Halifax with a portion of the *Circassian's* passengers and the *Royalist* arrived a few hours later with the rest of the passengers. The *Circassian* was eventually repaired and pulled from the beach.

After the grounding, the *Circassian* continued her normal duties on the high seas.[39] On February 7, 1872 the British ship *Elizabeth Fry* with Captain Mickle in command, was heading from "New Orleans for Liverpool, with a cargo of 3,100 bales of cotton," was burned to the water's edge. (*NYT*, 8FEB1872) Approximately two hundred miles south by east of Savannah, Captain Mickle

---

[39] According to other sources, the *Circassian* had run aground only twice during her career, the first grounding taking place "sometime during the war," on Cape Cod, Massachusetts and again in 1869 at Squan, New Jersey. (*NYT*, 31DEC1876) Clearly the *New York Times* article from October 21, 1865, provides insight into the possibility that she may have grounded a third time or that the "during the war" reference covered the grounding at Rocky Bay. Nonetheless, as reflected by Gary Gentile, the *Circassian* "having once gotten a taste for grounding…seemed bent on making a career of it." (Gentile, 40)

and his crew were rescued a few days later by the *Circassian* which was sailing from Rio Janeiro. Two years later in May of 1874, the *Circassian* would once again provide assistance to a vessel, her crew and passengers. On May 1st, the "steam-ship *Linda*, on her voyage from Barrow to Quebec, was sighted by the steamship *Circassian* of the Allan Line, in longitude 43 degrees west." (*NYT*, 7MAY1874) The steamship *Linda* was engulfed in flames with seventy-five cabin passengers, two hundred and sixteen steerage passengers and a compliment of officers and crew. The *Circassian* rendered aid and all of the passengers and crew were successfully saved. The *Circassian* traveled to Boston, Massachusetts to off load its shipwrecked cargo. The *Linda* was a total loss.

Her time as a commercial vessel was of mixed opinion. To those mariners and passengers rescued by the *Circassian*, no ill comments were probably stated. Her running aground on several occasions of course must have provided some concern, but she was nonetheless regarded as "A 1 by the Liverpool Maritime Exchange" for the majority of her career. (*NYT*, 31DEC1876)[40]

On December 11, 1876, nearing the end of his journey, Captain Richard Williams, his crew of 33 and the 13 passengers from the *Heath Park* found themselves amidst a terrible gale.[41] Heavy snow and winds "rendered it impossible to see more than the length of the vessel." (*NYT*, 15DEC1876) In an attempt to determine his position and nearness to land, Capt. Williams ordered the *Circassian* to be "turned to the windward and that lead heaved overboard." (*NYT*, 15DEC1876) As the crew clamored to toss the lead line into the water, the

---

[40] The term A 1, popularized and most known in our current day society as the name of a steak sauce, was an "old Lloyd's of London classification indicating that a ship has met the highest standards of construction. The term is now used colloquially to describe anything that is the very best." (McKenna, 1)

[41] In the first of eleven articles carried in the *New York Times* regarding the wreck of the *Circassian*, the Captain of the vessel is listed as Capt. Clark. Subsequent articles and most histories list the Captain as Capt Richard Williams. (*NYT*, 15DEC1876) Regarding the number of men on board the *Circassian* when she originally grounded, the tally was listed as follows: 47 men in total – *Circassian*'s Captain and thirty-three crew, *Heath Park*'s Captain and twelve crew. (*NYT*, 15DEC1876)

Circassian herself determined the depth of the water – shallow. The vessel slammed into an outer sandbar. The sudden jarring of the vessel against the bottom was met with quick orders and frantic yet determined action by the captain and the crew. But attempts to back the vessel into deeper water were met with stiff rejection. The pounding surf and the high wind pushed the *Circassian* closer and closer to land. The *Circassian* was hard aground, inching closer and closer to the beaches of Long Island, New York. She was approximately four hundred yards off shore as the waves crashed and the wind continued its howling call of destruction.

The men of the Station 10 Lifesaving Service were quickly assembled at the news of the grounding but their efforts were limited by the same storm which had assisted in the *Circassian's* predicament. Though the sea was "still high at daybreak...it began to lull sufficiently toward noon to render it safe to make preparations for landing the crew" of the stricken vessel. (*NYT*, 15DEC1876) Having gathered the necessary equipment on the beach during the early morning hours, the Lifesaving Service crew began firing rockets at the *Circassian* in an attempt to get a line aboard the ship. After five attempts, a line was finally passed to the ship. With the line finally in place, "a life-boat reached the ship and safely landed part of the crew." (*NYT*, 15DEC1876) Seven more trips through the pounding surf were made until all forty seven crewmen were safely ashore.[42]

Having survived the harrowing ordeal the crew of the *Circassian* and their once already shipwrecked passengers of the *Heath Park* were welcomed into Station 10 where they received dry clothes, shelter and a hot meal. As the men recounted their survival, the *Circassian*, which continued to be man-handled by the raging surf, "was thrown on her broadside, unprotected from the heave seas which repeatedly broke over her." (*NYT*, 15DEC1876) Most of the

---

[42] The number of those rescued also varies depending on the source utilized. Rattray states that forty-nine persons – "the ship's company of thirty-seven" and the twelve passengers from the *Heath Park* were aboard. It is possible that she did not include the two captains as part of her count. (Rattray, 121)

41

Circassian and *Heath Park* crews headed for New York over the next few days however some of the men remained to assist in the anticipated salvage attempt of the grounded vessel.[43]

As soon as the owner of the *Circassian*, S.S. DeWolf, was notified of the vessel's situation, the vessel was put under the charge of the Coast Wrecking Company. The tugs *Cyclops* and *Rescue* steamed toward her location and a wrecking crew comprised of men from the Coast Wrecking Company, the *Circassian*, the *Heath Park* and from the local Shinnecock Indian reservation, headed to the scene to salvage the ship. From the 16th of December to the 29th work continued on the vessel in an attempt to save her from destruction. With a third of her cargo removed by December 29th from her center cargo area, the *Circassian* was close to being able to budge from her sandy entrapment.[44] "All the water had been pumped out and everything was ready for a try at working the ship off the bar." (Field, 47) The lightening of the vessel coupled with an extremely high tide would hopefully prove a positive for the ship. Even though the vessel was backed off the bar almost a hundred yards up to that point, a storm was brewing and the time to save the vessel was fleeting.

By Friday morning, the 29th of December, the weather had turned from bad to worse. Gale force winds and raging surf battered the *Circassian* and its wrecking crew.[45] As the weather continued to deteriorate, C.A. Pierson, "the agent of the Coast Wrecking Company, left the vessel with 10 men, the water having become too rough to permit the continuance of the work of unloading." (*NYT*, 31DEC1876) Captain Lewis, who was in charge of the operation opted to

---

[43] Upon their arrival in New York City the crewmen "went directly to the British Consulate, who sent them to the Sailors' Home, No. 10, Cherry st." (NYT, 15DEC1876)

[44] The *Circassian* was carrying the following cargo: 332 tierces of soda ash, 110 tierces chloride of lime, 45 packages of merchandise, 100 cases sauce, 395 cases soda ash, 10 casks of gelatine, 41,660 Bath brick, 105 hogshead soda ash, 230 barrels soda crystals, 44 tons and 253 tierces dye-wood, 87 casks bleaching powder, 471 bales of rags, 281 bags hide pieces, 600 drams caustic soda, 15 cases of matches, and 600 Bath brick." The cargo was insured in New York City for $90,000 and the vessel insured for $100,000 in London. (*NYT*, 31DEC1876)

[45] The two schooners, *Cyclops* and *Rescue* "ran off before the storm to find a harbor, were yesterday [31DEC1876] heard from at Fire Island, whither they had sailed before the easterly gale began." (NYT, 2JAN1877)

remain on board the vessel to continue the salvage attempt. The lifeline attached from the mast of the *Circassian* and to the beach was ordered cut by Captain Lewis "afraid the crew and the Indians would use it to flee to shore prematurely." (Field, 47)

The Wreck of the *Circassian* – Courtesy of the Suffolk County Historical Society.

According to Captain Bennett of Southampton, he later quoted Captain Lewis has having said "We'll float tonight or we'll go to hell." (Field, 47) Captain Luther D. Burnett, who was one of the men hired "by the Coast Wrecking Company to take charge of the boats used to lighten the ship by removing the cargo," urged Captain Lewis and his crew to come back with him to the safety of the shore. But Captain Lewis, who had once before salvaged the stricken *Circassian*, passed on the offer.[46] The choice to remain aboard would prove to be gravely unwise and the Captain's premonition, all too close to reality.

---

[46] Captain Lewis had commanded the salvage operation of the *Circassian* earlier in the vessel's career when she had grounded. The location of the salvage operation however is clouded in confusion. Reports agree that he assisted with a previous incident but locations vary from on Cape Cod, Massachusetts during the war, Squan N.J. or off Sable Island. (*NYT*, 31DEC1876 & Gentile,

"The gale increased steadily until three o'clock in the afternoon when the cables were slipped to allow the ship to come on the beach. Owing to a strong current running to the westward and the heavy wind the ship's bow was kept up and she refused to come in as desired." (*NYT*, 31DEC1876) As the ship creaked and the waves pummeled the beached vessel she began to show signs of weakness under the constant pressure of nature's fury.

The *Circassian* was "suddenly observed by a gang of men who were watching on the beach to fill and sink to the level of the water. The mainmast went by the board at the same time, falling with a crash, and taking the mizzen-topmast with it." (*NYT*, 31DEC1876) Realizing that the vessel was slowing succumbing to the onslaught of the gale, the men on shore, coupled with the Lifesavers from Station 10 and neighboring stations began their second series of rescue efforts on the doomed vessel. The lifesavers began shooting lines from mortars to the vessel but all efforts failed. The seas were so rough that no small boats could be launched from the beach to attempt to reach the settling wreck. Soon after seven o'clock, the crew was seen having taken to the rigging in an attempt to survive. Holding on in the cold frigid surf and wind continued as minutes slipped into hours. By three in the morning however, the *Circassian* had taken all she could. "The ship broke in two amidships, and the men on board were driven into the mizzen rigging, shouting loudly for relief so that their heartrending cries could be distinctly heard on the beach." (*NYT*, 31DEC1876) "There were 10 Shinnecock Indians among the crew, and in the midst of the din and confusion which rose from the fury of the gale and the loud crash of the breakers upon the sinking vessel, the voices of those brave seamen could be heard chaunting[sp] religions hymns, until at length their songs were hushed forever." (*NYT*, 31DEC1876) The men on the shore could do nothing but watch through the howling wind and the storm-tousled surf in a sort of "torture of

---

47, respectively) A *New York Times* article indicates that Captain E.C. Perry, a fellow officer of the Coast Wrecking Company had been in charge of the *Circassian's* salvage at Squan, NJ. (*NYT*, 31DEC1877)

seeing lives lost within a stone's throw." (*NYT*, 31DEC1876) Two and a half hours later the mizzen-mast finally fell "when the wreck disappeared underwater with the exception of a small remnant of the forward portion." (*NYT*, 31DEC1876) The *Circassian* was no more.

The rescuers on shore began searching the shallows of the surf line for any of the wreckers or crew who may have been washed toward shore. "About 80 rods from the ship four men were discovered floating on a life-boat buoy. They were quickly taken on shore and were identified as Henry Morrell, first mate; John Rowlands, second mate; Alexander Wilson, carpenter, and Charles Campbell, a seaman, of the Coast Wrecking Company." (*NYT*, 31DEC1876)[47] The names of the lost included Captain of the *Circassian*, Richard Williams and eleven of his crew and Captain of the wreckers, John Lewis, and fifteen of his salvage crew.[48]

The search for those lost began immediately, but the churning sea and the "strong easterly current that prevailed" the majority of the day held on to her victims. Walking patrols of lifesavers, private citizens, fellow mariners and family members of the ten lost men from the Shinnecock Indian reservation trudged through the cold wet sand looking for any sight of the lost wreckers and crew. (*NYT*, 31DEC1876)[49] It would not be until the next day that the stormy

---

[47] Two *New York Times* articles published on the same day list two different first names for Mr. Rowlands (John and Thomas.) Though most reports and histories of the event indicate that four men survived the final sinking of the *Circassian*, Rattray states that "one of the four died afterward." (Rattray, 125) She continues to explain that "Mrs. Henry L. Cullum, 95, of East Hampton, says a cabin boy also survived and that she heard him lecture on the wreck later at the Clinton Academy." (Rattray, 125)

[48] List of the missing men as reported on December 31, 1876: Crew Lost: Richard Williams, Captain; Even Johnson, third mate; Horatio Johnston, steward; John Grant, cook; James Scott, boatswain; Henry Freewan, sail-maker; Thomas Orr, carpenter's mate; Andrew Logado, seaman; John McDermott, a stowaway; Frank Wright, Allen Nodder, Walter Hedges – all apprentices. Wreckers Lost: Captain John Lewis, foreman of the wreckers; Phillip Kearns, Luke Stillman, Patrick Donohue – all engineers; George Coffee, James Thurston, Warren Coffee, William Coffee, Oliver Killes, John Walker, Lewis Walker, Robert Lee, David Bunn, Russell Bunn, Mark Bunn, and Frank Bunn – all wreckers. (*NYT*, 31DEC1876)

[49] One of the persons on the beach looking for his fellow tribesmen may have been Shinnecock Indian Alphonse Elazer. He had left the stricken *Circassian* prior to the ship's destruction, under a

Atlantic surf would calm enough to allow for the recovery efforts to begin. Of the first three bodies found, some four miles east of Montauk Point, two were quickly identified as Shinnecock Indians and one appearing to be one of the *Circassian's* apprentices. At the site of the wreck, a small boat was launched to row around the still visible mizzenmast to see if any of the lost men were "entangled in the rigging." (*NYT*, 2JAN1877) "The water was clear enough to allow the boat's crew to see down to the shrouds, but no forms of men could be discerned" and an inspection of the forward part of the *Circassian's* bow section was also conducted with negative results. (*NYT*, 2JAN1877) Only in her time would the sea let go those she had claimed in the disaster.

By January 2, 1877, fourteen drowned men were found ashore "near Montauk, opposite Ditch Plain, four miles east of Montauk Light." (*NYT*, 3JAN1877) Of the fourteen men, one was identified as Captain Lewis; Captain Williams; Evan Johnson, third mate; two of the *Circassian's* apprentice boys; and five Shinnecock Indians.[50] The two other men were believed to be "Luke Stillman and Philip Kearns." (*NYT*, 3JAN1877) A representative of the Coast Wrecking Company was sent from New York City to help in the identification. By the seventh of January, many of the above had been buried.[51]

Even before many of the bodies of the men had been found, members of the Board of Pilot Commissioners held their regular monthly meeting. In addition

---

threat from Captain Lewis that if he left the vessel he would not receive pay for his work, nor would he be allowed "to work again," on the wreck. (Field, 49)

[50] The toll taken on the Shinnecock Indian reservation was devastating. As related in a *New York Times* article, the men who drowned "were about the only able-bodied persons of the community of two or three hundred remaining at home." The article then explained that the three Coffee's were cousins, two of which left widows and a total of six or eight children. Killes left a widow (his brother Andrew Killes had worked as part of the wrecking crew but had left a week before the tragedy to sail as a crewman on a whaling voyage), John Walker left a widow and eight children, and his brother Andrew also perished on the wreck. The Bunns, who like the Coffee's were cousins, left widows and a total of nine children. Robert Lee left a widow as well. (*NYT*, 1JAN1877)

[51] On January 7, 1877, the "bodies of Captain Williams, the mate, three apprentice boys, and two seamen of the wrecked ship *Circassian*, found on the Bridgehampton Beach, were buried" with "Reverend J. D. Stokes" preaching the funeral sermon. "The bodies of the Long Island wreckers belonging to the Shinnecock tribe of Indians, were also buried...at the Indian reservation." (*NYT*, 7JAN1877)

to other matters, the board launched an inquiry to the initial grounding of the *Circassian*. Though pilot Eugene Sullivan was aboard the vessel when she struck, it was determined that he was not in command and that it was Captain Williams who was in charge. "It is said that the spirit compass of the ship was rendered useless by the cold, the weather was thick, and neither Capt. Williams, nor Pilot Sullivan had the least idea of the true position of the vessel when she struck." (*NYT*, 3JAN1877) The inquiry was continued by the British Naval Court of New York City which convened and rendered their findings on January 18, 1877. "Taking into consideration all the facts, they are of the opinion that the pilot was mistaken in his calculation of the position of the ship, and that the standard compass, which there had been no opportunity of testing, may have indicated less than the allowed variation." (*NYT*, 19JAN1877) The report continued by stating that "the pilot is said not to have been in charge of the ship when she stranded, and had been below for about two hours before this. It is evident, however, that the master relied on the confident assertion of the pilot as to the locality of the soundings at 8 P.M., ignoring the similar soundings near Montauk, of which the pilot, also, appears to have been forgetful." (*NYT*, 19JAN1877) The report continued by stating "however confident the master may have been of his position at 8 P.M., still, considering the state of the weather, and the recent change of the standard compass, he committed a grave error in not having sounded at 9, or at latest, 10 P.M." (*NYT*, 19JAN1877) The findings were placing a significant amount of responsibility not only on the pilot of the vessel, but also Captain Williams.

The report concluded that "the court thinks it proper to call attention to the hazard of mistaking the soundings near Montauk for those of similar depth further to the south-west, when approaching the coast in thick weather, after having had no correct observation during several previous days. They also call attention to the fact of a so-called spirit compass being rendered worse than useless by the action of frost, whereby ships approaching the coast at night, and during intensely cold weather, may be stranded before the condition of the compass is perceptible." (*NYT*, 19JAN1877)

The *Circassian*, in her over twenty-six years at sea had proved to be a staunch vessel. She had performed duties during wartime, in commercial trade and had survived two groundings. Her third grounding, though harrowing proved escapable thanks to the bravery of the men of the United States Lifesaving Service. The want to save the ship however during her subsequent salvage attempt proved too much for the old vessel. Mother Nature, who had thrust the *Circassian* onto shore, with the assistance of seamanship error, finally was successful in dragging the vessel to the bottom.[52] The *Circassian*, like the crew and wreckers who unsuccessfully attempted to free the vessel from her sandy confinement on the bar, remain buried beneath the sands on the east end of Long Island.[53]

---

[52] Though the *Circassian* (1857) was lost, another *Circassian* was later launched and operated by the Allan Steamship Line. In 1884, the 2,356 ton steamer was heading from New York to Glasgow when she experienced a problem with one of her propellers. The situation was repaired by divers upon her arrival at Halifax. (*NYT*, 30JAN1884) Four years later, Capt. Barnett was bound from Liverpool to Montreal when her propeller shaft once again caused a problem. The *Circassian* was disabled and was towed to Halifax by the Steamer *State of Nevada*. The smaller 1,572 ton steamer towed the heavier *Circassian* for 72 hours to the safety of port. (*NYT*, 3MAY1888)
[53] Eventually a total of twenty-eight bodies would wash ashore from the wreck. (Field, 49, Rattray, 125)

The two physicians had done all that they could. With his wife at his side, Captain Charles P. Smith was suffering from Erysipelas and was in the final moments of his fight against the acute streptococcal infection in the bed of his home in Roslyn, New York.[54] It was the evening of July 24, 1881. Captain Smith has spent over twenty-five of his fifty-five years in command of various steamboats. He had piloted the *Croton, Ira Smith*, the *Jesse Hoyt* and the *Cygnus* during his years at sea. Though Captain Smith had finally succumbed to his injuries, he would always be remembered by those whom he had heroically saved as the skipper of the ill-fated *Seawanhaka.* Most specifically, his actions at the helm of the steamboat during her final moments would render an indelible impression on those who were aboard the vessel on her last day underway and had survived to tell of his exploits in the face of unimaginable terror.

A painting of the *Seawanhaka*. Courtesy of S.P.L.I.A.

The *Seawanhaka* was originally built in Keyport, New Jersey in 1866. She was 185 feet long and had a beam of forty feet. In 1874 she was rebuilt to an

---

[54] Erysipelas is an acute streptococcal infection characterized by deep-red inflammation of the skin and mucus membranes. Also known as St. Anthony's Fire.

overall length of two hundred and twenty-five feet when a forty foot section was inserted in the middle. Her draft was only six feet and had six hundred and eleven tons burden. With two decks and a salon that was "eloquently fitted up," the *Seawanhaka* was a popular vessel during her years on the water. (*NYT*, 29JUN1880) Her main operations were spent ferrying passengers from New York City to "various ports on the Long Island coast, leaving the Long Island villages in the morning and returning from the city at 4 o'clock in the afternoon." (*NYT*, 19JUN1880) The *Seawanhaka* made the almost daily pilgrimage for commuters calling at various landings including "Whitestone, Peat Neck, Sand's Point, Glen Cove, Sea Cliff, Glenwood, and Roslyn." (*NYT*, 19JUN1880)

On the afternoon of June 28, 1880, the *Seawanhaka* left from her pier in New York heading towards the north shore of Long Island for the last time. One of the passengers, Mr. V. Lopez of Sea Cliff, New York had completed his work day at No. 42 Pearl Street and was heading home. As the side wheel steamer churned through Hell's Gate something went terribly wrong.

The *Seawanhaka* as the fire spread. *Harper's Weekly* illustration.

Mr. Lopez later recounted to a reporter what happened next:

> *"I had started to go forward to see a friend who was in the forward part of the steamer. I had just passed the paddle-box when I heard a dull noise, much like a thud, which, I suppose was the explosion, though I thought nothing particularly about it at the moment. Just afterward smoke began to appear seemingly all around me; there was a cry from some of the ladies, and I felt myself pushed forward toward the bow by the crowd around me."* (NYT, 19JUN1880)

As quickly as the fire had started, so too had the panic. The *Seawanhaka*, its passengers, crew and captain, had but moments to attempt to survive the onslaught of the flames and subsequent destruction.

Capt. Smith at the helm. *Harper's Weekly* **illustration. Author's collection.**

Mr. Lopez was soon pushed towards the railing. Looking up he saw Captain Smith at the helm. As confusion reigned, "Capt. Smith stood at the wheel, with flames bursting out all around him, and it seemed almost as though he was turning a wheel of fire." (*NYT*, 29JUN1880) The Captain had little choice. Surrounding him in the narrow passage of water was a host of other vessels. He had to beach the vessel as soon as possible so that the passengers and crew, many of whom did not know how to swim, could attempt an escape. For several crucial minutes, with fire lapping at his hands and body, he pressed forward. Next to the *Seawanhaka* were the *Granite State* and several schooners. Once he was able to overtake them he pressed the *Seawanhaka* into the "sunken meadow between Ward's and Randall's Islands." (*NYT*, 29JUN1880) In a further effort to provide his passengers and crew the best possible opportunity to escape the burning ship was how he positioned the *Seawanhaka*. The way that he placed the boat onto the marsh was so that the vessel lay broadside to the wind, thus "keeping the fire as much as possible on one side of the boat" thus "giving those on board a better opportunity to save themselves." (*NYT*, 29JUN1880) As Captain Smith maneuvered the vessel, passengers began to drop overboard. Nearby vessels, aware at the raging inferno taking its toll on the *Seawanhaka*, immediately steered towards the stricken steamer. They began offering assistance and lowering their launches and life boats to aid in the rescue or recovery of those in the water as soon as they were able.

Medical personnel from Randall's Island and other boatmen immediately rallied to the rescue. One boatman, Mr. John Henry Bush was out on the water with his family when he saw smoke and flames on board the *Seawanhaka*. After dropping off his family on shore, he immediately proceeded to the area, eventually saving over twenty people who had jumped or had been pushed into the water. Over one hundred boats of all sorts eventually converged on the scene to offer help. The *Seawanhaka* continued to burn. Having done the best that he could, Captain Smith realized that he had to follow the passengers and attempt an escape. He exited the pilothouse, got to the side of the ship and dropped overboard into the water. From the water he watched as the *Seawanhaka* continued to go up in flames. It would burn well into the night. As the smoldering wreckage began to sink into the meadows, the death toll began to rise.

By July 1st over sixty persons were listed as either missing or dead. Divers, utilizing hard hat or surface supplied diving gear were soon on the scene and began the dreadful operation of victim recovery. Over the next few days the divers continued to pull up human remains from the muddy bottom and from the skeleton of the ship. Harbor policemen kept a close vigil on the wreckage as curiosity seekers and relic hunters attempted to take what they could find in the wake of the disaster.

The wreckage of the *Seawanhaka.* *Harper's Weekly* **illustration. Author's collection.**

As the public mourned the victims of the disaster, some private divers were hired by families to attempt to search for their missing loved ones. Various small boats converged on the site, their divers in the water bravely continued looking through the wreckage and surrounding water, but few bodies were retrieved. On the surface, wreckers utilized large chains and hooks to break away at various sections of the hulk. When small pieces of the starboard guard were removed, two bodies were felt with a boat hook, but the wreckers were unable to retrieve them. Another body was found under the port guard, another under the keep and yet another body was found in the mud. But the body in the mud was pinned to the bottom by a large and heavy iron rudder chain. (*NYT*, 25JUL1880) The search for bodies continued below and above the surface of the water. On shore, the firing of cannon from the "upper end of Ward's Island" was ordered. (*NYT*, 25JUL1880) It continued for almost an hour, the cannons booming their shells in the direction of the wreckage.[55] The attempts to retrieve bodies utilizing this effort proved fruitless.

On July 2nd, "a government tug brought a professional diver and a large number of dynamite cartridges" to the site. (*NYT*, 3JUL1880) The diver descended beneath the surface and placed the explosives around the wreck and in the adjacent waters. The flotilla of small boats, with their wreckers and divers were ordered out of the area. The charges were detonated. "The noise was terrific, and great volumes of water ascended to the height of many feet."(*NYT*, 3JUL1880) When the water calmed from the blast, "it was noticed that the surface of the water was covered with dead fish…and the killing of fish was all that was accomplished." (*NYT*, 3JUL1880) The diver, the dynamiting experiment not producing the intended results, was subsequently employed at the scene by a family member who had been vainly looking for his wife's body.[56] The husband of a missing passenger had been witnessed, day and night, at the scene of the disaster in his attempt to locate her body so that she could be properly buried.[57] The search, even with the diver looking through the sunken debris, continued.

The demolition experiment, cannonading, and other efforts concluded, the boatmen, wreckers and other divers under private employ continued their search efforts. Grapnel hooks splashed into the adjacent waters and were dragged along the bottom in their attempt to recover those still listed as missing. Divers

---

[55] The firing of cannon over the water of a shipwreck to recover bodies was a common practice. Scientifically a "waste of time" there were many who believed that the use of loud explosions would cause bodies to "surface." The practice would be utilized in another steamboat disaster, twenty-four years in the same waters when the *General Slocum* disaster occurred. Another reference of the use of cannon fire for the recovery of bodies is found in Mark Twain's *Huckleberry Finn*, Chapter VIII, "Boom! I see the white smoke squirt out of the ferryboat's side. You see, they was firing cannon over the water, trying to make my carcass come to the top."

[56] The diver, unhappy with the results wanted to conduct another round of detonations "but was overruled." He did go below the surface and retrieve several articles including "a brown checked gingham sack, with brown agate buttons; a pillow-slip, a woman's under dress, a shawl strap, a printed bandanna shawl." (*NYT*, 3JUL1880)

[57] Mr. Eugene Aucarigne "has devoted nearly all of his time since the burning of the vessel in attempting to find his wife's remains. He is almost constantly at the wreck on the sunken meadows. Sometimes in the night he is seen in the neighborhood of the Morgue wringing his hands and saying 'My poor wife! There she is in the water, dead, and I can't find her." (*NYT*, 3JUL1880)

descended into the murky depths, reaching, looking and vainly attempting to find those missing and dead to provide some sort of closure for the families. Some of those hoping that the men would find their family member's remains, kept a vigil on the shoreline. Others, who were too distraught over the tragedy and unable to remain at the scene, mourned in the company of friends and family as they anxiously awaited news regarding their loved ones.

On July 3rd, several city officials were beginning to get frustrated with the *Seawanhaka*'s owners over the state of the wreckage. Without movement of the wreckage, many believed that the remaining missing bodies could not be found and thus, interred properly. Mr. Kirk, who represented the steamboat company's interests, was to have arrived the previous day with a wrecking crew to break up and remove the wreck. Commissioner Thomas S. Brennan voiced his concern to a *New York Times* reporter stating that "It is terrible to know that, through some red-tape formalities between the owners of the vessel and the insurance companies, they [the bodies which were believed to still be in the bowels of the *Seawanhaka*] could not be retrieved." (*NYT*, 4JUL1880) Little progress was made on the wreck and the only bodies that were to be found were in other areas of New York's waterways. Funeral processions in Long Island and New York City continued over the next few days.

The frustration continued. Little work was completed on the wreck on the 6th of July, with the exception of a "few workmen [who] visited the wreck in the forenoon...took off the cap from the shaft...then quit work and left." (*NYT*, 7JUL1880) Two employees of the steamboat company maintained a watch on the wreckage, guarding the site from would be pillagers and harbor gangs who might pilfer anything of value from the scene.[58] The wreckage and the watch on the site

---

[58] The two men "spent their time in searching among the mass of debris for relics in the shape of coin, pocket-knives, &c., making an occasional find of no value. The search was very thorough in the part of the wreck where the office had been, and one man claimed to have found a half-melted gold coin." (*NYT*, 7JUL1880)

remained. As the summer progressed, so to did the investigation into what had caused the tragedy.

On July 12, 1880, a secret session of the United States Grand Jury was conducted. The Grand Jury had questioned several witnesses on the first day of their investigation. Over the course of the next week an a half, the members questioned crewmen, experts, inspectors and others in their efforts to determine the cause of the tragedy. Quickly the focus narrowed on the possibility that one of the boilers had exploded. The members of the Grand Jury also visited the wreckage of the vessel to learn more about the possible cause. The two experts were asked to "examine the boilers critically," and they did. (*NYT*, 25JUL1880) Based on their inspection of the wreckage area, the experts were able to remove portions of the boilers that raised suspicion. Utilizing drawings of "portions of the boiler shell and of some of the steam-pipes," the experts were able to show how the fourteen year old boiler materials had oxidized and "granulated."

(*NYT*, 25JUL1880) "The ordinary thickness of boiler plates," it was explained was normally "five-sixteenths or three-eights of an inch" thick," however their close inspection had determined that a "blow from a hammer would break" the shell of the boiler open. (*NYT*, 25JUL1880) Ultimately, some of the fragments recovered from the boiler's shell "were less than one-eighth of an inch in thickness," under close examination. (*NYT*, 25JUL1880)

The evidence provided to the Grand Jury, coupled with the statements of many of the survivors who had told investigators of their hearing a "dull thud" or explosion prior to the resulting fire, was enough to convince the Grand Jury that an explosion of some circumstance in relation of the boiler had caused the calamity.[59] But the investigation into the disaster was far from over. On the 29th of July, Coroner Brady began the inquest into the tragedy. Once again, members of the *Seawanhaka's* crew and many of the passengers were called in to testify. After two days of testimony, the jury "after a long deliberation, rendered a verdict. (*NYT*, 31JUL1880) The jury determined that the 35 passengers came to their death by injuries, the result of a fire which occurred on board the steamer *Seawanhaka* on the 28th day of June, 1880, on its passage from New-York to Roslyn. We find said disaster was caused by the bursting or collapsing of one of the tubes in the starboard boiler, whereby the flames were driven under the grate bars into the fire-room, thereby igniting the wood work, causing the destruction of the boat. We further find that the boiler had been duly inspected by the United States Inspector in March last, and that said boat was provided with all the appurtenances required by law, and the jury further believes that the loss of life in this disaster would not have been so great had the crew been disciplined and exercised to act in concert in case of a panic through fire or any other cause. In conclusion, the jury would strongly recommend, to avoid recurrence of a similar disaster, that the ceilings and walls, as well as the floors, of the fire-rooms of all steam-boats should be incased in metal at a suitable distance from the woodwork." (*NYT*, 31JUL1880)

On August 7th, the *Seawanhaka's* remains were put up for sale to the highest bidder. The auction was "pursuant to an order made by Judge Choate, of the United States District Court." (*NYT*, 8AUG1880) The auction, which had a "fair attendance of bidders," commenced at an opening bid of $1,000. Bidding increased in twenty-five dollar increments, the final sale going to Mr. Charles H. Gregory of Red Bank, New Jersey for the total sum of $1,410. The purchase price of the wreck included "the engines, tackle, apparel, and furniture" of the "burned steamer" as it lay." (*NYT*, 8AUG1880)

---

[59] "It is understood that in light of the testimony put before them, the Commissioners are also of the opinion that the hydraulic system of testing boilers is defective, and does not give a true and determinate test of the strength of the boilers – at least of old boilers." (*NYT*, 25JUL1880)

Three days after the wreck of the *Seawanhaka* had been purchased at auction the Grand Jury of the United States District Court presented its indictments. Eight persons, including "the owners of the vessel, the Captain and engineer, and the Federal Inspectors of hulls and boilers," were charged with manslaughter through criminal negligence. (*NYT*, 11AUG1880) In addition to the indictments, a larger picture of problems was brought to clarity regarding many of the steam vessels "plying to and from this port." (*NYT*, 11AUG1880) "Inspections of hulls and machinery are not made with any reasonable degree of accuracy and honest fulfillment…unseaworthy vessels are allowed to be crowded with passengers on dangerous waters; the required means of saving life are neglected as to kind, extent, and condition; machinery is not tested as the law requires, and the jurors, under the responsibility of their oath, declare that they believe that it cannot in any case, under the present uncertain and speculative practice, be satisfactorily determined that the boilers are well made of good and suitable material, or that other necessary requirements are complied with." (*NYT*, 11AUG1880) As pointed out by the reporter from the *New York Times*, the indictments and charges were an "indictment of the whole legal system for the protection of life on steam-boats."

The *Seawanhaka* disaster remained in the news and in the courts until the winter of 1881.[60] On October 27, 1880, it was reported that "the parties indicted for manslaughter in connection with the burning of the steamer *Seawanhaka*…withdrew their plea of not guilty…with their counsel announcing that they intended to move to quash the indictments." (*NYT*, 27OCT1880) A month and a half later, "Assistant United States District Attorney Fiero [had] expressed a desire to consolidate the indictments against the owners, Directors, and officers of the burned steam-boat *Seawanhaka*, and the United States Local

---

[60] The Irving Club, a committee made up of "prominent citizens of Harlem," presented three young boys of the Grammar School No. 68, gold medals for their heroic actions during the *Seawanhaka* disaster. The boys had been out rowing in a small boat when they saw the flames and tragedy develop. The boys collectively saved fourteen souls from the *Seawanhaka*, including Captain Smith. (*NYT*, 23OCT1880)

Inspectors of Steam-boats." (*NYT*, 1DEC1880) The Grand Jury was swayed by the consolidation request, "handed in a single bill against all the defendants, indicting them collectively instead of as individuals." (*NYT*, 1DEC1880) Eventually however, the courts decided to instead go after the two men of the United States Local Inspectors of Steam Vessels, Austin Jayne and John Mathews. The two men had inspected the *Seawanhaka* in March of 1880 including her life-saving equipment and most importantly, her boilers. Most significant and the basis for the charges was that the men had issued the *Seawanhaka* a "false certificate." The arguments continued from both sides of the courtroom until the jury was sent to deliberate the case. At this point in time, with all of the evidence explained and the charges pending against the two inspectors, the jurors were ordered to render a decision. For thirty-three hours, the jurors remained in deadlock regarding the charges which included manslaughter. The jury remained in deadlock and the case was dismissed. The *Seawanhaka* case then disappeared beneath the sea of legal documents. In many ways, the disaster with the exception of minor references in newspaper reports when other vessels faced tragic ends or circumstances faded in large part from public memory.

Captain Smith waited until the Spring of 1881 to return to his duties at the helm of a vessel. His new command was the *Cygnus*, "the first of the fleet of iron steamers built for the Iron Steamboat Company." (*NYT*, 25JUL1881)[61] Smith was in command of the new vessel for roughly two months when he began to suffer from a "cold and toothache." (*NYT*, 25JUL1881) He was found by Captain Longstreet, the Superintendent of the Iron Steamboat Company, "in bed in his room, with the left side of his face swollen and his left eye nearly closed." (*NYT*, 25JUL1881) Longstreet, a friend and colleague of Smith for thirty years

---

[61] "When the *Cygnus*, on May 25 last, made her trial trip to Coney Island, Capt. Smith made what might have been called his first appearance in public after the *Seawanhaka* disaster, and he was then heartily welcomed and congratulated by hosts of his old acquaintances and friends who were assembled upon the boat." (*NYT*, 25JUL1881)

urged him to go home and recuperate. Captain Smith dismissed the recommendation "and roused himself to take his boat out on time." (*NYT*, 25JUL1881) The next morning however, the Captain's condition has worsened and Captain Longstreet ordered him to return home amid his illness. A day and a half later, Captain Smith died.

On July 26, 1881, in Roslyn, New York, Captain Smith, the hero of the *Seawanhaka* disaster was laid to rest. Many of those who had survived the disaster were in attendance to pay their respects to the Captain and his family. "The funeral services were performed by three clergy men" and Reverend Hopkins, after a brief reference to the Captain's actions on the *Seawanhaka* stated that there were three "characteristics of Capt. Smith's life that deserved to be specifically noticed…courage, unselfishness, and humility." (*NYT*, 27JUL1881) Captain Smith was interred in the burial plot of his father, Stephen B. Smith, near the site of W.J. Bryant's resting place.

Two weeks after his passing, an additional memorial service was held at the Sea Cliff Tabernacle. Three thousand people attended the services to remember and reflect upon the Captain's heroic actions. Among the readings, Mr. Richard O'Gorman provided the following remarks to those in attendance:

> "It is very seldom that an assemblage so great as this can be got together for such a purpose as we desire to promote to-day A political this surely is not, and yet its purpose touches the highest pride of the Republic and the highest duty of the people. That in the generous plan of government under we live manhood has been freed from all hindrance of race and class and privilege; that all men, rich and poor, great and small, have equal rights, a fair field and fir play to win, if they can, wealth and power and honored names; this is the triumph of the Republic, which has made it beloved in all the myriad homes of all the earth and to see this grand rule of equality preserved, is the peoples highest duty and fairest hope. This rule we are here to-day to illustrate and apply. We are here to hear testimony to a gallant act done by a brave and gallant man, faithful to his duty at the risk of his life. Charles Smith was a man of the people, a sailor, a pilot, doing a pilot's duty skillfully day after day on Long Island

Sound...And so here, on this fair August day, with the sun shining on the waters over which our old pilot, Charlie Smith, used to steer us, we bid him our last farewell and lay the tribute of our grateful remembrance if it were a wreath of unfading flowers on his grave. What more may be done I know not...When we shall be all forgotten, men will see it [referring to his idea of the placement of a memorial obelisk] and learn the story and the less it should teach, that the faithful performance of duty is the highest virtue, and that even the simples life may be one gallant act be beautified and ennobled." (*NYT*, 15AUG1881)

The *Seawanhaka* disaster has been largely forgotten. The *General Slocum*, another steamboat disaster which occurred in 1904 and mirrored in many ways the previous tragedy would garner much attention as to the dangers of maritime travel in local waters. Capt. Smith rests in the Roslyn Cemetery. A mere hundred yards from his burial plot is the bustling Route 25A aka Northern Boulevard. Commuters of the modern era race to and from New York City utilizing this roadway. In some respects little has changed since the days of commuting by water. People still make the daily trip to the city; only most of them do so by car or train. The dangers are still there, however, in the present day as they were in days past. In seaborne commuting the captain was the eyes and ears for his clients. He had an awesome responsibility. Today that responsibility is present in every individual who drives his or her own vehicle. Inattentiveness can be deadly.

The crew and officers stood at attention on the main deck of the ship-of-the-line. The waves slowly lapped at the wooden hull as a deathly silence was broken only by the low sighs of those in attendance. Under the watchful eye of Squadron Commander, Commodore Thomas A. Catesby Jones, the final sentence for the two sailors was passed to all of those within earshot. The two seamen had attempted to jump ship. In their bungled desertion attempt the two men had assaulted and injured one of the ship's officers. The actions coupled together had left the United States Navy to the justifiable punishment – death. The two sailors "were strung up on the *Ohio*'s yardarms and their lifeless bodies left to dangle there as a warning sign to others." (Wood, 167) As the deceased sailors hung motionless, the *U.S.S. Ohio* swung lazily at her anchor. On the horizon lay the object of the sailors' unrequited lust; the shores of California and its gold rush. By 1850, with the *U.S.S. Ohio's* services no longer needed to patrol the territory of California's coast line, she sailed south around Cape Horn bound for the familiar waters of her launching.

The *U.S.S. Ohio* was originally built in 1817 at a cost of approximately $550,000. She was "one of nine ships to rate not less than 74 guns" and she was "authorized by Congress 29 April 1816."[62] (DANFS, Appendix IV) She was designed by Henry Eckford and was to carry sixty-eight guns, thirty-four thirty-two pounders, and thirty-four forty-two pound carronades.[63] She was a ship-of-

---

[62] The *U.S.S. Ohio* was "nearly identical to sister ships of the North Carolina class, which included the Alabama (renamed New Hampshire), Delaware, New York, North Carolina, Vermont, and Virginia." (DANFS, Appendix IV)

[63] The list of armament differs depending on the source and the years of her career being reviewed: According to the *DANFS*, Appendix IV, Volume IV, *Ships-of-the-Line*, "A record of *Ohio*'s original armament was not found. There is a partial indication in her deck log for 27 October 1838: ...received on board 64 breeches and carriages for the lower and main deck guns.' Bureau of Ordnance Gun Register shows her armament in 1845 as follows: Spar deck: two 32-pound cannons and twenty-four 42-pounder carronades. Main deck: thirty-two 32-pounder cannon. Lower deck: Thirty-two 42-pounder cannon. In January 1847 some new guns were received and her armament is recorded as follows: Spar deck: four 9-inch shell guns of 53 hundredweight, four 32-pounders of 42 hundredweight, four 32-pounders of 57 hundredweight and twelve 32-pounders of 42 hundredweight. Main deck: four 8-inch shell guns of 63 hundredweight, twenty-eight 32-pounders

the-line[64] and was one hundred and ninety-seven feet long with a fifty-three foot beam.[65] Her tonnage of 2,757 made her a formidable vessel and her complement of guns and armament illustrated that she was to be put to use as a military vessel. "Her decks were aft quarter, spar or main, upper gun, lower gun, orlop and main. At her stern was a light galley projecting aft."(Wood, 167) From below her bowsprit, an eight foot tall figurehead of the mighty Hercules looked forward to adventure and warfare on the high seas.

Her construction marked the first vessel to be built at the Brooklyn Navy Yard, but her timing, which was on the heels of the War of 1812 and prior to the advent of the American Civil War, did not provide her the ability to sail to sea and act in her capacity as a warship. She took three years to construct but in the end there was no rush to turn her loose to the sea as the fiscally strapped United States government had no military use for her upon completion. The ship though completed and ready for sea would not be commissioned formally by the United States Navy until 1838. For eighteen years she remained in "ordinary" which meant that she simply waited at her mooring to be called to service.

Once removed from ordinary, the *U.S.S. Ohio* received her first assignment as the flagship for Commodore Isaac Hull. For the next two years, the *U.S.S. Ohio* served in that capacity as part of the Mediterranean Squadron where she "protected commerce and suppressed the slave trade off the African Coast." (DANFS) Her years of non-use did not affect the performance of the vessel and many a sailor who shipped on her remarked as to her design and efficiency at sea. One officer who was stationed on the *U.S.S. Ohio* even stated that "I never supposed such a ship could be built-aship possessing in so great a degree all the

---

of 60 hundredweight. Lower deck: four 8-inch shell guns of 63 hundredweight and twenty-eight 42-pounders."
[64] A ship-of-the-line is defined by Edgar Bloomster as "a warship of three or more decks, carrying 70 to 140 guns (cannon), and usually ship-rigged." They were the battleships of their era.
[65] The particulars of the *U.S.S. Ohio* vary by source. Dr. Clarence A. Wood lists the total tonnage at 4250, length at 212 feet, beam 50 feet, draft 20 feet with a freeboard of 36 feet. (Wood, 167)

qualifications of a perfect vessel." (DANFS) Despite the positive attributes of the vessel, her use at sea by the United States Navy would be limited in scope.

Landing troops at Vera Cruz. Members of the *U.S.S. Ohio's* crew were part of this and other operations. Library of Congress Prints and Photographs Division, Washington, DC.

Upon her return from the Mediterranean cruise, the *U.S.S. Ohio* was placed once again into ordinary. She remained in the waters of Boston, Massachusetts and from 1841 to 1846 she acted as a receiving ship. As hostilities arose between the United States and Mexico, the *U.S.S. Ohio* was recommissioned on December 7, 1846 and set sail less than a month later for the Gulf of Mexico. Upon her arrival on March 22, 1847, it was realized that the vessel's draft was excessive for the gulf's shallow operating area. Though not utilized for coastal operations, "336 of her crew participated in the Tuxpan River Expedition. (DANFS)[66] While she remained in deeper water, Commodore Matthew C. Perry oversaw the battle which resulted in the capturing of three Mexican forts. The *U.S.S. Ohio*, in addition to providing personnel for the fight, also assisted in the retrieval of the guns from the brig *U.S.S. Truxton* which had

---

[66] Tuxpan is also spelled Tuspan. Both variations are found when referring to these specific U.S. Navy and Marine Corps engagements.

"foundered in a storm near Tuxpan" on September 16th of the previous year. (DANFS)

Having completed her duties in support of the naval activities off of Vera Cruz, the *U.S.S. Ohio* returned to the waters of the northeast, arriving in New York on May 9, 1847. Her activities continued as she then set sail on June 26, 1847 with the U.S. Minister to Brazil as a passenger to the waters of the Pacific. Attached to the Pacific Squadron, the *U.S.S. Ohio* plied the waters off of South America until the following November. As the California gold rush began, the vessel moved north and operated along the western coast of North America in an effort of "protecting commerce and policing the newly acquired California territory during the chaotic early months" of the migration westward for gold.

A drawing of the *U.S.S. Ohio*. Courtesy of S.P.L.I.A.

In 1850, the *U.S.S. Ohio* returned once again to Boston, Massachusetts. In 1851, the vessel returned to her duties as a receiving ship for the fleet. During the American Civil War, she was utilized to defend Boston Harbor in the unlikely event that the Confederate navy launched an attack on the northern harbor. While serving in this capacity, she was "temporarily rearmed with one 8-inch Parrott rifle, four 100-pounder Parrot rifles, and twelve 32-pounders." (Gentile, 162)

After the cessation of hostilities, she returned to her activities as a receiving ship. In 1875, she was placed in ordinary for the last time of her career. She was sold at Boston to Israel L. Snow of Rockland, Maine on September 27, 1883 for $17,000. The vessel was then sold to a group of men from Long Island, New York for $20,000.[67]

The *U.S.S. Ohio*. Courtesy of the Ward Melville Heritage Organization.

On October 28, 1883, the vessel left the Boston Navy Yard for the last time. She was towed by the tugboats *Luther C. Ward* and the *Germania* under the command of Captain S. Truman Preston. Bound for the eastern end of Long Island, her last trip would be quite eventful. Capt. Preston and the members of his

---

[67] The men who purchased the *U.S.S. Ohio* were Thomas F. Price, John T. Gallup, Samuel P. Hedges, Samuel Salata, David S. Vail, George W. Cooper and J. Henry Perkins. (Wood, 171)

salvage crew encountered a terrible storm. "Off Cape Cod…the ship rolled so heavily during the gale that the mess hall tables were swept clear of dishes." (Wood, 171) But the *U.S.S. Ohio* marked a significant investment so the tugs trudged through and survived the onslaught of the storm. "Between Christian Light and Pullock Reef" a huge humpback whale began following the ship. (Wood, 171) Considered a bad omen by the sailors involved in the voyage, they had to turn a blind eye to their superstitions and push forward to their final destination.

Finally, on November 1, 1883, the *U.S.S. Ohio*, almost sixty four years old arrived in Greenport, New York. For many months, the old ship-of-the-line remained at the town's dock. The new owners charged admission so that interested locals and visitors could "examine her innards." (Wood, 171) In early summer, with her valuable wood, metal and other parts having been stripped including the figurehead of Hercules, she was towed to Conklin's Point. Utilizing dynamite charges, Samuel Salata, Robert N. Corey supervised as a "gang of men proceeded to prepare her funeral pyre." (Wood, 171) On July 26, Robert N. Corey lit the dynamite's fuse. The *U.S.S. Ohio* however had one last fight left in her. "Spectators later reported that the old hulk looked especially grim," and her planned demise would not be without incident.[68] (Wood, 171)

The fuse lit, its spark racing towards the dynamite charges, Corey "ran to join a group of fellow workmen crouching some eighty paces away. And there, as the initial explosion occurred and the *Ohio*'s sides were ripped asunder, an iron bolt from the ship struck Corey on the head." (Wood, 171) He would only survive three hours and died at his home.[69] The *U.S.S. Ohio*, stripped bare to her

---

[68] "One imaginative onlooker claimed to have heard an angry snarl issuing from the vessel's deserted hold," prior to the detonation. (Wood, 171)

[69] According to an article published in *The New York Times* on November 21, 1895, Mr. Israel Snow was a victim of the *U.S.S. Ohio* while in Greenport when he "was killed during the dismantling of the vessel by the fall of block which struck him on the head." (*NYT*, 21NOV1895) I have been unable to verify this statement in any other source regarding the history of the *U.S.S. Ohio*.

skeleton, settled slowly into the dark waters. She would remain, for the next eighty-nine years, a memory.

The Hercules figurehead. Courtesy of the Ward Melville Heritage Organization.

In 1973, the remains of the *U.S.S. Ohio* were discovered by a group of scuba divers who were part of a North American contingent of the British Sub Aqua Club.[70] Initially, their identification of the wreck site was kept to a small circle, but when it was learned that the Mobil Oil Corporation was planning on placing pilings in the vicinity, the group of divers "protested and in doing so gave away the wreck's general location." (Berg) Once the area had been identified, other divers began their search and subsequently located the wreck of the *U.S.S.*

---

[70] I attempted to find out more about this specific group but the British Sub Aqua Club in England was unable to provide further information.

Ohio. After contesting access in court, it was determined that the wreck's location could not limit the ability for recreational divers to visit the remains.

Scuba diver Bob Auteri has dove on the *U.S.S. Ohio* site for over thirty-five years, starting when the site was re-discovered in the 1970's. During his explorations of the wreck site, he has located various items including a large bronze spike with U.S. stamped on each end. Other items recovered at the site include nails, a pipe, a washer and a small wooden section of the vessel's remains.

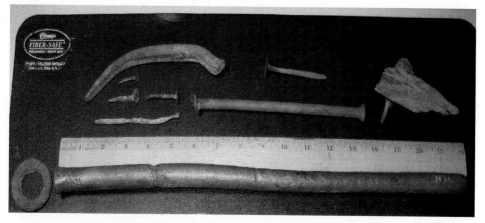

Artifacts recovered from the *U.S.S. Ohio* site by Bob Auteri. Courtesy of B. Auteri.

Not much of the former ship-of-the-line exists to be found and explored on the bottom. Interestingly, the *U.S.S. Ohio*, or rather parts of her literally became part of the Eastern end of Long Island in one form or another. The Hercules figurehead originally constructed at a cost of $1,500, which had been made by the "well known wood carvers of New York City," Dodge & Sharpe had been removed prior to the vessel's final demise. (Wood, 172) It was purchased by a Mr. Aldrich, "a resident of Aquehogue, for ten dollars." (Wood, 172) Mr. Aldrich then sold the figurehead to Miles Carpenter for fifteen dollars. Hercules, standing eight feet tall was then placed at Carpenter's establishment, the Canoe Place Inn located near the Shinnecock Canal.[71] But he would not remain on the south shore. In the early nine-teen fifties, the figurehead was moved to Stony Brook. According to an inscription on a plague at her current location, it was "presented by Cornelius N. Van Pattern and Thomas L. O'Donnell to the Stony Brook Community Fund."[72] (Smithsonian) In a pavilion named in its honor, Hercules remains today, alongside Stony Brook Harbor.[73] Inside the same pavilion, an anchor, also from the *U.S.S. Ohio*, is on display.

The remains of the vessel also made their way into many homes located on the east end. According to a letter from Ezra Hallock Young to the editor of *The Long Island Forum,* published in the December 1951 issue, "many barns, outbuildings and houses on the East end have the secondhand lumber bought from the Old Ohio and my father's diary of 1884 shows numerous mentions like brought a load of lumber from the old Ohio." (*The Long Island Forum*, 228) She further speculated that the first name of Mr. Aldrich was probably "John Elliot Aldrich." (*The Long Island Forum*, 228) In addition to her planking and other assorted wood, much of the *U.S.S. Ohio's* metals were also sold locally and a lasting example is the bell at the Greenport Methodist Church which was cast from metal purchased from the vessel during her scrapping.

Still an active diving location, much of the burned and wrecked hull remains beneath the sand. The *U.S.S. Ohio*, approximately twenty feet below the surface, remains today as a reminder of the wooden fleet of the United States Navy. Her last vestiges, preserved in one way or another, remain in more recognizable forms, illustrating an interesting aspect of the rich nautical past of Long Island's east end.

---

[71] According to an article published in *The New York Times* on November 21, 1895, that to move the Hercules figurehead "four oxen were employed for a fortnight in carting it the forty miles from Greenport to its present resting place," in Canoe Place. (*NYT*, 21NOV1895)

[72] According to Wood's September 1950 article the inscription on Hercules' pedestal read "the maid who kisses his mighty cheek, will meet her fate within a week; the one who presses his forehead, in less than a year will wed. No maid, no matron ever taunted Him with refusing what he wanted." (Wood, 172)

[73] Hercules can be viewed at the Ward Melville Heritage Organization in Stony Brook, New York.

Chief Officer Matthews stood on the bridge of the Cunard steamship *Oregon*. In a few hours, the steamship was due to arrive at New York to offload its passengers. The voyage had left from Liverpool on Saturday March 6, 1886. Most of the 896 passengers and crew not on duty were relaxing or sleeping, anxiously awaiting the vessels speedy arrival in America. The baggage of the passengers was being brought up from the hold to expedite the transfer of passengers to the dock. In the distance, a set of lights were noticed by a few passengers who were walking the deck of the steamship. The lights indicated a vessel on a northern tack. No alarm was sounded and the *Oregon* steamed westward five miles off of Fire Island, New York. At 4:30 a.m. the majority of the passengers and crew were fast asleep. Others who were fighting bouts of seasickness or anxious about the pending arrival in New York would soon find themselves confronted with the reality and urgency of their own survival.

The *Oregon* under steam. Author's collection.

The *Oregon* had been constructed in 1883 by Elder and Company at Govan, Scotland. Built specifically for the Guion Steamship Company, the *Oregon* was the youngest of three sister vessels including the *Alaska* and *Arizona*. She was five hundred and twenty feet long, had a fifty four foot beam, a draft of forty feet, three quarter inches and had a total tonnage of 7,500 tons. The *Oregon's* hull "was of steel and of great strength, and was separated into a number of watertight compartments." (*NYT*, 15MAR1886) She was propelled through the water by twelve thousand horsepower three cylinder type engines that had one high pressure cylinder of "70 inches in diameter" between two low-pressure cylinders which had a diameter of 104 inches." (*NYT*, 15MAR1886) Nine boilers fueled by furnaces which consumed "240 tons of coal a day," provided the engines with the necessary steam to speed the *Oregon* through various ocean conditions. (*NYT*, 15MAR1886)

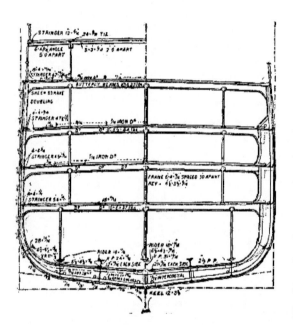

A drawing of the *Oregon*'s deck construction.

On her main deck were four masts and two smokestacks which towered into the sky. The vessel's large spaces were of the highest quality. The grand salon was eighty-five feet long and had a parqueteire floor with ceiling decorations in white and gold polished satin wood panels. On the promenade deck, a ladies' drawing room was located which had been "furnished in the most costly manner." (*NYT*, 15MAR1886) Above the promenade deck a smoking room was located which was paneled in Spanish mahogany. Artificial light throughout the vessel was provided by the "Edison incandescent electric light." (*NYT*, 15MAR1886) In keeping with the larger spaces of the vessel, the staterooms were tastefully appointed and of large size. The *Oregon*'s appointments for her passengers were as equally impressive as the ship itself. "She had accommodations for 340 first class, 92 second class and 1110 steerage passengers," which allowed her to provide transatlantic passage for over fifteen hundred and forty passengers in a single voyage. (*NYT*, 15MAR1886)

Her powerful engines and sleek design allowed the *Oregon*, an ocean greyhound, to make her maiden voyage from Queenstown to New York in seven days, eight hours and thirty-three minutes. Sold by the Guion Steamship Company on May 21, 1884, she made her quickest passage in August 1884 from Queenstown to the "bar off Sandy Hook in six days, nine hours and twenty-two minutes." (*NYT*, 21MAY1884) The Cunard Steamship Company, when confronted with the possibility of "war between Great Britain and Russia over the Afghan frontier," released the *Oregon* under government contract to be fitted out for naval service. (*NYT*, 15MAR1886) She was refitted as a cruiser and "took part in naval manoeuvres in Bantry Bay in July, being the only one of the chartered vessels…that was sent to sea." (*NYT*, 15MAR1886) After a peaceful resolution had been struck between the two countries, the *Oregon* was released from her naval obligation and soon returned to her passenger service between Liverpool and New York City.

The *Oregon* would remain a transatlantic steamer on the Liverpool to New York City route for the remainder of her career. In February of 1886, roughly a month and a half prior to the collision at sea south of Long Island, the Directors of the Cunard Steamship Company however decided to put the *Oregon*, in addition to the *Gallia*, *Bothnia* and *Scythia* on the Liverpool to Boston, Massachusetts route to send "the New-England outward bound travel through Boston Harbor," thus freeing up the congestion of New York Harbor and adjacent waters. (*NYT*, 2FEB1886)[74] The collision on the night of March 14th however would send the Board of Directors back to the drawing board.

The shock of the collision shook Captain Phillip Cottier from his early morning slumber. He immediately "rushed up from below and assumed

---

[74] The Cunard Steamship Company had decided to retire the *Cephalonia*, *Pavonia*, and *Catalonia*. The *Umbria*, *Etruria*, *Aurania* and *Servin* would handle the Liverpool to New York bound travel under the initially publicized plan. (*NYT*, 2FEB1886)

command of the deck." (*NYT*, 15MAR1886) He was soon provided a report from Chief Officer Matthews and other members of his crew regarding what had transpired. An unknown coasting schooner had slammed into the "mammoth steamer on the port side, directly abaft of the foremast." (*NYT*, 15MAR1886) The impact of the collision caused the unknown schooner to rebound "from the iron sides of the Cunarder," and it slowly "drifted into the darkness," a victim as well.

Below decks, the damage was extensive. The schooner had struck the *Oregon* creating a hole in the steamship "so large that a horse and wagon could have easily driven through it." The waters of the Atlantic rushed into the steamship. The point of impact was below the dining saloon and beneath the waterline. Captain Cottier ordered the watertight doors shut to stem the incoming rush of water. The *Oregon* had been built with watertight compartments, so initial thoughts must have been optimistic. Upon further examination however, it was determined that the "point of impact was right on the edge of a watertight bulkhead, with the result that two adjacent compartments were flooding, and much faster than the pumps could eject the overflow." (Gentile, 174) Attempts were made by the crew to plug the holes in the hull, but the final placement of a collision mat only slowed the inevitable. Water continued to pour in through the gashes in her hull and the *Oregon* was "quite a bit down by the head and listing perceptibly to port." (Gentile, 174) It was not if the *Oregon* would sink, but rather when. The *Oregon*, like the vessels of its era did not carry enough lifeboats and safety equipment to safely remove all of the passengers and crew.

The continued influx of water eventually reached the boilers and extinguished them. With the loss of the boilers, the *Oregon* had no power or electricity. The hot coal in the fires, now dampened by the sea sent a cloud of steam throughout the vessel and the fireman up the ladders to the main deck. The *Oregon* was now drifting, under no power, and taking on water at an alarming rate. Well aware that his vessel had possibly received a death blow, Captain Cottier immediately ordered his men to fire distress rockets in an attempt to attract the attention of possible passing vessels. For the next two hours as the *Oregon* continued to list, several attempts were made to plug the damage and stem the incoming waters. It was at this time that he ordered the officers and crew to launch the lifeboats.

Awakened by the terrific collision, passengers had hurriedly gathered on the main deck awaiting orders and clarification of what had occurred. Once the eight lifeboats had been launched, only half of all of the passengers and crew were able to leave the *Oregon*. This left over four hundred and fifty passengers and crew on the decks of the sinking vessel. By most accounts, everyone acted appropriately under the stressful conditions. The unknown schooner was witnessed to be in an equally significant state of damage. The coaster "drifted about in the neighborhood of the *Oregon* throughout the morning, her head gears all gone and her cutwater stove in." (*NYT*, 15MAR1886) The mystery schooner's crew was no where to be found and no boats from her davits appeared on the horizon.

Though two steamers had been seen in the distance when Captain Cottier had ordered the signal rockets fired, it was not until eight o'clock in the morning that the first of two vessels arrived on the scene. The pilot boat No. 11, known as *Phantom* appeared, having responded after sighting the red signal rocket. The crowded lifeboats began transferring their passengers to the decks of the *Phantom*. On the horizon another vessel was sighted. The second vessel to arrive, about an hour after the *Phantom*, was a schooner named *Fanny A. Gorman*, under the command of Captain Mahoney.[75] The loaded lifeboats were rowed to the two vessels and the passengers were taken aboard. The lifeboat crews then returned to the *Oregon* for the remaining passengers. This process continued until every last

---

[75] The *Fanny A. Gorman* (spelled as it originally was reported by the *New York Times*. It is spelled *Fannie A. Gorman* in later reports) initially hesitated in offering assistance. Captain Mahoney allegedly stated upon Captain Cottier's request for assistance that he didn't have enough provisions. Absurd as it sounded, Captain Cottier allegedly responded by stating, "I'm not asking for provisions, I'm asking for transportation." (Gentile, 177)

passenger and crewman were accounted for. The last man to leave the *Oregon*, the once "unchallenged mistress of the seas for fleetness," was Captain Cottier.

SINKING OF THE STEAMSHIP **OREGON** OF THE CUNARD LINE

A Currier and Ives illustration "Sinking of the Steamship *Oregon*."
Courtesy of Mark Silverstein.

At ten-thirty in the morning, now six hours after the initial impact by the unknown schooner, a new vessel arrived on the scene. Captain Ringk, in command of the North German Line steamer *Fulda*, immediately provided assistance. Over the next few hours, the complement of the *Oregon* which had been taken aboard the *Phantom* and *Fanny(ie) A. Gorman* were transferred to the much larger *Fulda*. After the last of the survivors had been hoisted aboard, "the Cunard liner made her last bow." (Gentile, 178)

The passengers and crew watched from the decks of the savior vessels as the sleek Cunarder sank beneath the waves a little before one o'clock in the afternoon. She had remained afloat for eight hours, providing enough time for the entire human cargo to be saved from the frigid waters of the Atlantic. The Cunard line had not lost a single passenger or crewmen thanks to the actions of Captain Cottier, his crew and the assistance of the rescue vessels.

The *Fulda* steamed for the last leg into New York. The initial saviors, *Phantom* and *Fanny(ie) A Gorman* continued on their initially planned voyages. The only visible remains of the once proud legacy of the *Oregon* were her main, mizzen and jigger masts. The *New York Times* reporters had scooped the story and interviewed Captain Cottier in the smoking room of the *Fulda* at midnight on the day of the collision. Amongst the male passengers of the *Oregon*, he recounted the chain of events and remarked that the captain and crew of the *Fulda* had provided excellent assistance to his crew and passengers. Remarking on the losses of the day, he was happy to announce that all of his passengers, including "three dogs – a terrier, a bull, and a skye" were saved. From another part of the room however, a fellow survivor remarked that there had been something lost, "a Chicago man lost two magpies." (*NYT*, 15MAR1886)

Ultimately however, the loss of the *Oregon* was quite significant. In addition to the value of the vessel, the belongings of the crew and passengers, there was also a full cargo of mail, packages, and other assorted items. As much of the cargo was on deck ready to be dispersed upon the vessel's intended arrival in New York, much of it had floated freely to surface when the ship sank into the murky Atlantic Ocean. In the March 16, 1886 edition of the *New York Times*, it was reported that the loss of the *Oregon* represented "over three millions lost." The article explained that though "it is impossible to compute…an approximate estimate can be made of the sunken treasures." The value of the vessel was estimated at over one and a quarter million dollars, registered mail of which she was carrying almost six hundred bags at one million dollars in value, over seven hundred thousand dollars in cargo and another two hundred thousand in passenger property and crew uniforms. The registered mail was of significant concern as it carried a large "consignment of American securities" and one lot of "10,000 shares of Reading, representing a par value of $500,000."[76] The cargo, which included silks, cloths, dry goods, machinery, earthenware, liquors, books,

---

[76] The *Oregon* was carrying 598 bags of mail. These bags of mail would have included letter mail, newspaper mail, two dispatch bags, and more. (*New York Times*, 16MAR1886)

dyestuffs, hardware, jewelry, tin plate, building materials and fruit at a total estimated value of over seven hundred thousand dollars. But on the bottom the *Oregon* rested. Only the items that floated would be initially found and salvaged.

By the 16th, wreckers were already on scene attempting to determine for the Cunard Line what, if anything, including possibly the *Oregon* her self, could be salvaged.[77] As vessels continued to pick up the myriad flotsam of luggage, mail bags, deck chairs and life preservers, no evidence was found of the vessel that had struck the *Oregon* and had sent her to the bottom. Captain Merritt on behalf of the Cunard Company had sent a schooner and the steamer *Rescue* to the scene with three divers.[78] On the 19th, the divers would descend into the depths to determine the condition of the wreck, to determine the feasibility of raising her to the surface and to retrieve cargo and personal belongings.

Further investigation into the state of the *Oregon* befell some inclement weather. A gasoline lit buoy was placed at the site of the wreckage so that other vessels transiting the area would not become fouled in the remaining masts of the sunken ship. A lightship was then moored to the site in lieu of the buoy and that remained on "station until November 1, 1886." (Gentile, 187) Ultimately, the Merritt and Chapman crews broke down the masts and the last above the surface reminders, disappeared.

What did remain unresolved was the identity of the vessel that caused the *Oregon* to go to the bottom in the first place. Theories abounded at the initial collision. As this was well before the days of ship to ship and ship to shore radios, vessels that were "at sea" were unable to be reached until they reached port. Initial reports of "overdue" vessels abounded with several vessels being listed as the possible vessel in question. A listing of vessels was soon published including the *Abbot F. Lawrence*, *B.C. French*, *C.A. Briggs*, *Mabel Phillips*, *Job*

---

[77] One professional diver who dove on the wreckage on the 16th reported that he believed that "after he made a thorough personal examination of the steamer, is to the effect that she is broken in two." (*NYT*, 17MAR1886)

[78] Though not named in the *New York Times* article, the schooner that assisted the steamer *Rescue* was named the *Edwin Post*. (Gentile, 188)

Jackson, Eva L. Ferris, Taulane, Charles H. Haskell, Spartan, Maud Sherwood, Kloto, and lastly the *Charles H. Morse*, which was not posted missing until "ten days after the accident." (Gentile, 185)[79]

Diving on the site was not relegated to just salvage divers in surface supplied diving gear during the weeks following the sinking. In the late nineteen fifties through early sixties, many divers began visiting the wreck site. Members of the Oceanic Historical Research Society, including Commander Donald Ferrin, United States Navy, began researching the *Oregon* and other local wrecks in their efforts to retrieve artifacts for use in local museums.[80] By 1963, the society was focusing its research on three wrecks in local waters including the *U.S.S. San Diego*, the *Black Warrior* and the *Oregon*. During some initial dives in 1961, divers "Donald Marchese and Mr. Murray Seliger of Brooklyn got into a pantry and brought up ironstone chinaware, some of it with the Guion Line crests and other with the Cunard Line crest." (Dunn, 101) In addition to the efforts made by the Oceanographic Historical Research Society, during the 1960's other recreational divers, including Michael de Camp popularized the location. At the time, there was a "sheer abundance of artifacts which lay scattered about," including "portholes...great piles of china plates, bowls, and cups." The treasure trove was allegedly so great for divers that they were bringing up artifacts by the bagful. As with any wreck site however, those days are over. Artifacts are still recovered but just not in the abundance of the early days of the wreck's exploration.

The *Oregon* wreck remains a popular diving destination for many divers. Two divers who have made numerous dives to the site are Mark Silverstein and Capt. John Bricker. During their approximate two hundred dives to the site, the

---

[79] The *Kloto*, like the *Charles H. Morse* was never seen again, but as pointed out by Gary Gentile, "shipping circles were inclined to believe that the *Charles H. Morse* was the schooner in collision, and that the *Kloto* floundered." (Gentile, 185)

[80] Efforts to locate members of the Oceanographic Historical Research Society have been unsuccessful. The initial research and artifacts collected by members of this group would provide great insight into not only early dives on the *Oregon* but also how the wreckage has deteriorated since the pioneering days of SCUBA diving in the late 1950's-early 1960s.

men have brought to the surface many interesting artifacts from the vessel and from its cargo holds. In addition to china, glassware, sewing kits, portholes, egg cups, a smoking pipe and an inkwell, the two men have watched many others enjoy the vessel's remains. During the course of their underwater adventures, both divers have served as mates on dive boats that take other divers to the site. Over the course of their many dives, many stories can be related. One story, regarding the discovery and eventual successful recovery was a team effort separated by a tragedy on the wreck. On board the *Sea Hunter III*, diver Mark Silverstein serving as a crewman headed out to the popular dive site. It was Friday July 10, 1998 and on his first dive of the day, Mark discovered a dinner plate with the Guion crest. He had also made another exciting discovery that he would have to further explore on his second dive to the bottom later in the day. Excited at the finding of the plate, Mark began cleaning the plate with his knife to clearly show the Guion crest so that he could get a photograph of the discovery.[81] One of the divers also on board that day was Harvey Leonard, a Brooklyn, New York native and dive shop owner. According to Mark, he was "getting on in years and had multiple medical conditions which impacted his everyday life, but he was most happy when he was diving his favorite wreck," the *Oregon*.

The cleaning of the plate was going well and as the crud from the bottom began to fall away onto the deck, Mark decided to dip the plate in a bucket of water to rinse it off. Unknown to Mark, the bucket also contained someone's anticipated dinner. A lobster, which had been discovered on the wreck as well nipped at Mark's finger. The yelp from Mark that followed the bite brought Harvey to Mark's side. Harvey commented quickly "No, no, that's good. Now you'll never forget this day." To document the discovery of the plate, Mark asked Harvey to hold the plate while the two men posed for a photograph.

---

[81] Because the vessel changed ownership, the china of the *Oregon* is a mixture of both Guion and Cunard. The Cunard china is more prevalent on the site.

Harvey Leonard and Mark Silverstein.

While the *Sea Hunter III* bobbed with the motion of the Atlantic, the group of divers got ready for the second dive of the day. Mark was anxious to return to the bottom near the steering quadrant area of the site. During his first dive when he had found the Guion crested plate, he had spotted the ship's auxiliary helm stand lying upside down in the wreckage. Before returning to the bottom though he assisted the other divers into the water. Harvey Leonard excited about his second dive on the wreck as well, jumped into the water and descended to the bottom. With the divers in the water, it was now time for Mark to get ready to take his plunge to the bottom and attempt to secure and lift the auxiliary helm stand to the surface. Before he could enter the water however, a diver popped up in a "sea of bubbles some 50 feet off the boat, splayed out and motionless." Something had gone terribly wrong. Mark quickly realized it was Harvey Leonard, just fifteen minutes into his second dive. Mark jumped into the water, swam over to Harvey and began his attempts to revive him. The rest of the crew assisted Mark and the lifeless body of Harvey onto the deck of the boat and awaited the United States Coast Guard. Soon the rotor wash of the helicopter was overhead the dive boat. Harvey was airlifted from the deck of the *Sea Hunter III* and was pronounced dead at the hospital. As Mark recounts, "Harvey was right, as I will certainly never forget that day."

Upon the return of the *Sea Hunter III* to her dock in Freeport, New York, Mark informed Capt. John Bricker of the sad events of the dive trip. He also passed on the information regarding the auxiliary helm stand to his diving buddy. Mark was aware that the next day, John was heading to the site as first mate. Mark was unable to crew on the trip and figured that John should try and retrieve the artifact. According to Mark, "Capt. John made short work of rigging an airbag and sending this prize artifact to the surface." The helm stand was restored by John whose vocation is as a metal worker. Though the wooden ship's wheel had been eaten away by worms to "mere nubs of wood emanating outward from the center hub," John was able to construct a replacement ship's wheel for the artifact.

(left) Diver and Captain John Bricker with growth encrusted auxiliary helm stand. (right) The auxiliary helm stand upon restoration.

A collection of artifacts recovered from the *Oregon* by M. Silverstein.

Diver Mark Silverstein with a porthole recovered from the *Oregon*.

A Guion Plate (left) – M. Silverstein   A Cunard Plate – Tony Bliss

A wide array of artifacts recovered during numerous dives. From top left to bottom right: flask and goblet, a Guion Crest Egg Cup, Mark Silverstein displaying a recovered smoking pipe and ceramic inkwell, brass picture button, Cunard Crest saucer.

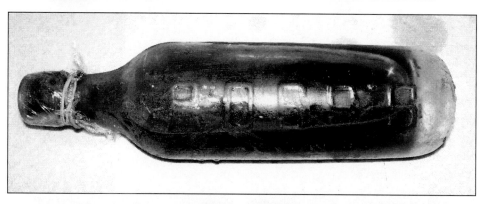

Assorted artifacts recovered during numerous dives on the *Oregon* wreck by Mark Silverstein and Capt. Bricker.
From top left to bottom right: still unidentified "face" tray or trivet, a close-up of a religious medallion, a Ross bottle, refurbished rudder indicator, and a cut glass salt dip.

The *Oregon* wreck site will continue to provide an interesting look at the era as divers continue to pull artifacts from her deteriorating hull. However, what still remains a mystery is the identity of the schooner that sent the *Oregon* to the bottom. Though still not positively identified as the vessel that struck the *Oregon* on that fateful night, many scholars and divers believe that the *Charles H. Morse* was the likely culprit. Located near the *Oregon* site, Joe Gallo, a diver from Center Moriches, Long Island states "that there is an unidentified iron hulled sailing vessel with the bow smashed in." (Field, 79) The wreckage, which has been searched for clues by other divers as well, has yet to yield a positive indicator that would link it to the *Oregon* collision or more importantly as the *Charles H. Morse*.

More dives will be required on the unidentified iron hulled vessel. Hopefully a shred of evidence will be unearthed by a diver that will finally provide the missing puzzle piece regarding the *Oregon* collision and subsequent sinking. Until that day, the final moments of the crew of the *Charles H. Morse* will remain as vividly unclear as the reason why the *Oregon*, steaming steadily towards New York, was struck a death blow by a mystery vessel. The *Oregon* ultimately whichever vessel struck her, slowly succumbed to her injuries at one hundred and thirty feet below the surface on that fateful night in March 1886, and to this day she remains.

The *John B. Manning* ashore. Courtesy of the L.I.M.M.

In the early morning hours of February 8th, 1895 the four masted schooner with a crew of eight men ran aground "between three and four hundred yards from the beach," near the Lone Hill Station. (Field, 114) Lifesavers from the Lone Hill and Blue Point United States Life-Saving Service stations responded quickly to the scene to assist. The weather conditions were terrible with high winds, near zero temperatures and ice-filled seas. With no ability to launch a surfboat due to the inclement weather a "line was shot to the stricken ship. Captain Sprague and his crew of eight men were brought ashore one by one by the breeches buoy apparatus." (Field, 114)[82]

As the Captain and crew of the Lone Hill United States Life-Saving Service station battled the storm, ice, and wind to rescue the men of the *John P.*

---

[82] The *John B. Manning's* mascot, a Newfoundland dog named Manny was also rescued from the vessel utilizing the breeches buoy. (Field, 114)

Manning, another schooner marked a northern course. She was encased in a tomb of ice, tossed in the wild and frigid sea, and she drew closer and closer to the shore line with every wave. A similar fate of grounding on the bar of Long Island's south shore was more than probable, it was planned.

The *John P. Manning* was one of many vessels that had fallen victim to the wicked cold and storm that had entombed the eastern seaboard with near zero temperatures, high winds and storm-mixed seas. "On the morning of the 7th the storm center was in the vicinity of Charleston, South Carolina, and twenty-four hours later it was off the coast of Massachusetts, with marked increase of intensity." (USLSS, 55-56)[83] "During the four days from the 6th to the 9th, inclusive, there were casualties within the scope of the Life-Saving Service to twenty-nine vessels of various descriptions, carrying crews aggregating one hundred and twenty-nine men, from none of which were any lives lost," with one vessel making the only exception.[84] Only a few hours after the *Manning* had grounded on the beach, another vessel, the schooner *Louis V. Place* found herself on the verge of disaster, yet another victim of the bitter cold and torrent weather.[85]

---

[83] According to the *Annual Report of the Operations of the United States Life-Saving Service for the Fiscal Year Ending June 30, 1895*, "The temperature in Florida on that morning (February 8) was the lowest ever recorded there by the United States Weather Bureau, while in New York City it stood at zero. Wind velocities were also very extraordinary, as high as seventy-two miles an hour having been reported at Wood's Hole, sixty-eight at Block Island, and fifty-three at Sandy Hook, and snow fell during the 7th and 8th all along the coast from North Carolina to Canada." (USLSS, 56)

[84] This might not be completely accurate. The storm wreaked havoc all along the east coast. A few days prior to the *L.V. Place* wreck, three souls were found encased in ice. At Lambert's Cove on the North side of Vineyard Haven, Massachusetts part of the schooner *T.P. Dixon*, which had left "New York Feb. 3 for Rockland," came ashore. The wreckage consisted of "only the vessel's main deck, broken off just aft the foremast, and the vessel's cabin." On top of the cabin, the "bodies of three men and a dog were found...incased in ice." How and why the *T.P. Dixon* befell such a disaster "will probably always remain a mystery." (*NYT*, 8FEB1895)

[85] By February 12th, a wrecking vessel of the "Merritt Wrecking Company" was already on the scene and was working on the recovery of the *John B. Manning*. It was refloated soon after. (*BDE*, 12FEB1895)

The *John B. Manning - Louis V. Place* in the background. Courtesy of the L.I.M.M.

The *Louis V. Place* had left the safety of Baltimore, Maryland on January 28th, 1895. She was bound for New York with a cargo of 1100 tons of coal. She had been built in 1891 and was a three masted schooner of 163 feet in length with a 36 foot beam and a draft of 14 feet. A seasoned sailor, Captain William Squires was at the helm and with him onboard were seven men. They had waited for two days in the Chesapeake awaiting favorable conditions and finally on the 28th, the order was given to get underway. But the favorable sailing conditions faltered soon after their departure and soon the *Louis V. Place* would find herself amidst a growing storm. "When they passed out of the capes at the mouth of Chesapeake Bay…the wind blew fresh west-southwest, but soon the rough seas commenced brought on by the shifting of the winds. Soon the onslaught of the weather marked a serious and severe storm. (Rattray, 145-146) The wind shifted to the north-northeast, dark clouds enveloped the sky. Captain Squires ordered "all the light canvas" furled and pressed the schooner forward north for the "rest of the day and that night under her lower sails only." (Rattray, 146)

"When Hampton Roads [VA] was reached she laid to for two days" the storm showed no sign of letting go of her death grip on the schooner and her complement of eight men. (*NYT*, 11FEB1895) The *Louis V. Place* pushed through the waves and rough seas, but the gale, a mixture of high winds, cold and bitter spray and snow began to overwhelm the coal laden schooner. Soon the *Louis V. Place* found herself in the middle of a mixed sea with a constant unwanted cargo of ice on her decks, rigging, and sails. "By seven a.m. On the 8th, the schooner was little "more than a drifting iceberg." (Rattray, 146)

The *Louis V. Place* reached the Long Island shores with "several feet of water in the hold, and though the steam pumps were kept going, she was sinking rapidly." (*NYT*, 11FEB1895) On the 7th, Captain Squires took a sounding as he had no way to tell his location due to the storm and blinding snow fall. He quickly learned that he was in eight fathoms of water. He decided to attempt to anchor the vessel and ride out the storm, but as the crew attempted to break loose the anchors, they found their efforts thwarted by thick ice.

With anchoring not a possible option, Captain Squires decided to call his crew aft to explain the situation. "Boys, I guess we have got to go ashore and trust in a kind of Providence to save our lives," he stated plainly. Based on his years at sea and the sounding he felt that the best option was to let the *Louis V. Place* run aground. (*NYT*, 11FEB1895) "Eat all you can, drink what brandy you think you need, and when we strike take to the rigging," he stated. (*NYT*, 11FEB1895) The men heeded his advice and as the gale and angry seas hurled the stricken and sinking schooner through the snow-strewn seas, the men prepared for their last respite in the icy rigging.

What took place on the outer bar after those final moments on the *Louis V. Places'* aft deck can only be imagined in awe. It is the type of situation that has befallen mariners since the first vessel sank far from shore. The separation between man and nature eclipsed only by wooden timbers was removed pitting man versus nature in a fight that seems one-sided and uneven. It is difficult to imagine the final moments on the aft deck, the eight sailors knowing that their only option to survive the weather and situation was to intentionally wreck the only thing that kept them from sinking below the cold grey sea. It surely must have been a moment of intense fear interrupted only by the biting cold of the storm.

Only two men would survive the harrowing event. One crewman, Soren J. Nelson, who survived the grounding perished as a result of his injuries a few weeks later. The remaining survivor was Claus Stuvens and the following quoted sections are his exact words provided in a sworn statement provided to a reporter for an article that was published in the *Brooklyn Daily Eagle* newspaper published on February 17, 1895. The statements describe in graphic detail the final moments before the schooner slammed her keel into the bottom of the bar and the entire course of events from the survivor's recollection.

91

Claus Stuvens in oilskins. Courtesy of the L.I.M.M.

After the men had dressed in their warmest clothing and had taken a bit of the brandy, Captain Squires ordered the men "to cut the halyards to bring down the sails. The order was obeyed, but these were frozen stiff and would not come down. It was but a few minutes after that when the schooner struck the beach on the crest of a big wave. We knew that was her deathblow. She bumped twice or three times, edging a little further in shore each time and finally settled with a slight list to port nearly broadside to shore and with the bow pointing up to westward." (*BDE*, 17FEB1895) The *Louis V. Place* was in the worst possible situation. With her largest surface area exposed to the crashing surf, the strength and staunchness of the vessel was at the whim of the continuous onslaught of the powerful wave action. The *Louis V. Place* now jammed into the outer bar. The men climbed into the rigging of the masts in an attempt to survive. Claus Stuvens continued his recollection of the incident.

"Big seas broke over the deck and the schooner plunged to every wave that leaped upon her. It was death to stay on deck and be swept away, while it was a more lingering death to go a loft, but we chose the latter. Captain Squires mounted to the crosstrees on the foremast with Olsen and myself. Nelson, Morrison, Allen, Ward and Jaiby were in the rigging on the other masts. We were all warmly clad, but nothing could keep such cold out of our bones. We didn't talk. We couldn't. In the first place it would not do any good. The wind howled through the rigging and the schooner plunged up and down in the surf. We were frozen up so tightly that we could scarcely open our eyes or mouths or move our arms or legs for numbness. We had been for two hours hanging on for dear life, not knowing at what minute the masts would by the board when I saw Captain Squires, just below me, fall with a rattling sound down the shrouds and his body was swept out by a wave. Next went Morrison, the cook. They made no sound or cry, but dropped into the boiling surge like logs. I firmly believe they had been frozen to death standing in the ringing and that it was a lurch of the vessel that sent them off their center of gravity and called my attention to them. All that Friday the men who remained stamped their feet on the crosstrees and moved about as well as we could and threshed our hands and arms around our bodies. The life lines fire from shore fell across the rigging but we were all too much benumbed to go down and pull them in. It grew frightfully cold again at night. It seemed beyond human endurance. Suddenly about 8 o'clock at night Engineer Charles Allen let go and went tumbling down into the sea. Soon after Jaiby, the big mate, died and went overboard. Ward, a seaman, I had lost track of, but when the sun rose Saturday morning I saw Ward hanging with his left hand to the ratlines, half way between the crosstrees and the bulwarks. He had died there alone in the night.

Nelson and I were enabled to live through that terrible night by making a shelter. We got on the mizzen crosstrees and cut the lashing of the mizzen top sail that had been furled. Into this hole we crept, and were enabled to keep out of the wind, but the cold was frightful. Poor Olsen tried to get into our shelter with us, but he was under the crosstrees and was unable to get around the mast and on to the crosstrees. We tried our best to save him, but we could not get to him and he could not get to us. He was stiff from cold and so were we.

About 2 o'clock Saturday morning Olsen died, sitting where he had been for hour after hour, still apparently trying to get around the mast to find a haven from the gale. Nelson and I kept life in our bodies and our blood moving a little, by beating our limbs and stamping our feet. Several lines were fired across the vessel at low tide. Nelson was too stiff to move, so I climbed down to the deck and managed to get a hold of one of them, but I could not haul it in because I was benumbed and could not handle the line. Ice formed on the line faster than I could haul I and it go so heavy I had to drop it. Then I climbed back to our perch and beat Nelson and myself some more and waited for the weather to moderate. We had not had anything to eat since the morning of Friday, and it was now Saturday night and growing colder. It was as much hunger and thirst as it was the cold that weakened us. In fact, if I had had a good meal of pork and beans and coffee I might have endured the strain longer than I did, as the fiercest part of the blizzard was over. But without food I couldn't have stood it much longer. It was about midnight, Saturday night, when I could see by the light of a fire built on shore, the men coming out to us with a life boat. We were both badly frozen. Nelson the worse, and it was with the greatest difficulty that we contrived to get down to the half submerged deck. We tumbled, any fashion, into the life boat, and in a few minutes were on shore. Everything possible to be done was done for us. It required hours of rubbing to bring back the circulation."

As Captain Squires and his men clung to the icy rigging breathing their last frozen breaths before tumbling into the tumultuous torrent of the sea, the men of the United States Lifesaving Service from the Lone Hill, Blue Point and Point of Woods stations fought in vain to assist the stranded mariners. The intrepid rescuers, some having been entrenched in a successful rescue attempt only hours earlier at the scene of the grounding of the schooner *John B. Manning*, tried in vain to reach the men. As their efforts continued to be thwarted by the below zero temperatures, high winds and ice filled oceans, they watched through the snow as the crew of the *Louis V. Place* slowly fell one by one from their frozen rigging refuge to the icy waters of death.[86] The bodies now nothing more than human icicles clinging to the crosstrees were tortured by the frigid tentacles of the waves spraying and lapping at them until their bodies finally gave way. The frozen bodies, the breath of life snuffed from their lungs, fell into the abysmal abyss.

Captain James Baker of the Lone Hill Station recounted the frustrated efforts of his the lifesavers in the same *Brooklyn Daily Eagle* article published on February 17, 1895.

"There was a blinding snowstorm on the morning the Place struck. I had come from the rescue of eight men, with the breeches buoy, from the schooner John B. Manning, a mile or more to east'ard, when Thomas Swanson informed me that at 8:30 o'clock, half an hour before I arrived, the three masted schooner had struck. We dragged our beach gear, planted the gun carriage in the sand and fired a line over the vessel that was pitching in the surf that was piled high with running ice. No boat could have lived an instant in those waters. The crew were all in the mizzen rigging o the vessel and they paid not the slightest attention to the lines. If there were any cries back at forth, as has been reported by some, I am sure I would have heard it. The fact is the crew were stupefied with cold and fright. That day, Friday, five lines were fired across the schooner, but without any result whatsoever. The men seemed chained in the rigging. A cry of horror went up on shore as Captain Squires fell and went overboard. We watched with agony the other men die and wondered if we would be able to rescue even one of them. It was impossible to launch the boat; the slush ice was 2 feet thick along the shore.

I should have said that when the schooner struck the beach, in our absence while working at the John B. Manning, our cook, John Ketcham telephoned west to Captain Miller of the Point o'Woods station, five miles distance to send men and gear, telling him the situation here. Captain Miller sent quickly in response the gear with Robert Albin, Sidney Welsh and John Smith. The mend had to drag the apparatus through the snow and across the wind swept beach hills. I sent men to the west to meet and help them. Blue Point station, five miles eastward, was telephone to, and those who

---

[86] Witnesses "reported seeing twenty-foot breakers" therefore the launching of a surfboat would have been impossible as well as foolhardy, for the rugged rescuers of the U.S.L.S.S. (Field, 117)

responded were Captain Frederick Rorke, George E Goddard, Peter Payne, Morris Baker and Edward Sweezy. Our own crew consisted of John Reynolds, George F. Swanbach, Frederick Sanders, Thomas Swanson, substitute, and Joseph B. Wicks, watchman. That made all together sixteen men. I noticed when I first ran down to the shore and sighted the schooner that there were four men hanging in the rigging.

The surf was washing over the vessel and sending spray over their heads. Every drop that struck their clothing froze as it alighted and soon the men were incased in a sheet of ice. I was convinced that the vessel was unable to get up any farther toward shore. The four men I saw provide to be the captain, mate, cook and a seaman. We saw them drop into the sea one after another and we were powerless to help. It was an awful experience to see men dying where we could almost put our hand upon them. The hull of the schooner all this time, you should remember, was completely submerged and the gale that howled along the shore was difficult to stand up against. We continued our efforts to get a line to the vessel, in the teeth of the gale, until the crew was exhausted and their faces were partly frost bitten. When night fell over the scene we went to the station to get something to eat and some hot coffee. A big fire of logs was built on the beach and a watch was kept up all night, hoping against hope that there would be some chance of saving the men. Fire on shore helps to keep courage, too, in a man off shore in such plight.

At daybreak on Saturday we began work again with the wreck gun and landed a line across the vessel. No attempt was made to grasp it. The line was hauled in and another fired at the masthead of the mast on which the men were standing. We thought surely that would make the men start, but they paid no attention to the line. They seemed in a sort of lethargy. At 2 o'clock the tide had run out so that some part of the submerged hull was visible. Then a whip line was fired across the deck and we saw Stevens [sp] slowly descend to the deck. We were on tip toe with anticipation, but after Stevens had pulled in a few fathoms he let go. We made signals to him to go back up the rigging, get his mate and bring him back to the deck. Then we saw that the other man, Nelson, couldn't be of any use in pulling. Puzzling over what to try next we thought of trying the breeches buoy and made signals, but the men paid no attention.

The tide rose again and we feared he would be washed off and made signals to him to go a lot to his topsail shelter. Late in the afternoon the surf boat was run down through the wash and slush to the breakers and Captain Rorke, Reynolds, Ketcham, Swanbach, Sanders, Swanson and myself tried to get it through the rolling breakers. After the boat had been upset several times we gave up the attempt. It was sundown and the fire on the beach was lighted again. It was low tide at 11:30 and we made another and this time a successful attempt to ride through the breakers. When we got to the side of the schooner we yelled and shrieked, 'Come down; come down.' The sea was running across the vessel and the deck was filling every minute. It was a question of seconds whether the men would be saved, after all. We sent two men up and they took the men along the icy decks from the ratlin[sp] shrouds. We got them ashore in a few minutes, cut their boots off – which, by the way, have been grabbed and cut into bits by citizens as souvenirs – and got something warm into them. They were hustled into dry clothing and made as comfortable as possible. Nelson's hands and feet were very badly frostbitten. Stevens' hands and ears suffered most from frost. The whole night was spent between Saturday and Sunday first applying snow to Nelson's hands and feet to take the frost out and afterward putting the men to bed and keeping Nelson awake. We feared if he went to sleep he would never awaken again. We rubbed him, encouraged him and talked to him. He was not allowed to sleep, only in little cat naps, until Sunday night. Both the men are now in the Marine hospital, Staten Island and both of Nelson's feet will probably have to be amputated. Nelson was taken on a stretcher.

The sea was smoother on Sunday that it had been, and we launched a surf boat to go and cut down the two men in the rigging. One was Ward, who had hung by one hand, frozen stiff as a statue, from the ratlines. His death grip by one hand had held him all through the storm. The feet were loosened from the ratlines and they dashed back and forth and rattled against the shrouds with every lurch of the vessel. We could not release the clutch of the hand and hat to cut the ratline to get the body down.

Capt. James Baker, U.S.L.S.S. Courtesy of the L.I.M.M.

It was another task to get down the body of Olsen. It was perched below the crosstrees, with one arm around the mast, while the other hand was hanging down. One boot was on the puttock shroud and the other on the iron bar under the crosstrees. It took a long time to disengage the arm from the mast. It was as rigid as iron and remained so until taken to the undertaker's in Patchogue."

As the *Louis V. Place* remained on the bar and as the weather finally abated, Mr. C.B. Parsons of B.T. Petty & Company of 72 South Street, New York arrived in Patchogue.[87] On the 12th of February he viewed the wreck. In a report published in the *New York Times*, he stated that the *Louis V. Place* was "valued at $30,000, with little insurance. The cargo, which was valued at $3,000, was insured." (*NYT*, 12FEB1895) As the wreck was surveyed, the two survivors were transported to a hospital for further treatment. Onlookers traveled from far

---

[87] C.B. Parsons, according to a *Brooklyn Daily Eagle* article published on Feb. 12, 1895, traveled to the "wreck with the brother of the lost commander of the Place." (*BDE*, 12FEB1895)

and wide to view the two ships wrecked on the shore. The search for the remaining crewmen continued.[88]

The ice-encrusted *Louis V. Place*. Courtesy of the L.I.M.M.

---

[88] The *New York Times* article published on Feb. 12, 1895 stated that "Capt. Squires's[sp] body had washed ashore at Southampton. An unknown body was ashore at Forges River, opposite Moriches, this afternoon [Feb. 11, 1895]." Later reports would indicate that the Captain's body had not been found and the report was erroneous. (*NYT*, 12FEB1895)

On the 11th, the body of one of the sailors washed ashore at Forge River, opposite of Moriches. Undertaker Ruland traveled twenty miles to retrieve the body. A determination of the identity was quickly made once letters and other items were found on his person. "On the body were found letters and papers which indicated that the man was Jaiby, the mate of the schooner *Louis V. Place*." (*BDE*, 12FEB1895)[89] Mate Thomas Jaiby and his two shipmates who had been retrieved from the *Louis V. Place*, seaman Fritz Oscar Ward and engineer August Olsen, were prepared for burial. As the wooden box containing his body was being taken out for the funeral procession, a "young woman dressed in deep mourning appeared and asked to see the body of the mate, who she said was her father." (*BDE*, 12FEB1895) The undertaker stopped the procession and ordered the box containing Thomas Jaiby opened so that the bereaved daughter could view her father. Though the "girl seemed much affected and cried bitterly…when asked to sign papers releasing all claim to the body the woman exclaimed: 'Why, that is not his name' meaning the name Jaiby which appeared on the blank. Becoming excited she again burst into tears and exclaimed as she saw a crowd of bystanders outside the door: 'What are those people doing here?" (*BDE*, 15FEB1895) Believing that something was afoot, the undertaker ordered the woman out of the shop. As she was leaving, Policeman Davis identified the woman as a "Miss Kirby, who had been arrested some time ago in Patchogue for keeping a disorderly house," and that her claim was completely false. (*BDE*, 15FEB1895)[90] The three men were buried on a plot at the Lakeview Cemetery which had been "furnished by Mrs. Augusta Weeks." (Field, 121) On the evening of the 15th, a memorial service was held at the Methodist Church under

---

[89] "A letter addressed 'Dear Father' dated October 21, 1894, asked the addressee to write and inform his poor wife whether he was dead or alive and to send some money or the landlady would put their family out on the street. It was signed Mrs. Julia Jaiby, care of Mrs. Samuelson, 125 Dikeman street, South Brooklyn." (*BDE*, 12FEB1895)

[90] Obviously it was possible that the woman was related to Thomas Jaiby, but the undertaker was probably suspect as he had met the son of Jaiby previously. The young man who was 18 years old had informed the undertaker that he and is mother was in extreme need and that they had not "heard from Jaiby since September. The boy had just been able to scrape enough money together to pay his carfare to Patchogue, while his mother was unable to come." (*BDE*, 15FEB1895)

100

the religious leadership of Pastor Ferguson and Rev. A.E. Colton.[91] While Stuvens and Nelson were attended to for their injuries, the remainder of the men of the *Louis V. Place* remained missing.[92]

The cemetery plots purchased by Mrs. Weeks. Courtesy of the L.I.M.M.

On February 23, 1895, a body came ashore at Shinnecock. The body was found by members of the Life-Saving Service and an inspection of body and person revealed by "his name in ink tattooed on the arm. His gold watch and papers were found in his pockets.[93] The body showed no signs of decomposition, as it was partially encased in ice, which had to be cut away." (*BDE,*

---

[91] Though many prayed for the lost souls during the service, morbid curiosity also ran rampant throughout the rescue and recovery operations. When the two crewmen were cut from the rigging of the masts they were brought ashore for proper burial. Throngs of onlookers and curiosity seekers (rubber-neckers) lined the beach in the severe cold to watch the tragedy unfold. A reporter for the *Brooklyn Daily Eagle* told of two young female curiosity seekers. "When the lifeboat with the dead bodies returned from the wreck the crowd rushed toward the surf and carried the boat to the upper beach. At the ghastly sight of the bodies many were overcome, but the girls stood without wincing." (*BDE*, 11FEB1895)

[92] "On February 19, 1895 the managing owner [C.B. Parsons] of the *Louis V. Place* wrote to the Ruland funeral home of Patchogue thanking them for taking care of the burials of the crew." (Field, 121)

[93] According to Mr. Field, H.B. Squires was quoted as follows, "I have the gold watch that was on my father when he was washed ashore two weeks after the disaster, some 32 miles eastward and opposite his birthplace Good Ground (Hampton Bays). It was presented to him by another ship's owner for his good seamanship and great ability in sailing their three masted schooner *John R. Bergen* into Nassau, British West Indies." (Field, 121)

23FEB1895)[94] Captain Squires, the first man of the *Louis V. Place* to fall from the frozen rigging, had finally been found.[95] Captain Squires was buried in a family plot once an inquest had been completed.[96] Four days later, another body washed ashore.

"About a quarter of a mile west of the Moriches Life-Saving station," a body was found by Frederick Tuttle of the Shinnecock Life-Saving station. (*BDE*, 27FEB1895) Though not immediately identified, by March 1, it had been determined to be the body of Charles Allen. He was buried with his shipmates at the plot donated by Mrs. Weeks. Only one member of the crew remained missing. The cook, Charles Morrison was committed to the deep during the tragedy and his body was never recovered.

Ten days after Charles Allen, the engineer, was buried, another shipmate was also reported having passed. Soren J. Nelson, who had been rescued from the rigging of the *Louis V. Place* due to the heroic efforts of Claus Stuvens and the men from the Life-Saving Service, succumbed to his injuries.[97] He was lavished with many posthumous honors and was buried in the Lutheran cemetery with a large Norwegian flag pinned to the coffin during the funeral procession. (*BDE*,

---

[94] The identification of the body by his tattoo illustrates a longstanding practice by many mariners. Sailors for many years had "marked" themselves so that if they were lost at sea and later recovered, they could be identified. In addition, others utilized religious symbols as tattoos so that they would be properly buried, etc.

[95] Capt. W. H. Squires mailed a letter to his brother Theron Squires of Bridgehampton, New York, prior to his departure aboard the *L.V. Place* from Maryland. The letter read:
Baltimore, January 23. Dear Brother, I intended to have written you again before I left New Haven, but omitted it, but will say that I left there Thursday and go to New York Friday, left there Saturday and arrived Tuesday. We are loading coal for New York and expect to leave to-morrow. I was disappointed in not getting a Cuban business. There did not seem to be anything worth taking, but I hope to get something next time. I don't like coasting in winter. I only got three hours' rest from New York here. It is too hard work. I will write you in New York. Love to all, Yours, etc. W.H. Squires. The letter was delivered after Captain Squires had perished in the *L.V. Place* tragedy. (*BDE*, 12MAR1895)

[96] "Most accounts have Captain Squires buried in a family plot in the cemetery on Main Street in Southhold, L.I." However, in a *Long Island Forum* article written by Harry B. Squires, the son of Captain Squires, he states that his father is buried in the family plot in Hampton Bays." A memorial was erected at that site in 1939-1940. (Field, 121)

[97] According to Van R. Field, Nelson perished on March 2, 1895 of tetanus. (Field, 121)

11MAR1895)   In the end, only one member of the *Louis V. Place* lived to recount the tale of survival in the face of disaster – Claus Stuvens.

Stuvens, as it was later reported was no stranger to the perils of life at sea. In an article titled *A Hero of Five Wrecks* published on March 24, 1895 in the *Brooklyn Daily Eagle*, his harrowing survival at the mercy of the sea was explained. In addition to explaining his previous close calls and shipwrecks, the article reported that the lone survivor was "peddling pictures along the south side of Long Island," and that he was attempting to raise money "to get him back to Germany," where his mother lived. (*BDE*, 24MAR1895)[98] The ultimate fate of Stuvens remains a mystery as many alternate versions of events were recorded. "Harry B. Squires says that he went back to sea and later died in Providence, Rhode Island, circa 1900-1902." (Field, 122)[99] Another version states that Stuvens "stayed about Patchogue for a while making a meager living selling a photograph of him as he was supposed to look, coming from the wreck.[100] The strain of what he had been through evidently was too much for him and he ended up in an insane asylum (Central Islip) where he died. His body was later buried with his shipmates in the Lakeview Cemetery in Patchogue." (Field, 122)

---

[98] Claus Stuvens, who was "about 30 years of age" had survived five shipwrecks during his fifteen+ years at sea. In 1880 "he was wrecked in the North sea" when his ship the *Charlotta* was "struck by a snowstorm…off the coast of Heligoland[sp]." Due to his extremities being frozen he was "unable to work for three months." In 1885, he was shipwrecked on the "the coast of Jonilaw, Mexico," Several of his shipmates perished while they awaited rescue. He then shipped out on a "Merritt Wrecking Co." wrecking vessel and was once again shipwrecked off of Long Branch, New Jersey. Four years later, while working as s fisherman off the coast of Yarmouth, Nova Scotia, "the fishing smack sailed into a hurricane." For two days and a night, the shipwrecked men "lived on salt fish and freshwater" before they were picked up by a passing steamer. His storied years at sea were recounted in the *Brooklyn Daily Eagle* article. A previous article published by the same paper on February 12, 1895 had erroneously reported that Stuvens had survived eight shipwrecks.

[99] Harry B. Squires would go on to collect many artifacts and information regarding the wreck which claimed his father's life, as well as many other maritime shipwrecks. The cover image for many books regarding various New York shipwrecks and maritime disasters, including two books by Van R. Field and Jeanette Rattray's *Ship Ashore*, all utilize an image from the Harry B. Squires collection - the *Circassian*.

[100] "Claus Stuvens, the lone survivor of the *L.V. Place*" was photographed "wearing the oilskins bought for him by Martin Anderson who hired him to pedal" the photographs door to door. An original photograph is part of the Long Island Maritime Museum Collection. (Field, 115) Various images of the wreck were taken by Anderson and many copies of the vessel covered in ice contain a reference to Anderson as the photographer.

While Stuvens peddled his photograph door to door, the *Louis V. Place* continued to succumb to the elements. "The ship completely broke up within a few weeks. One of the masts was purchased from the owners by the village of Patchogue, and set up in the middle of the village as a flagpole." (Field, 120) The cargo of coal eventually washed its way ashore and "residents of the south shore procured all the soft coal they wanted by simply picking it up on the beach and transporting it home across the frozen bay. Most of it was sold." (Field, 120)

The *Louis V. Place* on the bar. Courtesy of the L.I.M.M.

The history of the *Louis V. Place* painfully illustrates the amazing fortitude of the human body and spirit. Both the men strung up in the rigging of the wrecked schooner and the rescuers of the United States Life-Saving Service pitted themselves against the very worst conditions imaginable in an effort to survive and to save.[101] The tireless efforts of the U.S.L.S.S., which has been

---

[101] Many members of the Lifesavers suffered from frostbite as a result of their efforts. One perished from his injuries. "Keeper Sim Baker never left his vigil at the water's edge. He had frozen hands and feet. He contracted double pneumonia from which he did not recover." (Field, 121)

recounted time and time again, as well as the physical and mental strength of the *Louis V. Place*'s crew, will remain as stark examples of man versus nature.[102]

---

[102] The list of the Captain and crew of the *Louis V. Place* varies depending on the source utilized. The following is a complete list compiled with variations from various sources. The name, position and age (if known) is included: Captain William H. Squires, skipper, age 58-59; Claus Stuvens (William Stevens, Claus Stevens), seaman, age 30; Soren J. Nelson (Nielson); Charles Allen, engineer, age 28; August Olson, seaman, age 28; Fritz Oscar Ward (Mard), age 21; Charles Morrison, cook. (Various sources including Field, *BDE*, *NYT*, & others.)

The barge *Maryland* had finally reached the last of her usefulness. Bound from Camden, New Jersey to Newark, New Jersey, the two hundred and thirty six foot by thirty eight foot wide barge had begun to take on water. The three men on board the barge watched as Captain Robert Moon and the crew of the tugboat *Hudson* cast off the tow line. Raging seas lapped at the coke laden barge. The hole in the hull was taking on water too fast and the three men realized that their only option may be to enter the frigid waters in an attempt to survive. After the towline had been pulled onto the deck of the *Hudson*, Captain Moon turned the tugboat around and headed for the floundering barge. After some tense moments, the three men tending the barge were removed to the safety of the decks of the *Hudson*. The *Maryland* continued its plunge to the bottom taking no human toll. It was December 4, 1911. The barge *Maryland* however had been to the bottom before, except her name was the *General Slocum*. The first sinking however was associated with one of the worst maritime disasters of all time.

It was about nine twenty-five in the morning on June 14, 1904 as two New York City policemen, officers Haslinger and Lang, were walking the beat on Recreation Pier on the East River. The *General Slocum* steamboat, packed with excursionists, pulled up the gangplank and steamed away from the dock. A young girl "apparently about nineteen years old," ran down the pier and began crying. (*NYT*, 16JUN1904) The police officers walked over to the young woman and consoled her. They learned that she was upset because she had missed the group on board the steamboat. After a few tears had fallen, the policemen explained another way that the young woman could join the picnic group by taking another ferry that was docked at East Thirty-Fourth Street. The young woman walked down the pier and the last time the officer saw her she was boarding "a Belt Line car toward Thirty-Fourth Street." (*NYT*, 16JUN1904) Moments before the young woman arrived on the pier and realized she had missed the departure, another young girl, dragging her tiny brother "had reached

106

the pier just as the gangplank was about to be hauled in." As recounted by Officer Lang, "thirty seconds later and she'd have been safe." The *General Slocum* steamed from the dock bound for disaster.

The *General Slocum* taking on passengers. Courtesy of the National Archives.

Frank Perditski was a fourteen year old boy who was with his family on a day long outing along the Long Island Sound. He was one of over twelve-hundred passengers and crew onboard the *General Slocum* and he saw something that he knew the Captain should be made aware of immediately. He rushed to the pilot-house with the news to which he received the following response from Captain W.H. Van Schaick: "Shut up and mind your own business!" (Casson, 37) The young boy had been playing on the steamboat and had seen smoke. Where there is smoke there is usually fire and this was no exception. The captain's course response to the young lad's information would be one of many poor decisions. The *General Slocum* steamed full ahead along the East River of Manhattan. On deck a band played "Ein Feste Burg ist Unser Gott" or "Our God is a Mighty Fortress." The passengers, mostly women and children were moments away from the onslaught of a ravaging fire that would leave many of them burned or drowned. The *General Slocum* steamed ahead. The fire spread.

The *General Slocum* had been built in early 1891 at the Devine Burtis shipyards, along the same lines and design of her sister vessel, the *Grand Republic*.[103] Miss May Lewis, "a niece of President Lewis," of the Knickerbocker Steamboat Company of Brooklyn, christened the craft in view of members of the company, sightseers, and others. (*NYT*, 19APR1891) Up until the christening the name of the vessel was unknown to the public and the press had speculated with two possible options including the *Columbus* or *Grand Union*.

The *General Slocum* was two hundred and thirty feet in length at the keel and two hundred and fifty-five feet at the water line. Her deck was two hundred and sixty-four feet long with a twelve foot, three inch hold. The hull was divided into "three water-tight bulkheads, and three decks, capable of carrying 3,500 hundred passengers." (*NYT*, 19APR1891) The vessel was constructed of white pine with the outside planking being comprised of "oak three inches thick." (*NYT*, 19APR1891) The engines and supporting machinery, which would be installed after the *General Slocum* had been christened, were built by W.A. Fletcher & Company. The paddle wheels were thirty-six feet, six inches "outside of buckets with a nine-foot face." (*NYT*, 19APR1891) The *General Slocum*'s christening ceremony went according to plan and the vessel entered the water where she "rested very easily and evenly." (*NYT*, 19APR1891) It would be one of the last times she would do either as her career in the waters around New York would be filled with accidents, groundings, fights and the eventual fire that ended her days.

The *General Slocum* was placed into service and plied the waters, initially around Rockaway, New York. Less than four months after her launching the *General Slocum* ran into a mud bank. After being pulled off of the bank by a fleet of tugs, she had to be placed into a dry dock so that a repair could be made

---

[103] General H.W. Slocum was a Union general who served with General William Tecumseh Sherman during the American Civil War during the famous March to the Sea Campaign.

to a hole in her hull. In 1894, the *General Slocum* again ran aground, but the situation was much worse than its first grounding. The tide was ebbing and as she was heading out of the inlet at Rockaway, she struck a bar as she was "going down in the swell." (*NYT*, 30JUL1894) As a result, "several of her stanchions were broken and the lights were put out." (*NYT*, 30JUL1894) Pandemonium quickly spread throughout the vessel with passengers scrambling for life preservers and women fainting. On board "it was said there were 4,700 passengers." (*NYT*, 30JUL1894) Less than fifteen days later on August 15, 1894, the *General Slocum* once again grounded. "When off the inlet, the storm struck the steamer with full force, and the wind drove her rapidly leeward, and before she could be gotten under control again she was hard aground," on the same bar that she had to be pulled off of two weeks earlier. (*NYT*, 16AUG1894) The passengers, which numbered only six hundred and thirty were transferred to a passing steamer named the *Angler* and returned safely to the pier at Fulton Ferry in Brooklyn.[104] The *General Slocum* remained on the bar for the evening and was pulled free by the efforts of the *Frederick Vosbert, Commander, Wallace B. Flint* and *Wise*. (*NYT*, 17AUG1894) Once under her own power again, the *General Slocum* steamed for her berth at the foot of West Twenty-Second Street where she was greeted by a *New York Times* reporter. The reporter asked Captain W.H. Van Schaick a few questions. As to the damage incurred in the accident the Captain replied that she was fit and ready for sea and that the vessel would return to her normal trips on the 17th of August. After a few statements regarding how cool and collected his crew reacted during the incident, he stated that the *General Slocum* was "the finest wooden steamer afloat."

Less than two weeks after she had grounded, while attempting to leave for her regularly scheduled excursion to Rockaway Beach, she collided with the *R.T. Sayre* tugboat. The collision occurred as the *General Slocum* was maneuvering. According to Captain Van Schaick the collision was due to the

---

[104] Out of the 630 passengers on board, twenty-five chose to remain on board the *General Slocum* until she was freed from the bar on the 16th of August. (*NYT*, 17AUG1894)

negligence of the tugboat skipper, Captain J. Slattery. The *General Slocum*, with a full crew, three hundred and fifty passengers and a band onboard, lost its steering capability as her rudder was severely damaged. Two tugboats, the *Wallace B. Flint* and *Jack Jewett* immediately came to the aid of the *General Slocum* so that they could return to Jewell's Wharf and disembark the passengers. (*NYT*, 2SEP1894) The *R.T. Sayre* took the brunt of the damage but was able to be towed to a dry dock for repairs. The *General Slocum*, having removed her passengers was then towed to a dry dock where she would have repairs made so that she could return to her normal service. The bad luck of the *General Slocum* would wane for a few years, but it would return with a vengeance.

In July of 1898 the *General Slocum* collided with the steam lighter *Amelia* off of the Battery. "The two vessels locked, and were being carried on the Battery rocks," when tugs came to and rendered assistance. (*NYT*, 16JUN1904) After being repaired, the *General Slocum* again made headlines on August 17, 1901 when while on its passage to Rockaway had to handle a riotous bunch of passengers. Some of the excursionists, which included eight hundred members of the Dougherty & Wadsworth Iron Workers Association from Paterson, New Jersey had become thoroughly intoxicated. A fight had broken out on the lower deck and as the vessel steamed through the Narrows, some of the "drunken men carried it to the upper deck, where the women and children were, and began throwing glasses and bottles about with reckless aim." Captain Van Schaick mustered the crew of the *General Slocum* and charged the rioters. A melee ensued as "beer glasses, camp stools and everything else handy were used as missiles." (*NYT*, 18AUG1901) The riotous bunch was subdued and the Captain ordered seven of the rioters be "bound with ropes and shackles and placed in the hold." Fifteen passengers, including women and children were provided medical assistance and the rioters were turned over to harbor police.[105]

---

[105] The rioters were fined $5.00 each for their alleged actions on board the steamer. (*NYT*, 18AUG1901)

The last time the *General Slocum* met with a near disaster was in June of 1902, just two years before the final disaster. On June 15th, the *General Slocum* was on her last trip to Rockaway when a sloop began closing in on the vessel. "There was a hurried clanging of bells in our engine room, and the boat took a sharp steer to starboard, just clearing the sloop by a close shave," but the *General Slocum* slammed straight onto a sand bar. (*NYT*, 16JUN1902)[106] On board, the four to five hundred passengers were eventually transferred to the *George H. Mott*, skippered by Captain Walter Frost. No one was injured and the *General Slocum* was off of the bar by the 17th. Exactly two years later Captain Van Schaick would face the last disaster behind the helm of the *General Slocum*.

Having dismissed young Frank Perditski's message of possible fire, the *General Slocum* steamed forward on its voyage of doom. Once the fire had begun to spread to more of the vessel, the befuddled crew began feeble attempts at fighting the flames. John Oakley, a deckhand on the *General Slocum* was also alerted to the fire during the initial stages. He had been busy at the bar and upon the completion of his drink, went aft where he quickly located the fire. "I encountered a heavy smoke such as comes from burning hay…I thought I could put out the fire with little difficulty," he later stated. (Weber, 29) Oakley grabbed a bag and attempted to put of the fire. The bag, upon his setting it upon the flames burst. Oakley notified another member of the crew. Captain Schaick was again notified of the fire. Instead of heading towards shore, he pushed forward.

The crew continued haphazard attempts at fighting the now growing fire. "At last a line was fastened to the standpipe and the water turned on. The flimsy hose promptly burst in three places, and tore itself loose from the standpipe." (Casson, 42) No other attempts, according to survivors were made to fight the fire. The majority of the crew, realizing that their efforts were futile, coupled

---

[106] The June 16, 1902 *New York Times* article includes statements from Capt. W.H. Van Schenck. The erroneous spelling of the name Schaick.

with their own pursuit of survival, left the passengers to fend for their lives.[107]

Fire quickly spread to more and more of the vessel. Small children were thrown from the decks of the burning steamer into the water by their mothers in an attempt to save them from the flames.[108] The mothers then leapt after them in vain attempts of survival. As panic ensued, passengers began grabbing life preservers. Women tore the life belts from one another, their rotten construction strewing cork dust and shredded cloth to the decks. Meanwhile Captain Van Schaick steamed forward. Fixed on getting the vessel to North Brother Island, he ignored vessels who offered assistance and to other areas where he could have grounded the *General Slocum*. As he pushed on towards his final destination, the wind fanned the spreading flames. By the time he was able to beach the *General Slocum* on North Brother Island the *General Slocum* was "a roaring furnace, with hundreds of frantic women and children clinging, like swarming bees, to every uncharred refuge." (Casson, 44) In her two mile wake, bodies thrashed and eventually sank beneath the surface.

Tugboat captains underway and aware of the vessel's distress charged at full power to aid the passengers. One tug boat, the *Wade*, owned and engineered by Jim Wade was skippered by Captain Robert Fitzgerald. The Captain slammed his "boat straight against the burning steamer," and was able to help over one hundred and fifty passengers from the inferno. (Casson, 46) In addition to tug boat captains, other watermen, nurses, doctors, policemen and others which were going about their daily lives were soon thrust into action. Risking their lives, the men and women waded out into the water to pull the drowning victims to safety, launched small boats and provided assistance. One of the original police officers,

---

[107] Purser Michael Graham jumped from the decks of the *General Slocum* with twenty six pounds of money which he had stuffed into his pants. The weight sank him to the bottom. (Weber, 29)

[108] Though outnumbered by women and children, there were male passengers on board the *General Slocum*. "Men struggling to save their families, cursed him. One, crazed by the death of his child, drew a revolver and fired twice at the Captain's head." (Casson, 44) I have not found any other reference to this alleged incident.

after having saved eleven persons, perished on his twelfth attempt at saving a passenger.

The terrible images that were burned upon the survivors and rescuers would be haunting. Captain Fitzgerald "saw a boy climb out on the rail in the rear of the *Slocum*. His clothing was on fire, and in some unaccountable way he remained upright, a living pillar of flame. [I] saw him roasted almost to a crisp when the charred remains toppled over into the river." (*NYT*, 16JUN1904) The image was just one of the many images of terrible suffering, tragedy and loss. More would follow as bodies continued to be found inside the hull, in the water and on shore.

The *General Slocum*, engulfed in flames, struck the rocks at North Brother Island. As she hit the bottom, "the supports of the hurricane deck burned away, and with a crash, the upper works came down." (*NYT*, 16JUN1904) Hundreds of the passengers dropped into the internal inferno of the vessel. Mothers on the remaining portions of the lower decks "waited until the flames were up on them, until they felt their flesh blister, before they took the alternative to of the river." (*NYT*, 16JUN1904) The *General Slocum* remained on North Brother Island for only ten minutes. It began to drift further and finally landed a mile away on Hunt's Beach. Once she landed, the *General Slocum* had burned to the water's edge, all of her upper decks, with hundreds of charred remains, having dropped into the steaming skeletal remains of the vessel. Burned and drowned victims were pulled from the water and placed on shore. Rescuers recounted how the oars of their small boats struck the dead as they attempted to get closer to the still smoldering vessel to look for any survivors. Bodies floated on the surface and just below. Few life preservers were found on any of the dead. Most life preservers were found on the bodies which were located or retrieved from the bottom. According to several reports of the incident, a layer of cork dust surrounded the wreck and the dead.

By one o'clock in the morning, 486 bodies had been recovered. An hour and a half later the number of recovered bodies had reached 606. Divers under the employ of the Merritt Wrecking Company were soon on the wreck and immediately began diving into the still smoldering vessel in an attempt to recover the remains of the passengers. Eventually twelve bodies were taken out of the hold of the vessel. Three divers worked around the clock to assist in the recovery process. Meanwhile, police officers using boat hooks pulled up "two and three bodies at a time," in the waters around the wreck. (*NYT*, 16JUN1904) The scene was nothing less than horrific. A happy excursion planned by the St. Mark's Church group had ended in a terrible disaster. An entire neighborhood, Little Germany, would never be the same again as entire families in many instances, were completely lost in the tragedy.

Amazingly Captain Van Schaick had survived the terrible ordeal. His actions at the helm to push the vessel forward at full steam to North Brother Island were immediately decried as a terrible decision by witnesses, the public and the press. As the city attempted to deal with the tragedy, many questions were being asked. Why had the captain not heeded the initial report of a possible fire? Why did he not run the vessel aground immediately? Why did he press the vessel forward thus allowing the head winds to fuel the fire? Were the life preservers and fire equipment useless? Had the crew acted heroically or cowardly?

The public and the press demanded answers not only from Captain Van Schaick, who had according to one *New York Times* reporter "told four different stories," while he was interviewed at the Alexander Avenue Station, but also the Knickerbocker Steamboat Company and the Steamboat Inspection Service. (*NYT*, 16JUN1904) As bodies continued to be pulled and dragged from the water, the dreaded process of identification continued. The death toll was astronomical. The majority of the deceased recovered in the initial efforts were placed on the shore line of North Brother Island. After they were tagged, the bodies were removed to a temporary morgue which had been established on the Charities and Corrections Pier at East 26th Street. Lined up so that relatives could walk through the macabre scene, the morgue would soon become a place of absolute despair, anger and despondency. Men, women and children viewed the bodies in an effort to identify and locate their relatives. Special attention had to be paid to those who, at the sight and awful realization that their love one or in some cases many loved ones had perished, needed medical attention themselves.[109]

The City of New York started an inquest on June 20, 1904. Headed by District Attorney Francis P. Garvin at the Second Battery Armory in the Bronx, the details of the incident were revealed as survivors and those in mourning attempted to learn more. Owner of the Knickerbocker Steamboat Company, Frank Barnaby "admitted that records of the purchase of life preservers had been falsified." (Weber, 55) Though his lawyers had recommended that Mr. Barnaby not speak to much detail, for obvious reasons, the lawyer did state that he [Mr. Barnaby] has "trusted the officers of the boat." (Weber, 55) It was quickly apparent that the president of the company had already shifted the blame and responsibility to Capt. Van Schaick. The Captain, who was still suffering from wounds including a burned and injured foot incurred during the incident, was "carried into the drill hall on a stretcher." (Weber, 55) During the questioning, the Captain stuck to his original statements. In addition to reaffirming that his actions were the best possible under the circumstances, he stated that "I figured up three or four years ago [1900] that up to that time I had carried about 30 million people, and not one of them received injury of any kind while they were in my charge." (Weber, 27) As pointed out by Harvey Weber in his article, *The Great Slocum Disaster*, the statement by the Captain, "taken under oath...was indeed an odd – and inaccurate – statement." (Weber, 27)

---

[109] The loss to families was significant. "There were four of the Strickroth family, five of the Dieckhoff family, six of the Gress family, ten of the Weis family, eleven of the Rheinfrank family, and so on." (Casson, 48)

His version of events was consistent with his previous statements which he had made at the Alexander Avenue Police Station on June 15, 1904.[110] "I started to head for one hundred and Thirty-fourth Street, but was waved off by the captain of a tugboat who shouted that the boat would set fire to the lumber yards and oil tanks there. Besides, I knew that the shore was lined with rocks and the boat would founder if I put in there. I then fixed upon North Brother Island." (*NYT*, 16JUN1904) In regards to the crew of the *General Slocum*, he recounted that they "did Herculean work with the fire apparatus. They were under the instruction and management of the mate, Edward Flanigan, and had, I believe, two streams at work. They did noble work, but it was of no use. The boat apparently was dry as tinder, and burned like a match." (*NYT*, 16JUN1904) He continued to explain that his plan was to lay the *General Slocum* sideways on the island so that passengers and crew could escape in the relatively shallow water.

Regarding his actions at his post, the Captain stated that he "stuck to my post in the pilot house until my cap caught fire. We were then about twenty-five feet off North Brother Island. She went on the beach, bow on, in about twenty-five feet of water. All the people at that time whom I saw jumped into the water and waded to the shore. I followed them." (*NYT*, 16JUN1904) The Captain must have been still in a state of shock when he gave his original statements to the police and reporters at the police station. "I do not understand how so many were lost. I thought that many waded ashore where I did. I am, of course, sorry for the accident, but I cannot see how any living man, could have done more than I did." (*NYT*, 16JUN1904)

As the inquest continued at the Armory, work continued on the remains of the *General Slocum*. After an initial disagreement between the City of New York, Merritt & Chapman Wrecking Company and the insurance company for the Knickerbocker Steamboat Company was rectified, the hull was finally raised

---

[110] As previously noted, Capt. Van Schaick's statements allegedly varied at the Alexander Avenue Police Station. The statements made by the Captain referred to in this chapter are from the *New York Times* article, *The Skipper's Story*, originally published on June 16, 1904

on June 23, 1904. Once freed from the bottom, it was "towed at once to the flats in Flushing Bay, off Riker's Island." (*NYT*, 24JUN1904) Though initial expectations believed that the hull would contain more bodies, few were found during the raising. "As the hull was raised from the mud one body floated to the surface," but a cursory inspection of the wreckage was "fruitless." (*NYT*, 24JUN1904)

While the deceased were taken to their final burial in a never ending procession of hearses and as the City of New York befell into a state of mourning, the inquest concluded with its indictments. In total, seven persons were indicted including, Capt. Van Schaick, President Frank Barnaby, Secretary James K. Atkinson, Treasurer Frank G. Dexter, Commodore Pease, and two United States Assistant Inspectors, Henry W. Lundberg and Thomas Fleming. As indicated in the initial inquest, the shift of responsibility fell upon the shoulders of Captain Van Schaick and the United States Inspectors. New York City Assistant Inspector of Steamboats, Henry Lundberg, "who had allegedly inspected the boat, took the fifth amendment," and it was not until the almost end of his testimony that he agreed "to answer a few questions." (Weber, 55) The answers to the questioned resulted in only his word that he had inspected the vessel in accordance with the law and "knew nothing of any irregularities." (Weber, 55)

Eventually, only Captain Van Schaick would be found responsible in court for his part in the disaster. On January 27, 1906, William H. Van Schaick was sentenced to ten years imprisonment for his "partial responsibility for the tragedy in failing to train his crew at fire drills and to keep his fire apparatus in shape." (*NYT*, 28JAN1906) Out of the three indictments, which included two counts of manslaughter and one for training negligence, the jury of his peers only decided to find him responsible for the one count of negligence.[111] Upon the jury's announcement, Capt. Van Schaick "turned and looked at them [mourners]

---

[111] The two counts of manslaughter were for causing the death of *General Slocum* steward Michael McGrann and an unknown woman, a.k.a. Rachel Roe. (*NYT*, 28JAN1906)

in a confused fashion, but betrayed no other sign of emotion." (*NYT*, 28JAN1906) When the sentence was handed down by United States Judge Thomas, members of the jury stated that they felt that the imprisonment for ten years was quite severe. As he sat in his detention pen, Van Schaick spoke to a *New York Times* reporter. Dejected and staring at the reporter with his one good eye he stated, "I have no fault to find with either the verdict or the sentence, but I was a victim of circumstances that I could not control and of an act of Providence. I did my best to save the passengers – nobody could have done more than I did. I am an old man now. I have followed the sea for more than fifty years."[112] (*NYT*, 28JAN1906) Van Schaick was transported to Sing Sing prison. He was sixty-eight years old. Of the other indictments, all were dismissed. Inspector Lundberg was tried three times but "each time the jury disagreed" and then he simply disappeared. (*NYT*, 28JAN1906)

Van Schaick would remain in prison for roughly two years. A petition with over one thousand signatures asked for clemency as many felt that Van Schaick was both too old and that the real blame of negligence should have been shouldered by the Knickerbocker Steamboat Company and its officers as well as the manufacturers of the vessel's safety equipment including life boats, fire hoses, and life preservers.

The disastrous fire, destruction and death did provide for a sweeping set of reforms regarding the steamboat industry. Over two hundred and sixty vessels were inspected and brought up to federal safety standards immediately following the incident. The "maritime laws were strengthened," so that incidents such as the *General Slocum* could hopefully be averted in the future. Unfortunately, over twelve hundred innocent passengers had to perish to push for reform. Wired lifeboats, iron-filled life preservers, rotten fire hoses, rusted stand-pipes, an ill-trained and mostly cowardly crew culminated in the chaotic disaster that sent to the bottom and to their death, innocent victims of greed and gross negligence.

---

[112] Capt. Van Schaick had lost the use of his left eye during the *General Slocum* incident. (*NYT*, 28JAN1906)

In the Lutheran Cemetery in Middle Village, Queens, a monument remains to present day. It is a continuous reminder to sixty one of the unidentified victims of the over twelve hundred lives lost in the *General Slocum* disaster. The monument and for that matter the entire history of the event will hopefully remain a part of the public conscious as man marches into the future. In an attempt to satisfy bottom lines and fiscal advantage, it is the public that suffers when something goes terribly amiss. Beneath the shifting waves and sands of the Atlantic Ocean, off of the New Jersey coastline, the *General Slocum* is no longer able to cause anymore death and destruction to its crew or passengers.[113] The important human obligation of man to look out for his common man, so horribly identified through the flames and later smoldering remains of the *General Slocum* in 1904, should remain as a constant reminder for future generations of how terrible and thoughtless man can be towards his fellow man, woman and child. Captain Robert P. Moon of the tugboat *Hudson* was one of the last persons to see the *Maryland* in her final moments as she sank off of the coast of New Jersey. Upon his arrival in New York he reported the loss. He stated that "ill luck had always followed the *Maryland*, and he had no regret now that the boat was lost." (*NYT*, 6DEC1911) In a way, Captain Moon was absolutely right.

---

[113] The search for the *Maryland* continued. In 1994, Wes Hall of Mid Atlantic Technology and Ralph Wilbanks of Diversified Inc. again looked for the remains off of Corson's Inlet on behalf of N.U.M.A. Following negative results, N.U.M.A. "located a document from the *Annual Report of the Chief of Engineers*, 1912, page 1620, item 7." The document explained that the Maryland had been dynamited in an effort to lower the obstruction. The demolition "began on February 12 and completed on February 18, 1912." this information was pivotal as it indicated that the *Maryland* would not be in one piece, but rather more likely be a broken up mass. In 2000, Wilbanks was provided additional information from Dolan Research, Inc. A new search then occurred in September and October of 2000. Utilizing side scan sonar and a cesium magnetometer, a target area was identified in 25 feet of water. During a survey the site exposed "large timbers, some splintered, and four fragments of coke-like material." Utilizing the magnetometer, a contour map was developed that showed that the magnetic of the test site were "217 feet by 38 feet." As indicated in the 1912 Corps of Engineers report, the *General Slocum* was to be "210 feet by 37." Further detailing the search, Wilbanks had a "gemologist and four professors from the College of Charleston Geology Department look at the best sample of the 'coke' fragments," all agreed that it was indeed coke. (Wilbanks, NUMA)

Many of the over eleven hundred officers and enlisted men of the U.S. Navy armored cruiser *U.S.S. San Diego* enjoyed the moment of frivolity and frolic of the ball that had been provided to them in their honor. Many were arm in arm with young ladies while others captured a moment of peace and quiet in an alcove or dimmed hallway to assure their loved ones that their upcoming sailing to war-torn Europe would be uneventful. Other men danced and enjoyed the female companionship under the red white and blue bunting and American flags that hung decoratively from the ceiling and walls of the hall. Later in the evening, a photographer asked all of those in attendance to stand for a photograph. The snapshot, which was later printed in the *New York Times*, showed officers in their dress white uniforms, enlisted personnel in their blue uniforms and ladies dressed to the highest of fashions holding bouquets of flowers. It would be a stark difference to the life changing event which lay ahead of them in the coming weeks. When they left the relative safety of port, anything, including the dreaded lethality of the German Imperial Navy's U-boats, was possible.

The *U.S.S. San Diego* was originally launched as the *U.S.S. California* on April 28, 1904 by the Union Iron Works in San Francisco, California. She was an armored cruiser of the *Pennsylvania* class.[114] She was five hundred, three feet, eleven inches in length with a sixty-nine foot, seven inch beam and had a total draft of twenty four feet, one inch. She displaced 13,680 tons and was heavily armed for the era with four eight inch guns, fourteen six-inch guns, eighteen three-inch guns, and two eighteen-inch guns. She was commissioned on the first

---

[114] The *U.S.S. Pennsylvania*, sister ship of the *U.S.S. California/San Diego* was involved with an interesting first for the U.S. Navy. On January 18, 1911, civilian pilot Eugene Ely landed on a 119 foot long temporary wooden platform on the stern of the *U.S.S. Pennsylvania*. After a short celebration with the Captain of the armored cruiser, Ely then successfully took off from the short platform in his eight horsepower aircraft. The *U.S.S. Pennsylvania* holds a significant place in the birth of United States Naval aviation. Ely would die later the same year and was awarded the Distinguished Flying Cross in 1933. (Van Deurs, Oct. 1956 & Sweetman. 124)

of August 1907 and was part of President Theodore Roosevelt's push for a stronger and more efficient U.S. Navy.

The *U.S.S. California's* first duty was to participate in a "naval review at San Francisco in May 1908 for the Secretary of the Navy." (DANFS) Over the course of the next few years, the *U.S.S. California* would spend the majority of her time at sea in the Pacific Ocean steaming to Hawaii, Samoa and along the west coast of the Americas.[115] In December 1911 she sailed for Honolulu and then in March of 1912, she "continued westward for duty on the Asiatic Station." (DANFS) After assisting in the flexing of United States naval might in the Far East, she was ordered to the waters off of Nicaragua and then Mexico to keep a "watchful eye" on political instabilities in those regions. (DANFS)

The *U.S.S. California* renamed *U.S.S. San Diego* – Armored cruiser number 6.

On September 1, 1914, the *U.S.S. California* was renamed the *U.S.S. San Diego*.[116] She then served as the "flagship for Commander-in-Chief, Pacific

---

[115] The United States Congress "in 1911 and 1912 ensured the fleet's unhampered access to the canal with a $5 million appropriation for fortifications," and the Navy pressed forward with "dredging the channel into Pearl Harbor, Hawaii, the fulcrum of defensive and offensive operations in the Pacific, and on 14 December 1911 the armored cruiser *California* became the first heavy warship to thread its way through the coral." (Hagan, 241)

[116] All of the *Pennsylvania*-class armored cruisers were renamed so that other vessels under construction could utilize their names. *Pennsylvania* became *Pittsburgh*, *West Virginia/Huntington*,

Fleet, intermittently until a boiler explosion put her in Mare Island Navy Yard in reduced commission through the summer of 1915."[117] (DANFS) As war began to rage in Europe, the *U.S.S. San Diego* returned to her duties as the flagship until the middle of February 1917 when she was finally placed into reserve status. Her time in reserve status would be limited and she was commissioned to full service, again as a flagship for "Commander, Patrol Force, Pacific Fleet, until 18 July," when she was ordered to report to the eastern seaboard. The *U.S.S. San Diego* was bound for Hampton Roads, Virginia.

Upon her arrival on the east coast, the *U.S.S. San Diego* joined Cruiser Division 2 and "later broke the flag of Commander, Cruiser Force, Atlantic." (DANFS) Her main duty upon her arrival at her new duty station was to escort convoys of vessels bound for Europe. While en route to New York Harbor for one of her convoy patrols, something went terribly wrong.

The official statement from the U.S. Navy Department ticked throughout newsrooms on July 19, 1918. "The Navy Department has received reports from the Third Naval District stating that the *U.S.S. San Diego* was sunk ten miles southeast of Fire Island at 11:30 o'clock this morning." Newspaper men clamored to find out more about the loss of the armored cruiser so close to America's shores. Questions abounded throughout newsrooms and on the streets. Was it at the hands of a German U-boat crew? Had a torpedo savagely ripped through the hull and sent the cruiser to the bottom of the Atlantic? Was it an accident...another boiler explosion? As details rushed across news desks, the survivors of the sinking warship slowly began to filter into New York City. Soon answers, speculation and a mixture of both began to be published for the world to read.

California/San Diego, Colorado/Pueblo, Maryland/Frederick, and *South Dakota/Huron.* In addition, their designator, ACR became CA with the same number listing.

[117] After completing a steaming trial on January 21, 1915, a boiler tube exploded. Eight seamen were initially injured and five were killed during the incident. A fireman, Darrell L. Varnardo, died on the 25th of January due to burns received during the explosion. On March 20, 1915, Secretary Daniels sent commendatory letters to two of the *U.S.S. San Diego's* crewmen who braved the explosion to fight fires, secure other boilers, etc. (*NYT*, 23JAN, 26JAN, & 21MAR1915)

Clinging to the statement, one reporter for the *New York Times* even interpreted the statement from the Navy Department. "So far as can be ascertained there appears to have been no loss of life. The cause of the sinking has not yet been determined." (*NYT*, 20JUL1918)The U.S. Navy Department and the American public would have to wait until the survivors were able to be questioned by the U.S. Navy so that some sort of determination could be ascertained.

Captain Harley H. Christy, U.S. Navy was in charge of the *U.S.S. San Diego* as she steamed from Portsmouth, New Hampshire bound to New York Harbor. The vessel had completed "seven round trips to France…and never sighted an enemy submarine." (*NYT*, 21JUL1918) Upon her arrival in New York she was to ship out on her eighth trip to Europe for convoy protection. Following the prescribed "Orders for Ships in Convoy," he was "steering a safe and proper course," as he steamed south of the Long Island coastline. She was heading on a course of 304 degrees true, zig-zagging across the blue waters of the Atlantic Ocean at fifteen knots. Lookouts manned their posts, officers on deck kept a sharp lookout ahead, abeam and astern for suspicious activity, and the crewmen went about their duties on board the ship. At 11:05 in the morning however, all hell broke loose. An explosion rocked the ship. The *U.S.S. San Diego* had received a mortal blow to her hull. The Atlantic Ocean, one second separated by the steel of the *U.S.S. San Diego's* hull, began rushing into a gaping hole below the waterline. The ship was sinking and sinking fast. She soon began to list to port.

"At about frame No. 78 on the port side and well below the waterline,' the explosion which had been caused by either a torpedo or a contact mine, was quickly sending the cruiser to the bottom. The "skin of the ship was ruptured in the vicinity of bulkhead No. 78 at the level of the port engine room, and bulkhead No. 78 was so deformed that watertight door No. 142, between the port engine room and No. 8 fire room, was opened to the egress of water." (*NYT*,

6AUG1918) With no ability to limit the influx of sea water to one or two compartments, the vessel's port engine room and adjacent compartments, including the No. 8 fire room, were soon completely filled with seawater. As the *U.S.S. San Diego* began to list, other dangers began to develop for the officers and crew. The listing to port to 9 ½ degrees provided free passage for the seawater into the gun deck and as a result, the rush of water added to the already precarious condition of the cruiser. "Water entered through the 8-inch guns port No. 10, which was justifiably open to permit using the gun." (*NYT*, 6AUG1918) This water, plus the flooded compartments from the explosion quickly pushed the *U.S.S. San Diego* to a port list of 17 ½ degrees.

Postcard view of the *U.S.S. California*. Author's collection.

Immediately following the explosion, gunners fired volleys of shot at suspicious objects in the water. Whether they had seen the culprit who had caused the explosion or were just firing at illusions, the smoke from the batteries soon clouded the decks of the vessel for the other crewmen and officers, with the exception of Captain Christy. It was clear to him that the *U.S.S. San Diego* would soon capsize. The radio room had no working equipment due to the explosion so there was no ability to send a message to other vessels or land units of the explosion. The Captain, aware of the situation had no other choice. An order soon rang out from the bridge – *"All hands abandon ship."* (*NYT*, 21JUL1918) The life boats were launched "in good order and excellent discipline prevailed," as the crew left their doomed ship. (*NYT*, 6AUG1918) "Boats were ordered lowered, and two sailboats, one dinghy, one wherry and two punts were launched, the life rafts were launched, and the lumber pile on deck was loosed and set adrift." (*NYT*, 21JUL1918) To provide additional flotsam to act as make-shift life preservers for the sailors, "fifty mess tables and a hundred kapok mattresses were thrown overboard." (*NYT*, 21JUL1918) Gunner's mates, who had remained at their posts to fire on possible targets, finally had to abandon the ship as well, as she began to capsize. "In accordance with the best traditions of the Navy...the last man to leave the ship," was Captain Christy. (*NYT*, 21JUL1918) "As the ship was turning over he made his way over the side to the armor belt, thence to the bilge keel, and jumped overboard from the docking keel, which was then eight feet from the water." (*NYT*, 21JUL1918)[118]

Upon his splash into the water, his officers and crew "cheered him and the executive officer. They cheered the ship as it went down. As the flag was raised on the launch the men in the boats sung 'The Star Spangled Banner." (*NYT*, 21JUL1918)[119] A little less than twenty minutes had elapsed since the explosion. The *U.S.S. San Diego* was no more.

In the water and in the life boats were the bulk of the vessel's crew and officers. Captain Christy, aware that he had not been able to have any radio transmission sent, ordered "Lieutenant C.J. Bright, USN...to Long Island to report the disaster," and to request the assistance of rescue vessels. (*NYT*, 20JUL1918) As the Lieutenant and the men under his charge rowed for shore, the other survivors waited. Bobbing in the Atlantic Ocean, the men and officers tried to figure out what had happened and if any men were lost or missing.

---

[118] The actions of Captain Christy were released in a statement by Rear Admiral Leigh C. Palmer who on July 21, 1918, was the acting Secretary of the Navy. (*NYT*, 21JUL1918)
[119] It was also reported that the sailors sang "My Country, tis of thee." (*NYT*, 21JUL1918)

Lieutenant Bright and his men landed their boat on the beach on Long Island, New York a few hours after the sinking.[120] According to initial reports provided by the thirty-four sailors who "landed at Point o'Woods L.I. [the loss of the *U.S.S. San Diego*] was due to a torpedo from a submarine," however as sailors who were quasi-interviewed upon their arrival in New York Harbor, they offered a different version. (*NYT*, 20JUL1918)[121] They said that "she either struck a coast-defense mine or had an internal explosion." (*NYT*, 20JUL1918) In an early *New York Times* article regarding the incident, a reporter had interviewed a naval officer on the condition of anonymity, who spoke to some of the survivors who were being held at quarantine in New York Harbor. He stated that "there was no truth in the report that the warship had been sunk by a German submarine." (*NYT*, 20JUL1918) The officer further stated that many of the first 100 survivors thought that the *U.S.S. San Diego* had been a victim of an internal explosion" of one of her boilers. (*NYT*, 20JUL1918)

Before Lieutenant Bright and his men had even reached the Point O' Woods station, rescue vessels were already on their way to help the survivors. "The sound of the explosions and of the fire which followed it however, was heard by naval aircraft in the vicinity, and one naval airman was the first to see what had happened. After catching sight of the sinking ship and seeing sailors and life raft in the water, he flew back to land," where he reported the situation. (NYT, 21JUL1918) According to a seaman interviewed after the incident, he stated that while in the water, "a hydroaeroplane flew over our heads and one of them landed near our raft. The pilot questioned us and then flew away." (*NYT*, 21JUL1918) Wireless operators quickly transmitted S.O.S. calls and soon "Naval ships from the Station at Sayville, Coast Guard cutters, and other ships," were

---

[120] In the "Sank After Explosion" article published in the *New York Times* on July 20, 1918, it was reported that "one officer and two boats' crews were landed at Life Saving Station 82 on Long Island."

[121] The first 100 or so survivors who arrived at Quarantine were not allowed to speak to anyone, however one naval officer who spoke to the men at Quarantine provided information to the *New York Times*. (*NYT*, 20JUL1918)

heading out to save the now adrift sailors of the *U.S.S. San Diego*. (NYT, 21JUL1918)

The *U.S.S. California*. Author's collection.

The first rescue vessel to arrive at the scene was the steamer *Malden*. The crew of the *Malden* was successful in picking up three hundred and seventy men from the water. Twenty minutes after the arrival of the *Malden*, a second vessel, the steamer *Bossom* arrived at the site and began loading sailors and officers aboard. The *Bossom* took on seven hundred and eight men with the third arriving steamer, *S.P. Jones* picking up the last seventy-eight men. The three vessels "searched the entire vicinity for survivors until 3 P.M.," and then steamed for New York Harbor.[122] According to Captain James Brewer, skipper of the steamer *Bossom*, the sailors were in good spirits in light of their ship sinking beneath them. He was of course frightened when while on his approach to the men when his vessel "passed a school of perhaps twenty sharks, which were feeding on the

---

[122] A fourth vessel arrived on the scene but did not take on any of the *U.S.S. San Diego's* crew. The Naval Court of Inquiry acknowledged the "courage and a splendid spirit in taking their ships into these waters, where a submarine had apparently been operating, and deserve commendation for their actions." The three vessels listed in the report and their captains were as follows: *Malden*, Capt. Brown, *Bussun*, Captain Brewer, and *E. P. Jones*, Captain Dodge. The spellings of the report and the original article of July 21, 1918 do not correspond. (*NYT*, 21JUL1918 and 6AUG1918)

body of a small whale." (*NYT*, 21JUL1918)[123] No sailors were reported of having been lost to a shark attack during the sinking of the vessel and the following rescue operations.

As survivors on board rescue vessels steamed to New York, speculation continued.[124] As expected, reports of the circumstances varied depending on who was questioned. Some sailors were adamant that they had "seen the periscope as they were launching the boats" or that it could not have been a mine because the explosion "had taken place almost amidships." (*NYT*, 20JUL1918) As naval airplanes and a dirigible flew from Long Island to the skies over the Atlantic Ocean, the men who had landed at Point O' Woods were picked up by a patrol boat and shuttled back to the New York Navy Yard. The line of rescue vessels continued to steam towards New York with their new passengers aboard. As the newspapers and public demanded more information the U.S. Navy began its investigation. Though the first group of sailors to land on Long Island had opened up and provided their versions of events to reporters and locals, the U.S. Navy quickly shut down the unofficial transmissions of information. As military aircraft, Navy destroyers, Coast Guard cutters and patrol boats launched into activity, reporters who attempted to gather information were referred to Washington for comment. Quickly the U.S. Navy issued statements regarding the incident. But to do so they too had to collect and disseminate the contradictory, confusing and often inaccurate information that was floating around in news, maritime and naval circles, much like the flotsam of the sunken *U.S.S. San Diego*.[125]

---

[123] Captain Brewer also told an interesting story that had been related to him by some of the *U.S.S. San Diego's* crew. "The men said that one of their number, a gunner, stayed until only a few feet of the hull was above water. He ran the length of that, called for a cheer for the old ship and the U.S.A. and dived overboard," prior to Captain Christy's ceremonial leaving of the ship. (*NYT*, 21JUL1918)

[124] In addition to the cause of the sinking, the other major point of speculation was the loss of life. Though some sailors stated that there must have been a "considerable loss of life," others were not sure. (*NYT*, 20JUL1918)

[125] The "Navy authorities took charge of all of the telephone and telegraph wires communicating with Fire Island and other points nearest the place where the explosions had been heard. Attempts

On July 21, 1918, Acting Secretary of the Navy, Rear Admiral Leigh C. Palmer authorized a more descriptive and narrative statement as to the events of the sinking and subsequent rescue of the *U.S.S. San Diego's* officers and crew. Palmer reported that "American naval vessels found and detonated five or six mines in that vicinity last night [July 20, 1918 – day after the sinking]" (*NYT*, 21JUL1918) In another statement released later on the 21st of July by Rear Admiral Palmer, "no wake of a torpedo was seen. The first thing Captain Christy noticed was, while standing on the wheel house eight feet above the forward bridge, he felt and heard a dull explosion." (*NYT*, 21JUL1918) Once the explosion had occurred, Captain Christy "immediately sounded submarine defense quarters and general alarm." (*NYT*, 21JUL1918) Captain Christy ordered the *U.S.S. San Diego* full speed ahead and "sent an officer to investigate the damage." (*NYT*, 21JUL1918)

Rear Admiral Palmer also was able to report what had happened in the engine room of the vessel when the explosion occurred. The starboard engine operated until "it was stopped by water rising in the engine room. Machinist's Mate Hawthorne, who was at the throttle in the port engine room, was blown four feet under the engine-room desk. He got up, closed the throttle on the engine, which had already stopped, and then escaped up the engine-room ladder." (*NYT*, 21JUL1918) As Hawthorne raced up the ladder, "Lieutenant Millen, on watch in the starboard engine-room, closed the water-tight door to the engine-room and gave the necessary instructions to the fire room to protect the boilers." (*NYT*, 21JUL1918)

Though speculation continued throughout the shipping, naval, and newspaper circles, Secretary Daniels issued a statement that "he believed a mine and not a torpedo was responsible for the sinking of the cruiser *San Diego*." (*NYT*, 21JUL1918) Daniels continued by stating that "the sinking of the vessel, aside from the loss of life, was of no significance from a military standpoint."

of civilians to use the wires were blocked, and information regarding the nature of the vessel was prevented from being disclosed by the survivors." (*NYT*, 20JUL1918)

(*NYT*, 21JUL1918) The loss of life the Secretary of the Navy was referring to was, like the cause of the explosion, still up for conjecture as well.

Because men were picked up by a variety of vessels, some landed on the beaches of Long Island, and some were missing, it was difficult for the U.S. Navy to determine who had been lost due to the explosion and subsequent sinking. As some naval officers speculated as to culprit of the naval mines off of Fire Island, the Department of the Navy was working to determine which sailors had lost their lives.

By the 23rd of July, the list of fifty-nine missing men had been lowered to eight sailors.[126] The following day, Secretary Daniels announced that the number had been lowered once again by two. The following sailors were reported as killed as a result of the explosion and sinking of the *U.S.S. San Diego*:

> Engineman Second Class Clyde Chester Blaine
> Fireman First Class Thomas Everett Davis
> Seaman Second Class Paul John Harris
> Machinist's Mate Andrew Munson
> Engineman Second Class James Francis Rochet
> Machinist's Mate Second Class Thomas O. Frazier

As the country learned of the fate of the *U.S.S. San Diego* and her crew, the U.S. Navy sent out a vessel to investigate the condition of the wreck. "On July 20 *USS Bagley*, a torpedo boat, arrived on site with a Navy diving party." (Gentile, 67) When it was determined that the *U.S.S. Bagley* was not an appropriate diving platform, a small boat from the *U.S.S. Perkins* was utilized instead. Diver William Williamson, rigged in surface supplied diving apparatus, descended on the recent wreck.

Over the course of two dives, Williams reported "the wreck to be lying in 18 fathoms (108 feet), bottom up, with the smoke pipes bent to one side."

---

[126] Several U.S. Navy officers provided the opinion that a German submarine had not laid the mine responsible for the *U.S.S. San Diego* explosion but rather that the mine had been delivered by a "neutral ship." The officers stated that "steamships had been captured off the River Mersey in England and the entrance to Kigstown Harbor, Ireland, flying Norwegian and Swedish flags with their holds ostensibly full of fish under which a number of mines were found concealed." (*NYT*, 23JUL1918)

(Gentile, 67) Williamson, who in addition to finding the "jagged hole five feet in diameter on the portside," also found "numerous holes, dents, sheared rivets: the results of a plethora of depth charges dropped on the *San Diego* in mistaken believe that she was a submarine." (Gentile, 67) Other divers soon followed Williamson's lead.

On July 27, 1918, a second group of divers arrived on over the remains. Two divers, "Joseph Rouleau and John Gardner," from the *U.S.S. Passaic* were sent over the rail to the bottom to investigate. (Gentile, 68)[127] In addition to determining that the "*San Diego* pointed approximately north; the hull was inclined about twenty degrees from vertical with the starboard side uppermost," diver Gardner also found "an unexploded depth charge lying on the hull adjacent to the boiler rooms." (Gentile, 68)[128] The vessel was eventually deemed unsalvageable but possibly a hazard to navigation, so a buoy was placed over the site. The *U.S.S. San Diego* was in approximately one hundred and ten feet of water, hull up. The superstructure was therefore not protruding at any dangerous height below the surface. The *U.S.S. San Diego* was to remain on the bottom.[129]

On August 5, 1918, readers of the *New York Times* and other newspapers learned that a German submarine had taken responsibility for the mine that had struck the *U.S.S. San Diego*. "The United States cruiser San Diego was sunk off Fire Island last month by a mine laid by the German submarine *U-56*, which captured and burned the Canadian schooner *Fornfonstein* in the Bay of Fundy," the short article reported. (*NYT*, 5AUG1918) "According to statements made by members of the crew of the U-boat to sailors from the sailing ship who were

---

[127] Several available histories of the *U.S.S. San Diego's* salvage operations include the *U.S.S. Passaic* as the *U.S.S. Passaio*. A review of the U.S. Navy's *Dictionary of American Naval Fighting Ships* lists no such vessel of that name. The *U.S.S. Passaic* YT-20 was originally laid down as the *Right Arm* in 1891, then she became the *U.S.S. Pontiac* (II), being renamed *Passaic* on April 11, 1918. She was purchased by the U.S. Navy from Merritt & Chapman Company in 1898 and after WWI she was sold to John Kantzler & Sons, Bay City, Michigan. (DANFS)

[128] Author and diver Gary Gentile explains that he believes that the 'mine reported by the Merritt and Chapman divers eventually detonated, not only peeling back hull plates, but initiating the process of decay by further loosening beams and rivets." (Gentile, 95-96)

[129] The *U.S.S. San Diego* was struck from the U.S. Navy on August 26, 1918. (Gentile, 69)

taken on board the submarine." (*NYT*, 5AUG1918) The article was accurate with one exception; there was no way that it was the *U-56*.[130] Eventually, it would be reported that the submarine that was responsible for the laying of the mines was the *U-156*.

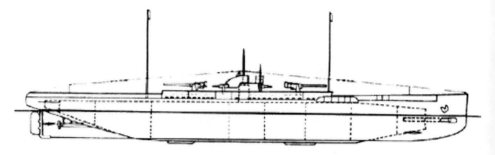

A U-151 type German U-Boat.

The *U-156* was a *U-151* type submarine. She had been built at the Atlas Werke shipyards in Bremen, Germany. Ordered on November 29, 1916, she was launched on April 17, 1917 and commissioned five days later. Her second commander, Richard Feidt would have been the officer in charge of the *U-156* when she laid the mines in the waters south of Long Island, New York. During her career she sunk forty-two ships, damaged three and sunk one warship – the *U.S.S. San Diego*. Most histories report that the *U-156* and her crew of seventy-seven men never returned to home port though her remains have never been found.[131] It is mostly accepted that she was lost in the North Sea in 1918. From

---

[130] It was impossible for the German submarine *U-56* to have been the submarine responsible for the destruction of the *U.S.S. San Diego* because the *U-56* had been reported missing prior to the events of July 19, 1918. The *U-56*, a *U-51* type submarine was commissioned on June 23, 1916 and during her brief career of only one patrol, she had been successful in sinking four ships for a total of 5,374 tons. On November 3, 1916 she put ashore the crew of the Norwegian vessel *Ivanhoe* at Lodsvik and then simply disappeared. Her eventual fate is unknown, but the fact that she did not surface for any additional supplies, rearming, etc. is worthy of note. Most likely, the article simply was missing a 1before the 56. (www.uboat.net)

[131] The WWI *U-156* should not be confused with WWII *U-156*. The second U-boat also has an interesting history. On September 12, 1942, she torpedoed the British troop ship *Laconia* (a converted Cunard White Star Liner – a former line from the same line with the same name had been sunk by a German torpedo in WWI on February 25, 1917) Werner Hartenstein, the commander of the *U-156*, after torpedoing the vessel began to assist the 2,732 passengers and crew that had been forced into the water. He requested assistance via Admiral Donitz who then sent the *U-506* and *U-507* to assist in the rescue operation. In addition to two Vichy French surface ships,

June to September 20, 1918, U.S. Navy forces working with the Royal Navy completed the first phase of a massive minefield across "240 miles of open sea from Scotland to Norway." (Sweetman, 139) The U.S. Naval operation placed a "total of 70,263 mines...including 13,562" from the British in the waters with the objective of "penning Germany's U-boats inside the North Sea." (Sweetman, 139) Five days after the first phase was completed, just two months after her successful mining and sinking of the *U.S.S. San Diego*, the *U-156* was lost. (www.uboat.net)[132]

As the report was issued in the black and white pages of newspapers across the country, the Naval Court of Inquiry was holding its proceedings in Washington, DC. The Naval Court of Inquiry had been quick to investigate the incident. "The court is of the opinion that the loss of the United States ship San Diego was due to an external explosion of a mine. That the loss of the ship, loss of life, and injury to personnel incurred was in no way due to any negligence, failure to take proper precautions, or inefficiency of the Captain, or any of the personnel of the ship. That the loss of life and injury to personnel was incurred in the line of duty and in no way to due to their own conduct." (*NYT*, 6AUG1918) The Naval Court of Inquiry continued by stating "that at the time of the disaster

---

the survivors of the sunken troop ship were being rescued when a Liberator aircraft circled above and left. Upon the Liberator's return the pilot bombed the *U-156*, ignoring "flashing signals, radio messages and a Red Cross Flag." The *U-156* was damaged and Hartenstein was forced to return those whom he had saved back into the water. Though they were eventually saved by the other vessels, the *U-156* had to limp back to port for repairs. "As a result of the Liberator's attack, Donitz ordered all U-boats henceforth not to rescue survivors." Interestingly, during the Nuremberg war trials, Admiral Donitz was charged with murder because of this order. Though he was found responsible for other war crimes he was acquitted on this charge "on the ground that the Allies themselves had waged unrestricted submarine warfare and had rarely rescued survivors." (Pitt, 155)

[132] The *U-156's* involvement in the mine laying operation and sinking of the *U.S.S. San Diego* as a result were questioned in a 1999 article by Mark Briggs. The article, "Why She Sank, was published in the *Endeavor Magazine*, "a publication of the University of North Carolina at Chapel Hill." The article was about the work of Dr. Russell Van Wyk, a professor at the institution and his research into a seventy page Soviet Report that included "German documents." According to the article, the professor found "a 1945 interrogation of German Spy Kurt Jahnke and his Johanne-Dorotheja." The report included a statement that "Jahnke had arranged for one of his agents to place explosives in the boiler room of the *U.S.S. San Diego*, which caused the sinking of the Armored Cruiser." A historian at the Naval Historical Center in Washington, DC however stated that he felt that the professor's "findings appeared extremely apocryphal" and stated that 'it's pretty generally accepted wisdom around here that it was a mine laid by *U-156* that got her." (Albert)

and thereafter, the conduct of the Captain, officers, and crew was in the highest degree commendable, and that the remarkable small loss of life was due to the high state of discipline maintained on board." The report stated that "at or about 11:03 A.M.," the explosion occurred. Lastly, the Naval Court of Inquiry stated that "no officer should be held responsible for the loss of funds or property for which he was unaccountable, and that no further proceedings should be held in the case." (*NYT*, 6AUG1918)

The *U.S.S. San Diego* deemed unsalvageable by previous dives on the wreck was once again visited by the U.S. Navy and her divers. A follow up investigation on the wreckage by the crew and divers of the *U.S.S. Resolute* on October 15, 1918, after taking another sounding, found that "the wreck had settled slightly" and therefore there was no need to take fulfill their intended orders of dynamiting the wreck. (Berg)[133] Approximately one year later on October 21, 1919, "the buoy was discontinued, and the wreck symbol on the U.S. Coast and Geodetic Survey charts was removed." (Gentile, 69)

On December 8, 1918, Secretary of the Navy Daniels, even though the war was over, "strongly urged" that the U.S. government continue its policy of the "upbuilding of the American Navy in further extension of the policy adopted in 1916." The annual report highlighted various aspects of the U.S. Navy's accomplishments and losses including the ships sunk during the Great War. "Four naval vessels were lost as a result of submarine activity – the destroyer *Jacob Jones*, the converted yacht *Alcedo*, the coast guard cutter *Tampa*, sunk

---

[133] The *U.S.S. Resolute* was actually the third of five U.S. Naval vessels that would serve under that name. The *U.S.S. Resolute* was a wooden salvage tug that had been built in 1916 as the *S.S. Sarah E. McWilliams*. The original owner of the vessel was Merritt & Chapman Co. of New York and the U.S. Navy purchased her on August 8, 1918. She was based at "Central District Salvage Station, Stapleton, Staten Island, New York…and she performed local towing duty, took part in several salvage operations, and assisted in patrolling the local anchorages into 1919." Decommissioned on May 15, 1919, the tug was sold back to the Merritt & Chapman Co. the next day. The *U.S.S. Resolute* would again serve in the Navy in early 1942 and then again returned to commercial operations until scrapped in 1955. (DANFS)

with all on board, and the cruiser *San Diego* sunk in home waters by striking an enemy mine." (*NYT*, 9DEC1918)[134]

The *U.S.S. San Diego* was of course, largely forgotten in the press until an issue of the crew's Liberty Bonds surfaced on January 14, 1919. When the ship had sunk to the bottom of the Atlantic, she took with her over $100,000 of Liberty Bonds which had been purchased by the officers and crew of the ship. The issue was that the Controller of the Congress has ruled that "there is no provision of law authorizing the issue of duplication in lieu of lost coupon bonds." (*NYT*, 14JAN1919) The officers and crew had purchased the bonds in 1917 while in San Diego and had "no opportunity after receiving their bonds to send them ashore for safekeeping. They agreed to take their bonds (of first issue) while the *San Diego* was on the Pacific Coast in the Spring of 1917," but that never happened because they had not yet received the bonds from the government. (*NYT*, 14JAN1919) "A year later, when the *San Diego* entered New York Harbor to join the convoy service, the Liberty bonds were finally delivered on board and came into the physical possession of the subscribers who had lent their money to the Government. The exacting nature of convoy service precluded the taking of the bonds ashore by the owners, and the securities could not be safely transmitted to relatives because it did not provide for the registration of packages." (*NYT*, 14JAN1919) Soon after, the *U.S.S. San Diego* was sent to the bottom. Along with the vessel went the Liberty bonds and the savings of many of the officers and crew. "Navy officials have informed the Treasury Department that the cruiser cannot possibly be raised...and that she will always stay at the

---

[134] The vessels listed as being lost by submarine activity included the *Jacob Jones*, sunk on December 6, 1917 near the Scilly Isles, the yacht *Alcedo* sunk on November 5, 1917 off the coast of France, and the U.S. Coast Guard Cutter *Tampa* sunk with all hands on September 26, 1918 in the Bristol Channel. Interestingly, Secretary Daniels also mentioned the *U.S.S. Cyclops*, deeming its disappearance "one of the unsolved mysteries of the seas." The *U.S.S. Cyclops* usually finds mention in many of the Bermuda Triangle theories and conspiracies. The remains of the *U.S.S. Cyclops*, a collier carrying a crew of 280 which left from Barbados on March 4, 1918, have not yet been found. (NYT, 9DEC1918) (Sweetman, 137, 138, 142)(Berlitz lists the *Cyclops* having lost 309 passengers & crew at the time of her disappearance. The *Cyclops* was 500 feet in length and 19,000 tons)

bottom of the sea, and no one can ever present the lost Liberty bonds to the government for redemption." (*NYT*, 14JAN1919) As pointed out by the writer of the article, "a refusal to reimburse them [the officers and crew who had purchased the bonds originally] in view of the unavoidable loss of the bonds at sea during the war, and considering the inability of the subscribers to send the securities ashore for safekeeping, would be a hardship." (*NYT*, 14JAN1919)

It would take several months for a decision to be made regarding the lost Liberty bonds. State Senator Martin Saxe assisted in the claim put forth by the officers and crew of the *U.S.S. San Diego* and on July 17, 1919, just two days shy of the first anniversary of the sinking of the vessel, the men learned that they would be able to submit their individual claims to the Treasury Department for the issuing of duplicate bonds. The Treasury Department had originally denied the application for the duplicate bonds, but a committee had sought a review of the denial. Chief Water tender James H. Poteet, a crewman on the *U.S.S. San Diego* was the test case. He explained that he had over "$350 worth of Liberty bonds in his locker when the ship went down," and that there was no way they could have survived the destruction. (*NYT*, 17JUL1919) But the Treasury Department was not swayed because the *U.S.S. San Diego* was on the bottom of the Atlantic Ocean. It was not until they were informed by various sources, including Assistant Secretary of the Navy, Franklin D. Roosevelt, that the U.S. Navy had "dropped thirty depth bombs on the wreck," after the Navy Department had decided against salvaging the vessel. (*NYT*, 17JUL1919)[135]

After the Liberty bond debacle was rectified, the wreck of the *U.S.S. San Diego* remained relatively forgotten, but not for very long to those who saw a virtual goldmine on the bottom of the Atlantic Ocean. The first company that requested salvage rights from the United States Navy was the "New York based Saliger Ship Salvage Corporation" in May of 1921. (Gentile, 70) Though the

---

[135] To my knowledge, no one has ever recovered any of the Liberty bonds from the wreckage of the *U.S.S. San Diego*. Of course the only way any could have survived is if they had been placed in some sort of watertight case or package.

U.S. Navy was skeptical at the corporation's methods and financial backing for the project, they nonetheless granted permission to the plans to be assumed at their own risk. Ultimately, no salvage attempts were completed on the *U.S.S. San Diego* by the Saliger Ship Salvage Corporation. The next plan to salvage the wreck would not be for over thirty-six years.

In 1957, Maxter Metals Corporation paid the U.S. Navy "1,221.00 for scrapping only," of the *U.S.S. San Diego* wreck. (Gentile, 72) While the company waited for a rise in the salvage market, other parties began to realize that it was more important that the *U.S.S. San Diego* stay on the bottom. In 1962-63, the issue came to a head between those who saw profit with the remains coming up from the depths and from those who saw her place on the bottom as an important part of the eco-system and fishing industry. In 1962, "a great hubbub ensued when the salvage rights," of the vessel, "were sold to a professional salvage firm." (Rattray, 196) "The company planned to blow up the 503-foot, 13,400-ton cruiser for its scrap metal. They paid an initial $1,200, plus another $1,200 for a performance bond. The company agreed to give up the job if they were compensated for $15,000 already spent on surveys, equipment, and negotiations." (Rattray, 196)

The debacle of the proposed salvage caused much debate and various groups including the American Littoral Society, "a nonprofit organization of skin-diving enthusiasts and anglers," asked for legislation, the National Party Boat Owners Alliance, who explained that the destruction of off-shore wrecks would be an anchor on their profits. (Rattray, 196) The salvage company never completed its planned destruction and salvage job on the wreck. But others with plans to salvage parts of the wreck for financial gain would follow.[136] Another type of diver would also begin to explore the wreck.

---

[136] Capt. Dan Berg recounts another commercial attempt at salvage. A "Long Island diver attempted to raise the one remaining, 18 foot in diameter, 37,000 pound bronze prop. He succeeded only in sinking his own barge mounted crane which now rests on the bottom a short distance from the Diego's stern." Interestingly, as pointed out by Capt. Berg, "someone else made off with the

The other divers and explorers of the wreck were those who wished to visit and explore the wreck site due to the historical value of the *U.S.S. San Diego*. One of the groups was the Oceanographic Historical Research Society. In an article, *Underwater Research*, published in the May 1963 issue of the *Long Island Forum*, author Charles D. Dunn explained the various dives completed on the *U.S.S. San Diego*. According to the article, members of the group had begun researching the vessel and had started diving operations on the site in 1961. "One brief penetration was done by Herb Cutting of Flushing and Don Marchese late that year. Based on their findings, we started work in earnest last summer [1962]." (Dunn, 117) The group, aware that wreck penetration was a dangerous activity had utilized the use of safety lines, powerful five hundred watt lamps, and back up divers on the outside of the entrance site of the hull. The hope of the group was to recover "many artifacts exemplary of Navy life in World War I." (Dunn, 117-118) Though what artifacts were retrieved by the group is unknown, divers followed their lead and began to bring to the surface a myriad of artifacts.

The artifacts that were raised during the sixties through the eighties varied from personal effects of the officers and crew to portholes and other parts of the vessel. In addition to china, brass items and lanterns, some divers also recovered some artifacts that could go "bang." In June 1982, "the *N.Y. Post* reported that the bomb squad had been tipped off that a local diver had recovered a two foot long, five inch diameter artillery shell from the *San Diego*. The diver had planned to sand blast it and stand it next to his fire place." (Berg) The shell was confiscated by the Suffolk County Police Department who then transferred it to the U.S. Army for detonation.

Captain Dan Berg recounts that in October of 1987, he and other divers diving from the Research Vessel *Wahoo* conducted dives on the site in an effort to highlight the rich history of the wreck. Diver George Quirk "had located in the bow of this WW I cruiser...a newly discovered storage room...full of china,

---

valued prop." (Berg) Gary Gentile provides an in-depth accounting of this and other salvage attempts made on the *U.S.S. San Diego* in his book on the subject.

some bowls and silverware." (Berg) In addition to video and still footage collected from the dives, artifacts were recovered and donated to "local museums, used to decorate area dive shops…aimed at increasing the public's interest in diving and shipwrecks." (Berg) The heady days of artifact recovery however were dwindling.

During the major artifact recovery era, many items from the *U.S.S. San Diego* were recovered. Mark Silverstein and Capt. John Bricker have made numerous dives to the site and have recovered a host of artifacts. Some of the items that they have recovered include both personal effects of the sailors who served on the *U.S.S. San Diego* as well as parts of the vessel. They include: a skylight, a porthole, a cage lamp, a drop light, a bronze cleat, a sound phone, a pressure gauge, a brass bell shaped lamp, a brass big gun firing indicator panel, a torpedo firing key, an oiler, a coal bin light, a brass valve, a brass round ship's clinometers in working condition and more. In addition to aspects of the vessel, the following personal items have also been recovered from the site: a souvenir spoon, a glass inkwell, a cut class salt shaker, a set of nickel plated keys, officer's china, a Watermann's Ideal fountain pen, a brass optometrists testing lens, various coins, brass uniform buttons, a stainless steel capsule case for pencil leads, a Autostrop safety razor, a brass flashlight, brass padlocks of various types, a brass officers' shaving kit with case, and much more. The vast collection illustrates the myriad of items that "went down with the ship." The *U.S.S. San Diego*, like its brethren of the deep is a virtual time capsule of a long lost era of our history. The retrieval of the items provide an insight into the past and have provided divers like Mark Silverstein and Captain John Bricker with the ability to touch history in the murky depths of a vessel that was sent to the bottom during the War to End all Wars.[137]

---

[137] All of the items listed were located and retrieved by Mark Silverstein and Captain John Bricker prior to the establishment of United States Navy restrictions against the removal of any items from a ship or aircraft wreck site.

Capt. Bricker with a recovered porthole.   **A refurbished porthole.**

Captain John Bricker and Freddy Belise with a host of artifacts.

Refurbished sound tube (left) and bell light (right).
All photographs courtesy of Captain John Bricker.
All artifacts recovered prior to 1998.

Electrical Communication box.   **Brass lamp.**

An intact shaving kit recovered from the *U.S.S. San Diego*.
Exterior view showing great detail. Interior view showing the shaving contents as
they would have appeared the day of the sinking. All photographs courtesy of Mark
Silverstein. All artifacts recovered prior to 1998.

141

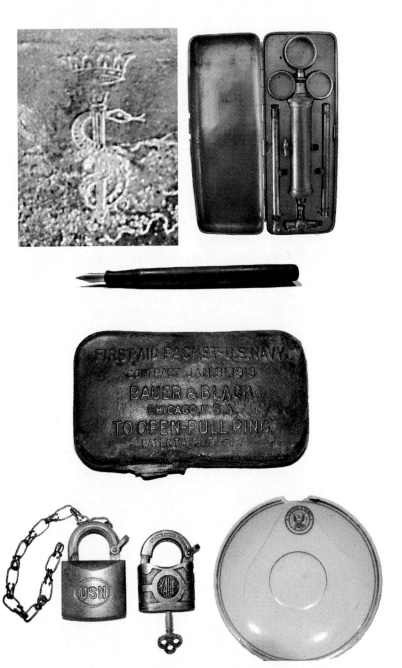

Various artifacts recovered from the *U.S.S. San Diego* by Mark Silverstein.
Top left: A case for a hypodermic needle. Top right: interior view of the case. Top
center: a Watermann pen. Center: Military First Aid case. Bottom left: U.S. Navy
Locks one with chain and one with key. Bottom right: A saucer from the *U.S.S. San
Diego.* All artifacts recovered prior to 1998.

The *U.S.S. San Diego* was eventually placed on the National Register and is currently a protected site. As a result, it is illegal for explorers to the *U.S.S. San Diego* wreck site to remove any artifact. The Department of the Navy Naval Historical Center website states that "ship and aircraft wrecks are government property in the custody of the U.S. Navy." A further review of policy shows that "through the sovereign immunity provisions of Admiralty law, the Department of the Navy retains custody of all of its naval vessels and aircraft, whether lost within U.S., foreign, or international boundaries." Salvage rights and diving access however are two different issues. "Divers may dive on Navy ships and aircraft wrecks at their own risk…however, federal property law dictates that no portion of a government wreck may be disturbed or removed. Unauthorized removal of any property from a U.S. Navy wreck is illegal."

Painting of the *U.S.S. San Diego* in her final moments - Francis Muller. U.S. Navy.

The *U.S.S. San Diego* is still a popular diving location, notwithstanding the regulations against artifact recovery. Author and diver David Rosenthal recounts many of his dives on the wreck in *Scuba Diving the Wrecks and Shores of Long Island, NY* and continues to descend upon the wreck to learn more about

143

its history and condition. In April of 2008, at the start of the diving season, a group from the Long Island Divers Association dove on the wreck to see how, as president Bill Pfeiffer said, "she weathered the winter." Though artifacts are not to be removed from the site, the ability to dive in local waters on "the only large American warship lost during the war," still enthralls many divers. (Massie, 762)

The *U.S.S. San Diego* remains on the bottom of the Atlantic Ocean and will remain there until she finally disintegrates away. Throughout the eighty plus years that she has been dove on and explored, a host of artifacts have been recovered which provide an interesting glimpse into a turn of the century naval vessel. In less than thirty minutes the armored cruiser, once known as the *U.S.S. California*, succumbed to the ravages of man kind during a time of war, taking six souls with her to the bottom. The flag of freedom that flew from her mast was saved, as were over eleven hundred sailors.[138] No matter how many ships and sailors are sent to the bottom during peacetime and wartime operations, the sacrifices made by United States Naval personnel must never be forgotten. Surely the *U.S.S. San Diego* will remain a popular diving location for many reasons. Hopefully, the most important reason will be the ability for the divers to quietly pay their respects to those who did not return home from the *U.S.S. San Diego's* last voyage.

---

[138] The U.S. ensign of the *U.S.S. San Diego* had been struck prior to the vessel's sinking. The flag was reported as having been carried for safe keeping by one of the sailors who had landed at Point O' Woods on Long Island, New York. The final fate of the flag is unknown. (*NYT*, 20JUL1918)

The lookout kept a sharp watch on the barren rolling seas of the North Atlantic. He and the rest of the crew of the *Life* magazine expedition were scanning the horizon for a yellow oil drum that had been placed as a marker. On deck, the divers, now on their third attempt to locate the site, were anxious and excited for an opportunity to descend upon the wreck. Bob Dill, Earl Murray, Ramsey Parks, Peter Gimbel and Kenneth MacLeish had already prepared their diving gear and photographic equipment, but as darkness began to eclipse the day, their small vessel headed back to port. One diver remarked, "If the sea were a woman, she'd be a bitch." (*Life*, 17SEP1956) Somewhere beneath the boat on the cold bottom of the ocean was the object of their quest. The divers, on assignment for *Life* magazine would have to wait to attempt to gather color photographs of the sunken ship. The grand dame of the sea was not willing to accept wetsuit clad visitors that day.

Twenty four hours later, the intrepid men took to the air to try and locate the dive site. The oil drum, they reasoned, had disappeared, but a trail of oil bubbles finally appeared. Following the spots, the airborne searchers finally located the source of the oil and the wreck. After returning to land, the men again gathered on their boat and headed out to the spot. Armed with the most up to date "surface and subsurface gear," the men would spend another two days on the rough seas waiting for the seas to calm. (*Life*, 17SEP1956) Finally, the weather cleared to permit diving on the site. The divers rigged their gear and mentally prepared for their descent into the deep. For all but one of the divers, this would be their first time descending to the sunken ship. Peter Gimbel held a distinct advantage. He and fellow diver Joseph Fox had dove on the vessel the day after she had plunged to the bottom. Even though he had visited the wreck prior, the dangers of the site still loomed. The divers donned their thick black rubber wetsuits and diving equipment. Then, one by one, the divers jumped into the cool waters to begin the over two-hundred foot descent to see, explore and photograph the pride of the Italian line, the *Andrea Doria*.[139]

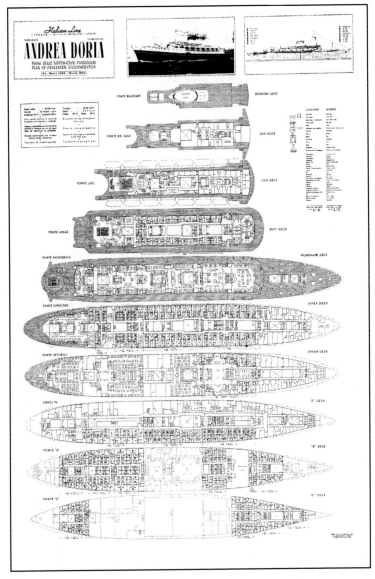

The deck plans of the *Andrea Doria*. Courtesy of S.P.L.I.A.

---

[139] The team made several dives to the *Andrea Doria*, exploring various parts of the vessel, recovering small items, and taking multiple pictures. The article, including the front cover photograph of Peter Gimbel holding a suitcase recovered from the wreck, appeared in the September 17, 1956 edition of *Life* Magazine. The suitcase and its contents were returned to its owner, Mrs. Justine Messina of Valley Stream, New York.

★ At his studio in Conca, Salvatore Fiume, world famous Italian muralist, is painting "The Legend of Italy" for the Main Lounge of the Andrea Doria.

These men are building a ship...

How do you build a ship? With tons of steel and copper and brass? With winch and crane and riveting gun? With calloused hands and well-trained minds? No . . . you build a ship with your heart.

When every bolt that's driven home is sent there by a man who loves to build a ship . . . when every mural is painted by a man whose life is painting . . . when every piece of tile and glassware, every tapestry and rug and chair . . . every menu served and every detail of the thousands in your vessel is the product of men's

hearts . . . then you have built a *ship*. This is the tradition of Italia. This will be the *Andrea Doria*.

The lovely, completely air conditioned Andrea Doria enters transatlantic service from Genoa, arriving New York in December. Special West Indies Cruise January 30, 1953 . . . 17 glorious days.

Italian Line
"ITALIA"—Società di Navigazione—Genova

See your Steamship Agent or
American Export Lines (General Agents)
39 Broadway, New York 6, N. Y.

ANDREA DORIA · SATURNIA · VULCANIA · CONTE BIANCAMANO The "Sunny Southern Route" to LISBON · GIBRALTAR · BARCELONA · PALERMO · NAPLES · CANNES · GENOA

Circa 1952 advertisement of the *Andrea Doria*. Author's collection.

The *Andrea Doria* had begun her life in February of 1950 with the laying of her keel. In less than one year, she was launched at a length of seven hundred feet (656.5 feet at the waterline), ninety feet, two inch beam and a forty-five foot, four inch depth. She was built by the Ansaldo Shipyards at Sestri, Italy and was owned by *Italia*. The *Andrea Doria* was powered with six steam turbines which were "fitted for oil fuel." She could operate at twenty-three knots and was manned by a complement of five hundred and seventy-five crewmen. Her accommodations provided 1,241 passengers. The *Andrea Doria* set sail on her maiden voyage in January of 1953.

The vessel was a floating palace. No aspect of the vessel was overlooked during her construction and fitting out. The *Andrea Doria* was the Italia Lines' attempt to reestablish her transatlantic service between Genoa, Italy and New York. The cost of the construction of the hull and machinery amounted to "$30 million dollars" and her "sumptuous furnishings and prize works of art were worth, according to several estimates, an additional $10 million to $28 million." (Gentile, 19) The artwork included some of "Italy's finest works of art," including a "sixteen hundred square foot mural by Salvatore Fiume, covering eight walls, paintings by Luzzati, Predonzani, Zuffi, Ratti, Bragalini, and Felicita Frai," as well as ceramic pieces, "mosaics, frescoes, fabrics, crystals, and panels of rare woods." (Gentile, 19) One of the showpieces of the ship was a "full sized bronze statue of the sixteenth century Admiral Andrea Doria who had been sculpted by Paganin." (Gentile, 19) [140]

The *Andrea Doria* had ten passenger decks. Starting from the top mast downward the decks included: Belvedere, Sun, Lido, Boat, Promenade, Upper, Foyer, A, B, and C decks.[141] The B and C decks were fore and aft, separated by the "engine room where the power of fifty thousand horses spun two thick axles, each turning a three-blade propeller that was nineteen feet in diameter." (Hoffer, 35) The B-deck, in addition to the Tourist Class cabins, also "housed the garage."

---

[140] The sculpture had been donated to the ship by a descendant of the Admiral, Marquis Giambattista Doria. (Gentile, 19)
[141] The Boat Deck, aptly named, was the location of the *Andrea Doria*'s sixteen lifeboats.

(Hoffer, 35)[142] Beneath C, the last passenger deck, were cargo, fuel and water holds.

The Norseman. Courtesy of the Imperial Club

Throughout the ship, amidst art and elegant attentions to details, various compartments, cabins, a gift shop, purser's office, three pools (one for each type of passenger – First Class, Cabin Class and Tourist Class), lounges, bars, ballrooms, a ten-room hospital, recreational areas, provided comfort, relaxation and entertainment for the transatlantic trips. The vessel, though not the fastest, nor the biggest, was a floating palace that provided for her passengers, albeit only for a few days crossing, with an elegant voyage across the Atlantic. By 1956 however, "the golden age the transatlantic passenger liner was in its dotage." (Hoffer, 35) The advent and growing popularity of air travel was taking a toll on the sea-going method of travel. The *Andrea Doria* would not need to worry about

---

[142] Nine automobiles were aboard the *Andrea Doria* on her last voyage. In addition to a Rolls Royce owned by "Miami Beach socialite Edward Parker," there was also an experimental car aboard. The one of a kind prototype was designed in conjunction between the Chrysler and Ghia companies. The concept car, named the Norseman, was built based on the drawings of Virgil Exner, Chrysler's Chief Designer. The vehicle featured a cantilevered roof which meant that the entire roof was supported from the rear of the vehicle. The wrap around glass windshield had no forward supports. It took over a year to construct the vehicle from "sketches and models created by Exner's studio." Completed without engine, the Norseman was stored in a wooden crate and had been placed in the number 2 cargo area of the vessel. Accomplished diver, researcher and *Andrea Doria* historian David Bright located the remains of the vehicle while looking for a lost diver in the early 1990's. "The crate had disintegrated and the car was in very, very poor condition. The ocean's salt water invaded the Norseman's metal and most of the car is rust, corrosion and a heap of undistinguishable junk. The tires are still there and have assisted to its identification." (Bright) David Bright unfortunately perished after completing a dive on the *Andrea Doria* on June 8, 2006.

ending her days due to the increased use of aircraft travel. On her last day, her only worry was another passenger liner.

A model of the *Andrea Doria* built by Joseph F. Kearney.

The *Andrea Doria* had completed "one hundred incident-free crossings" during her three years of service. (Gentile, 12) Her record however would forever be remembered by one tragic event. On July 25, 1956, the *Andrea Doria* was off of Nantucket and was under full power as she sped through the waters toward her destination - New York. A thick fog enveloped the ship and on the bridge, the radar, fully powered and in operation sent out its waves searching the unknown for contacts. A vessel appeared on the screen. The contact was reported at sixteen miles in the distance. The *Andrea Doria*, Captain Piero Calamai in command on the bridge, pressed forward at near full speed through the fog. There were 1134 passengers and her complement of crewmen on board the vessel as her bow cut through the water and the fog on her voyage with destiny.

A bow and stern view of the *Andrea Doria*.

Close-up images of the upper decks and bow of the *Andrea Doria*.

A closer view of the starboard side of the *Andrea Doria*.

A close-up of the impact site.

Andrea Doria – Ship Specifics

Length	700 feet
Beam	90.2 feet
Depth	45.4 feet
Tonnage	29,083

This replica of the Andrea Doria is eight feet long. It is an amazing work of art that in itself has an interesting history. See the Getting Involved page for the builder's website to learn the story behind the building of the replica.

Outbound from New York was the Swedish passenger liner *Stockholm*. Under the command of Captain Gunnar Nordenson, the vessel was heading eastward for Scandinavia, carrying seven hundred and fifty passengers and crew. Once the *Stockholm* passed the *Nantucket* lightship, her course turned from east to northeast. Though this maneuver was not in keeping with the 1948 "International Convention for the Safety of Life at Sea," which had recommended "an eastbound course twenty miles to the south, [of the *Nantucket* lightship]" the *Stockholm* pressed forward on her course at eighteen knots. (Hoffer, 227) The recommendations however, were only voluntary and even though "several shipping lines had an agreement to follow the southern route," the *Stockholm* and her parent company had not formally agreed to the recommendations. Later that evening, as passengers settled in to their temporary shipboard routine, a blip appeared on the radar screen on board the *Stockholm*. At the time, it was reported that the vessel westbound [the *Andrea Doria*] was two degrees north of the *Stockholm*. As the miles decreased between them, a constant bearing - decreasing range or CBDR type of situation began to develop. A collision course was on the horizon if action was not taken by the vessels.

Instead of steering clear of one another, both vessels, inadvertently made navigational changes and in effect, began to shorten the distance between one another. In a series of misinterpretations committed by both vessels' officers, the vessels were on a collision course. Churning through the waves and out of the fog, Captain Nordenson saw the *Andrea Doria* when it was too late. On board the *Andrea Doria*, Captain Calamai realizing that he was too close to the mystery vessel ordered the ship's rudder hard to port, "relying on his vessel's high speed to take him out of the path of the *Stockholm*." (Keatts, 87) Ultimately, his order to turn to port exposed the *Andrea Doria*'s starboard side instead of her bow, which would have provided a "smaller target and minimize impact." (Keatts, 87) Captain Nordenson, on the bridge of the *Stockholm* swung hard to starboard, but the collision was inevitable. Both vessels' speed and stopping distance proved too great. The ignorance and misinterpretation of radar equipment, grossly neglected by both vessels' crew on duty on the bridge, had turned both vessels in a direct line of one another. Both crews braced for the impact.

At 11:22 P.M., the *Andrea Doria* and the *Stockholm* collided. The *Stockholm* slashed into the starboard side of the liner. The reinforced icebreaking bow of the *Stockholm* sliced into the hull of the *Andrea Doria* causing instant carnage to the vessel. On board the *Stockholm*, the crewmen who were berthed in the bow were either instantly killed or gravely injured. "A gash below the bridge 40 feet wide and a third through her vitals," had killed several of the Italian Liner's passengers and had, in an instant, set into motion the slow, agonizing death knell of the *Andrea Doria*. (*Life*, 6AUG1956) As the Atlantic Ocean began to claim the seven hundred foot vessel, the passengers and crew of the *Andrea Doria* focused on their effort to survive the collision.

On board the *Stockholm*, Captain Gunnar Nordenson took immediate action and backed his vessel away from the liner. He issued an announcement to his passengers and crew informing them that their vessel, just hours out of New York, had collided with another vessel, but that the *Stockholm* was okay. The bow of the *Stockholm* was a mixture of wreckage, metal, wood, and debris. The vessel looked like a prize winning boxer with a smashed nose. Physical ailments, such as a broken nose can be repaired. Gaping holes in hulls in a vessel underway at sea is a different scenario altogether. Though the *Stockholm* had managed to survive the collision, the *Andrea Doria* was not as lucky. The *Andrea Doria* began listing almost immediately after the collision occurred.[143]

SOS calls rang out on the airwaves. Assistance was needed because the *Andrea Doria* had taken a severe list, rendering her port side lifeboats useless. The *Stockholm*, having determined her seaworthiness, offered assistance. As the fog began to lift, those on board both vessels realized the gravity of the situation.

---

[143] The *Stockholm* cut into the *Andrea Doria* below the "waterline to [the] main deck, destroying watertight integrity of [the] bulkhead deck. Starboard fuel tanks, nearly empty at end of run, flooded, causing list." (*Life*, 6AUG1956)

The *Andrea Doria* was never going to reach port. Instead she was heading to the bottom of the North Atlantic. Over sixteen hundred souls had to be rescued. Over the course of approximately five hours, one of the greatest maritime rescues of all time would take place. Fifty-one passengers and crew however, would be lost as a result of the collision.

As the crew of the *Stockholm* began to lower its lifeboats to assist in the offloading of the *Andrea Doria*'s passengers and crew, vessels began responding to the SOS calls. The *Pvt. William H. Thompson*, a U.S. Navy transport, *Ile de France*, a passenger line, *Cape Ann*, a freighter, *Robert E. Hopkins*, a tanker, *Laura Maersk*, a freighter, all reported that they were en-route and would arrive on scene as soon as possible. The United States Coast Guard station at East Moriches heard the frantic calls for assistance and "immediately notified the supervisor of the watch, who passed it on to the Coast Guard Rescue Coordination Center in New York City." (*Life*, 6AUG1956) Almost simultaneously, eleven Coast Guard vessels were ordered to get underway to assist in anyway possible.[144] The *Andrea Doria*, the majority of her passengers reporting to the Boat deck on the high side of the ship, prepared to lower themselves onboard the lifeboats. The ship, her lights going dimmer, was taking on water with each passing moment. Her time on the surface was dwindling.

Once other vessels arrived on the scene, a flood of lifeboats were launched to aid in the rescue of the *Andrea Doria*'s passengers and crew. By 4:58 in the morning, "the master of the *Ile de France* told the Stockholm: All passengers rescued. Proceeding to New York full speed." (*NYT*, 26JUL1956) The *Stockholm*, with a large number of the rescued passengers and her own passengers and crew aboard would follow her lead and begin to limp slowly

---

[144] The Coast Guard immediately recalled reinforcements. One Coast Guardsman, "Mel Abbot, was racing along the deserted Belt Parkway from his Brooklyn home at 70 mph when a traffic cop screamed up and made him pull over. Abbot explained the emergency, but the cop gave him a ticket anyway." (*Life*, 6AUG1956) The rules of the road, both on land and at sea were not to be tread upon lightly.

toward the same port. However, those who had survived and had been rescued would watch as the *Andrea Doria* spent her last moments on the surface. "Nearby

The *Andrea Doria* during her final hours. Courtesy of the U.S. Coast Guard.

a thousand survivors gathered at the rails of the *Stockholm, Cape Ann, Pvt. William H. Thomas*, and other ships to watch the writhing vessel." (Hoffer, 186)

She had remained afloat for almost eleven hours and in her last moments, "the *Andrea Doria* finally acquiesced to an inevitable fate." (Hoffer, 186) Newspaper men and photographers filled the sky, snapping pictures of the vessel's last moments, Captain Calamai "watched unbelievingly from a late arriving tugboat…[trying] to disguise his grief, but Third Officer Giannini could see that the captain seemed to be dying with his proud *Andrea Doria*." (Hoffer, 186)[145] By 10:09 in the morning, the *Andrea Doria* slipped beneath the surface

---

[145] The round-trip of the *Andrea Doria* was supposed to be Captain Calamai's last voyage in command of the ship. He was slated to take command of the *Andrea Doria*'s sister ship the *Cristoforo Colombo*. "A strange combination of circumstances was to decree that the beautiful

and sank to the bottom of the Atlantic. For fifteen minutes a whirlpool spun "additional bits of wreckage to the surface," the *Andrea Doria* was no more.

As the rescue fleet headed for port, questions were being raised by reporters and the public alike. How could two vessels, both equipped with radar, have been involved in a collision?[146] For those who perished in the tragic collision, the answer was moot. For those who survived, it was a question that needed to be answered. As news of the tragedy began to fill newspaper columns and magazine articles, two men heard a calling from the sunken liner. For one man, the call from the deep would become a lifetime passion and pursuit. For the other, it almost ended his life. The *Andrea Doria*, on the bottom for less than a day had already become a siren of the deep for those who yearned to hear her call.

Peter Gimbel and Joseph Fox were the first two divers to see the *Andrea Doria*. Gimbel, who in addition to being an investment banker, was "also an accomplished underwater photographer." (Gentile, 57) MacLeish, a *Life* magazine editor assured Gimbel that they "would purchase any underwater photographs that Gimbel might take of the sunken liner." (Gentile, 57) Soon after, Gimbel, Fox and a small entourage convinced a skipper on Nantucket Island to venture out to the site. Twenty-eight hours after the *Andrea Doria* sank, Gimbel and Fox descended to gather photographic images. Using "double tanks with no pressure gauges, breathing off double-hose regulators, and wearing rubber exposure suits over woolen underwear," the two divers explored the vessel. (Gentile, 58) After shooting several photographs, Fox indicated to Gimbel that he was having problems. "He was suffering from carbon dioxide build up; he felt dizzy and uncoordinated" and Gimbel recognized the signs of a diver in peril. Quickly Gimbel assisted Fox to the surface. The action saved Fox's life. Fox

---

Doria would never return and Captain Calamai would be denied command of the *Colombo*." (Keatts, 86)

[146] On the front page of the *New York Times*, beneath the main articles concerning the collision and impending sinking of the *Andrea Doria*, an article, "Cause of the Crash Puzzles Radar Men," highlighted what would remain the continuing question regarding the incident. (*NYT*, 26JUL1956)

would never dive on the wreck again; Gimbel however was "hooked for life." (Gentile, 59) He would return to dive the wreck a few weeks later, this time with Editor Kenneth MacLeish and a team of divers.

Life magazines from August 6 & September 17, 1956. Author's collection.

Left: "Divers Explore the Sunken Doria" article by Kenneth McLeish. Above the September 17, 1956 article is the front cover of the August 6, 1956 issue of *Life* magazine. Above the article to the right is a copy of the *New York Times* front page when the *Andrea Doria* and *Stockholm* collided. Author's collection.

While the second set of photographs, many of which were in color, was being viewed across the globe in the glossy pages of the September 17, 1956 issue of *Life* Magazine, another group of divers were gearing up for their descent on the *Andrea Doria*. Hoping to photograph and film the sunken vessel was a team which included James Dugan, Frederic Dumas, and Louis Malle. Along with "back up divers, support personnel….compressors, and French dive equipment," the men were on their way to the wreck site by September 13, 1956. (Gentile, 60-61) Over the course of two months, the expedition was plagued with bad weather, personnel changes, and equipment shortages. Though some footage was attained of the *Andrea Doria*, there was not enough to utilize the film commercially. The expedition ended when cameraman Louis Malle suffered an eardrum injury.[147]

As divers continued to descend upon the wreck in various expeditions, the question of how the two liners struck continued. "Four months of hearings established that both vessels shared responsibility for the collision." (Keatts, 88) The *Stockholm*, not adhering to the recommendations set forth in the 1948 International Convention for the Safety of Life at Sea, was well north and was in a way, "was legally driving in the opposite direction on a wide, but potentially dangerous one-way street." (Hoffer, 227) However, the *Andrea Doria*, with fully functional radar equipment, should have recognized the potential problem and effectively took action to steer clear of the approaching vessel. In addition, the *Andrea Doria* was in a dangerous status due to her empty fuel tanks and her rate of speed in a thick, patchy fog bank. Both vessels and their crews however were responsible because had the radar readings "been plotted to establish the course of each oncoming vessel, the converging paths would have been evident to the officers of both liners in adequate time to avoid collision." (Keatts, 88) Hindsight however is always twenty-twenty.

In the fifty-two years since the *Andrea Doria* plunged to the bottom, divers have braved the conditions of the sea, sharks, the dangerous depths and the unimaginable hazards to visit the shipwreck. Initial thoughts of salvage

---

[147] The groups attempts to gather film was unsuccessful. "The total accomplishment of nearly two months' work was twenty seconds of test film." (Gentile, 61)

eventually faded and instead, divers began to explore the wreck more intimately as their equipment increased in efficiency and effectiveness. From well planned and financially backed expeditions with plans to enter and remove safes and other valuable items, to amateur technical divers, the *Andrea Doria* has played host to many adventurers. Some of the divers and adventurers wished to find evidence that would assist in the determination why the *Andrea Doria* took such a significant list upon the initial collision. Others wanted to retrieve interesting artifacts from her gift shop, her china closets, or other areas of the vessel. In August of 1973, former U.S. Navy divers Don Rodocker and Chris DeLucchi utilized an undersea capsule named *Mother* to remain submerged on the *Andrea Doria* site for over a week as they attempted to access and procure the bank's safe. During their saturation dive the men breathed a "mixture of 5.4 percent oxygen and 94.6 percent helium through umbilicals – long hoses" while they cut through the hull doors to gain access to the foyer of the vessel's bank. (Graves, 95) By day eight the two men had successively removed the doors and gained access to the area of the ship. Unfortunately, they were greeted by a tangled amalgamation of rotted wood paneling, electrical cords, light fixtures and other disarrayed debris. The men decided against going into the maelstrom of wreckage determining that to do was in an effort to retrieve the safe would have been "suicide." (Graves, 95)[148]

To date, many pieces of the vessel's artwork, including the statue of Admiral Doria, a ship's bell, tons of Italia line embossed china plates, cups, saucers, trinkets, souvenirs, and more have been recovered.[149] Divers, like Mark

---

[148] Though unsuccessful in their attempt to remove the *Andrea Doria*'s safe, the two men who had formed a company, Saturation Systems, Inc., were "besieged with requests from insurance and salvage firms to put *Mother* to work retrieving millions of dollars' worth of sunken cargoes." (Graves, 95)

[149] The recovery of the stern bell of the *Andrea Doria* is included in Gentile's book, *Andrea Doria – Dive to an Era*, pages 121-147. Gentile recounts his and the team's adventures in vivid detail of the successful mission to locate, identify and recover the stern bell. In addition, Gentile provides an intimate look at the mystery of the *Andrea Doria*'s bow bell. "Long before the *Andrea Doria* took her nose dive to the bottom of the cold Atlantic, her bow bell went missing. Had it been removed prior to her last trip…had it been knocked off its mount by the force of the collision…had it been

Silverstein and Captain John Bricker have completed numerous dives on the site and have recovered a host of artifacts from her dark remains. Each of their artifact recoveries required extensive penetration into the *Andrea Doria's* jumbled interior. This is a world where tables, stools, staircases and wash basins jut out at crazy angles owing to the wreck's starboard-side-down position on the ocean floor. Since no ship is built to withstand loads in that position, nor years of salt water immersion, the *Andrea Doria's* structure continues to deteriorate which makes navigating her insides hazardous for all but the most experienced divers. Many divers have become disoriented or trapped within her interior spaces in their quest for *Andrea Doria* "souvenirs". Both divers take the utmost care and precaution when planning their dives to the *Doria* which has been called the "Mount Everest of shipwreck diving" owing to her 250-foot depth and harshness of sea and weather conditions.

Bricker and Silverstein have retrieved china, glassware, silverware and brass fixtures from the wreck. In addition, Silverstein has shot video of the *Andrea Doria* on days when the visibility has been exceptionally good. Interestingly, very few recovered artifacts actually bear the name "*Andrea Doria*" because of the money-saving custom of applying the company name to shipboard items rather than the name of a specific ship. This way, items can be more easily shared between ships of the line. That is why most *Andrea Doria* artifacts likely bear the inscription "ITALIA". Silverstein has one item in his collection which actually bears the name "T/N ANDREA DORIA" - a latex rubber balloon which may have been part of the decorations during the eve-of-arrival party that fateful Wednesday night. But his most-prized artifact according to Silverstein is a jar of still-preserved liquored cherries which he found amongst the remains of a bar

---

removed by crew members before the sinking?" Ultimately, the bell was not lost, but instead, somehow ended up in the garage of Edward Rowe Snow, a "ship historian and prolific writer of sea tales," who stated that "the story of how I acquired this bell is still classified material, and cannot be told for several years." Snow died in 1976 and with him went the secret of the bow bell of the *Andrea Doria*. (Gentile, 147)

located in the stern and from which he adventurously sampled the contents upon returning to the deck of the dive boat *Sea Hunter III*.

Top Left: A Jar of cherries recovered from the wreck by Mark Silverstein.

Top Right: Silverstein sampling the forty+ year old cherries on the dive boat.
Left Center: A sampling of items recovered by Peter Halabatros from the giftshop.
Bottom Left: #3 from the Shuffleboard court recovered by Silverstein.
Bottom Right: ID Tag.

China has always been a popular item recovered by divers. The *Andrea Doria* had three types of china which were utilized for the three types of passengers.

Top left: Italia Goblet.

Top right: First Class coffee cup.

Center: Assorted glassware. All china and glassware shown was recovered by Mark Silverstein.

Bottom left: A balloon recovered by Mark Silverstein. Upon close inspection it reads T/N Andrea Doria. T/N is the Italian version of "Motor Vessel."

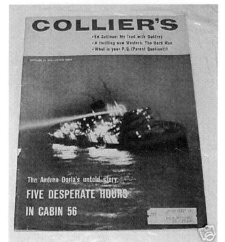

September 28, 1956 issue of *Collier's* Magazine. Author Cornelius Ryan's article, *The Andrea Doria's untold story: Five Desperate Hours in Cabin 56* tells the harrowing fight by passengers and crew to save others. Author's collection.

Always willing to answer the call of the sunken liner was Peter Gimbel. Though he took an almost decade hiatus between his dives - three sets of dives in 1956 and 1957 - he returned on multiple occasions to film, to explore the wreck, and to further investigate claims of internal causes, such as design flaws which resulted in the *Andrea Doria*'s quick list after the collision.[150] Gimbel returned in 1975 and again in 1981 where he found crucial evidence regarding the damage caused by the collision and to retrieve the bank safe.[151] After the Bank of Rome safe was topside, Gimbel and Ted Hess focused in on determining the cause of the *Andrea Doria*'s significant list. "A massive breach never before suspected led out to the sea. The bulkhead separating the generator room from the deep tank compartment had been smashed open by the *Stockholm*'s pivoting bow; the existence of the watertight door was incidental." The discovery by the two divers indicated that "with three compartments torn open by the collision, the luxury line had suffered a blow with which she had been unable to cope." (Gentile, 75)

---

[150] During Gimbel's dive with Ramsey Parks in August of 1957, a large blue shark paid the men a visit as they ascending their anchor line. "As the shark veered in too close for comfort, Gimbel stabbed it in the snout; his blade went in to the hilt. Although the knife evidently missed the brain, the shark swam away and did not return. Gimbel got away, and *Life* got the photos." (Gentile, 62)

[151] The safe was opened on live on television on August 16, 1984. For three years after its retrieval the safe had been kept in a tank "where the water temperature was maintained closed to freezing." When the safe was opened, "bundles of U.S. and Italian currency were found in a remarkable state of preservation after nearly three decades of sea water immersion. The rubber bands holding the money together still retained their elasticity." The currency, "American Express travelers checks, and a leather pouch containing secret bank codes," were eventually preserved and sold to the public. (Gentile, 76-77) Many maritime museums have these items in their collections. Occasionally items from the safe will come up for public sale at auctions.

Some men have spent large amounts of money, effort and personal sacrifice to answer the *Andrea Doria*'s call from the deep. Others, over fifteen, have answered the call and perished as a result of her charms. Like a siren of the sea, the *Andrea Doria* will continue to call to divers who are willing to risk their lives to see her one last time. The *Andrea Doria*, slowly succumbing to the effects of the elements and of the sea will eventually disintegrate and become one with the ocean, as many of her brethren wrecks have done. But the *Andrea Doria*, will always remain ingrained in the hearts, minds, and souls of those who have descended upon her decks, peered through her crumpled hull and passageways, retrieved artifacts, artwork, and other souvenirs. Those who have braved nature, diving physiology, physical and mental stress however, did not see a twisted skeleton. Rather they caught a glimpse of one of the most beautiful and alluring ladies of the sea. As a result, the beckoning call of the grand dame will surely still be heard by those who choose to listen.

The Coast Guardsmen and members of the Suffolk County Marine Patrol had made a gruesome discovery. A lifeboat, its metal bottom "smashed on both sides of the keel" was found on the cold and barren winter sand on the Sand City Peninsula "about 1000 feet from the Hobart Beach Pavilion." (*LI*, 24JAN1963) The lifeboat contained the body of only one man who was "wedged under the seat, cast in a solid block of ice." (*LI*, 24JAN1963) The body's "left wrist lashed to the craft" was later identified as Hugh Reid, an engineer. (*LI*, 24JAN1963) The only way to remove the poor soul was to chip his remains out of the ice that had solidly formed around him. As the detectives and Coast Guardsmen investigated the lifeboat, a determination was made to have the lifeboat removed from the beach and transported to the Eaton's Neck Coast Guard Station. As the truck pulled away from the beach, the stark black letters of the white lifeboat could easily be read – *Gwendoline Steers*.

The *Gwendoline Steers* was a ninety-six foot long tugboat that had been originally built in 1888.[152] The vessel was roughly one-hundred fifty tons and utilized combustion engines to tow and push cargo barges to and from various business commitments. "She was a wooden/steel jacketed tug...was always well maintained" and "with brass bells, custom fittings and teak floors," the tugboat was a beautiful vessel. (Carr, 36) Throughout a large part of her career on the New York waters, she had been owned and operated by the Steers Sand and Gravel Company of Northport, New York.[153] On December 22, 1962, the *Gwendoline Steers* was off of Greenwich, Connecticut when "it ran aground on a

---

[152] Information regarding the *Gwendoline Steers* is vague. As illustrated in previous chapters, specifics of the vessel vary depending on the source. Length (96 to 100 feet) – Beam (20 to 42 feet – not logical) and tonnage (149-150 tons). (Glick, LI, Carr, NY, & Wreckhunter) Carr indicates in his book that she had been constructed in 1886. In addition, Wreckhunter.net lists several previous names for the *Gwendoline Steers* including *J. Rich Steers, Melrose, Triton* and *Douglas H. Thorne*.

[153] The Steers Sand and Gravel Company had a long history on the north shore of Long Island. In 1911, Henry J. Steers reopened Port Eaton, a sand mining operation and "rechristened the area Sand City" "In 1923, the Steers Company moved its operations to Northport and Sand City was abandoned." (Carr, 84 & 85 respectively)

small island."(*LI*, 10JAN1963) The hull of the vessel had been damaged by the grounding, but according to the maintenance supervisor for the Steers Sand and Gravel Company, the vessel had been repaired a few days after the minor accident at a Hoboken, New Jersey shipyard.[154]

The *Gwendoline Steers*. Courtesy of the Monmouth County Historical Society.

After her repairs had been completed, the *Gwendoline Steers* was deemed fit to return to her various duties on the waters of the Long Island Sound. On December 30, 1962, the tug received orders to leave her mooring. She weighed her anchor and "left New York about 11:30 Sunday morning," on a "routine trip to Northport Harbor." (*LI*, 3JAN1963) The plan was to head east to Northport, "spend the night, and return the next day with loaded barges from the Steers Sand and Gravel Co." (*LI*, 3JAN1963)[155] "At the time, the company was mining the high bluffs west of Ocean Avenue," and the *Gwendoline Steers* had been transporting "sand filled barges to New York City. (Carr, 36) On board the

---

[154] According to one of the company's spokesmen on January 9, 1963, "the bottom of the ship [*Gwendoline Steers*] was not punctured, only dented." (*LI*, 10JAN1963)
[155] The reported "plan" of the tugboat came under suspicion after her loss. "After the tragedy, it was widely believed that the *Gwendoline* was sent to Northport to pick-up company officials for a gala New Year's Eve party on board." (Carr, 36)

tug was the crew of the *Gwendoline Steers* which included Captain Herbert Dickman, who had thirty years of experience of working on the sea on various vessels and tugboats. His crew consisted of eight men including Robert E. Nolan, his mate, Ray Harrison and Hugh A. Reid both engineers, Robert E. Knox, Roy L. Burnett, Rasmus Nordvik, and John Iverson, all which served as deck hands. Claude A. Markell was also on board and serving in the capacity as the ship's cook.[156] The voyage through the water of the Long Island Sound had started out routine enough, but as the day progressed, a divergence from the routine is exactly what happened to the men and the tug boat.

As the vessel churned through the frigid waters, the "weather began to turn sour." (*LI*, 3JAN1963) The *Gwendoline Steers*, no stranger to the cold and rough weather, plowed through the building seas as she pushed toward Huntington Harbor. "At about 4:30 in the afternoon, Coast Guardsmen at the Eaton's Neck Lifeboat Station picked up a radio signal from the tug boat. The radio watch-stander was informed by the *Gwendoline Steers* that she was "an hour overdue for its Northport destination and that it was shipping water." (*LI* 3JAN1880) In addition, the vessel reported that "the pumps and engines were working properly." (*LI*, 3JAN1963)

Because no "emergency" was declared by the *Gwendoline Steers*, Chief Warrant Officer George C. Bannan, the commanding officer of the station, told the skipper that the he would "attempt to launch rescue craft," if the tug's situation deteriorated. (*LI*, 3JAN1963)[157] But at the time, no call for assistance was made, and instead, Chief Warrant Officer Bannan and Captain Dickman "agreed to repeat radio contact in one hour in order to keep check on the ship's progress." (*LI*, 3JAN1963) After the hour had passed, the Coast Guard's radio watch stander attempted to contact the *Gwendoline Steers*, but there was no

---

[156] Throughout the investigation, various spellings of the crewmen's names were published including Iversen and Nordvick.

[157] According to Carr's research, "only days before, the Coast Guards squadron had been hauled from the water and laid up for winter repairs. Only a 36-foot motorcraft was available, which was no match for the frigid, and now white-capped waves." (Carr, 37)

response. Repeated hails on the radio to the tug boat were not met with an answer. The *Gwendoline Steers*, her skipper and crew of eight men were never to be heard from again.

The Coast Guardsmen continued to attempt to make contact with the overdue vessel as the weather deteriorated sharply. "Waves turned to giant proportions...reports from Long Island and Connecticut claimed 10-to12 foot waves...gusts of wind up to 90 m.p.h." (*LI*, 3JAN1963) No contact was made and the weather conditions were limiting Coast Guard Station Eaton's Neck ability to launch their own craft into the maelstrom. Instead it was decided that a "125-foot search and rescue vessel from New London, Connecticut," be launched in an effort to locate the tugboat. But because of the weather conditions and distance, the search and rescue vessel would not be on the scene until the next morning. (*LI*, 3JAN1963) Radio calls continued, but no contact was made. The little light left of the day disappeared and waves "just off the point were recorded as nine-feet high and winds were listed as 55 m.p.h." The temperature was three degrees above zero," and the *Gwendoline Steers* was missing. (*LI*, 3JAN1963)

As night fell, the mystery of the *Gwendoline Steers* began. After the lifeboat was found on the beach and the body of the engineer recovered, the Coast Guard continued its efforts to locate the tug and the remaining crewmen. Flotsam and bodies were soon found along the beaches of various north shore communities, but what had happened to the *Gwendoline Steers* in her final moments remained up for speculation. On Friday January 4, 1963, a body was found on the Nissequogue town beach. The body was later identified as Capt. Herbert Dickman. The following day, the body of engineer Robert Knox, was discovered and identified on West Meadow Beach in Stony Brook.[158] Other flotsam was found as police officers, Coast Guardsmen and locals braved the cold winter weather to walk along the hard sand of the beaches. One Eaton's Neck resident "recovered frozen lines and an oar from the boat on the beach in

---

[158] Robert Knox "was found among reeds with his hand still entwined in a life ring." (Carr, 38) This graphic image was included in a *Life* magazine article about the loss of the *Gwendoline Steers*.

front of his home." (*LI*, 10JAN1963) A life preserver, marked with the vessel's name was "fished out of the waters at Eaton's Neck," during the same time frame, "within site of the Coast Guard Station." (*LI*, 10JAN1963) Though an oil slick had been discovered by Coast Guardsmen near the strip of beach where the life boat had been found, further investigation determined that the area was considered inconclusive due to large formations of rocks beneath the water. The search for the missing crewmen and the tug continued in earnest.

The Coast Guard, its search and rescue and later recovery operations continuing, also launched an investigation to attempt to gather as much information regarding the *Gwendoline Steers*. Several eyewitnesses had reported that they had seen a tug boat during the time frame that the *Gwendoline Steers* was in the vicinity. Unfortunately, none of the eye-witnesses could verify that the vessel that they saw was the *Gwendoline Steers*. Nonetheless the eye-witnesses who had come forward were quickly questioned by the authorities. It was hoped that their testimony could help locate the tug boat and her missing crewmen. Five eyewitnesses provided testimony to the lead investigator United States Coast Guard Captain Frederick K. Arzt.[159] In addition, two former crewmen and a shipyard worker who had supervised the repairs made to the *Gwendoline Steers* a few days prior to her disappearance were also questioned.

Sitting in front of a huge American Flag at the Eaton's Neck Coast Guard Station, Captain Arzt questioned the five witnesses as to their account of what they witnessed and what might have happened to the *Gwendoline Steers*. Mrs. Richard Streb of North Creek Road in Eaton's Neck, on January 3, 1963 stated that she saw the boat "a little bit from the end of Eaton's Neck, but a little off of Lloyd, not quite a mile east, a little nearer Lloyd than Eaton's." (*LI*, 10JAN1963) Mrs. Streb was re-questioned a week later on the 10th of January

---

[159] Captain Frederick Arzt's name is spelled three different ways depending on sources. I have utilized the Arzt spelling throughout this chapter and Appendix C. It should be noted that Captain Arzt was familiar with the Steers Sand and Gravel Company and had investigated the loss of one of her fleet in January of 1958. See Appendix C.

again by Captain Arzt. During this session, Mrs. Streb, according to at least one newspaper account, was the "key witness" to the vessel's disappearance when, during the session she was witnessed "pointing in the direction of Lloyd Neck from her home," stating "that's the exact spot where she went down." (*LI*, 17JAN1963) Mrs. Streb continued stating that "I didn't even realize it was in grave danger." When questioned about her previous testimony, she stated that she had not made a previous statement testifying that she "could see three or four men at one end of the tug. You could tell from the way they moved their arms that they were working desperately. Then all of a sudden, it all vanished." (*LI*, 17JAN1963) She clarified the previous statement for the investigator and other witnesses by stating that "the part about the vanishing is true, the part about the men is not true. I didn't make that statement." (*LI*, 17JAN1963) Another problem with her testimony was that she was confident that she had witnessed the vessel, not necessarily the *Gwendoline Steers*, at three-thirty in the afternoon, but the Coast Guard did not receive a radio call from the tug boat until an hour later.

Another witness was Kuno E. Hamann, who also resided on North Creek Road, in Eaton's Neck. He "testified that an anemometer at his home showed wind velocity at 58 to 60 m.p.h. at about 3:30 on the afternoon the *Gwendoline Steers* disappeared. He said at 4:00 he noted the temperature was two degrees above zero." (*LI*, 17JAN1963) Mr. Hamann continued and testified that "at about 4:00 he looked out a window in his home and saw a tug off Lloyd Neck near buoy six. He said however, he could not tell the color of the ship through his binoculars." (*LI*, 17JAN1963) He then remarked that he "had said when he saw the tug he remarked, 'You wouldn't think any job was that important to be out in this kind of weather.' Then he went out of his house to walk his dog. When he returned, he said, he again looked to Lloyd Neck for the tug. He said that he thought he saw the tug off Target Rock but that he could not be sure as his view was obstructed by salt spray on his window." (*LI*, 17JAN1963) Lastly, Hamann stated that he "could not say if the tug was covered with ice or not. The time was then about 4:30." (*LI*, 17JAN1963) According to the newspaper report, Hamann had previously stated that "I saw her trying to get into the harbor, but I didn't see her sink. I looked away a minute and when I looked again, she was gone." (*LI*, 17JAN1963)[160]

A nine year old boy, Steve Bayne, of North Creek Road in Eaton's Neck, also testified at the session. "He testified that he spotted a tug at about 4:30 in the afternoon. He pinpointed the location of the tug he saw on a chart of Long Island Sound. The boy said he watched the tug for about 10 minutes. He said he turned away. Five minutes later he came back and didn't see it anymore." (*LI*, 17JAN1963) His mother, Annette Bayne, followed her son's testimony. "She told the board, 'I saw a tug pulling barges at about 3:00 or 3:30. There was some equipment on the barges.' She said later she saw two tugs off Target Rock. 'I wasn't too sure which way they were going." (*LI*, 17JAN1963)[161]

The next eye-witness was a history teacher from Northport High School and a three year United States Navy veteran of the Second World War, Mr. Richard Streb. He "testified that he saw two tug boats, one coming out of the harbor, the other in the Sound headed south.' He said he saw the first boat off Target Rock between 3:00 and 3:30. 'I couldn't tell the color,' he said. He testified he could not identify the boat by name or company." (*LI*, 17JAN1963) Streb continued his detailed testimony. He "saw the second boat off Lloyd Point. 'It was low in the water at the bow,' he said...the boat was not making progress, but because it was holding the same position against heavy seas and winds it must have been under power.' According to Streb the tug he first spotted came from Northport Harbor, reached Target Rock, then turned around and went back

---

[160] Capt. Arzt asked about Mr. Hamann's original statement. Capt. Arzt told Hamann that the statement "inferred that the tug boat sank." Hamann responded "I didn't make that statement." Arzt then asked another question, "Did you see a tugboat sink?" Hamann responded, "No." (*LI*, 17JAN1963)

[161] Clearly, the eye-witnesses had seen multiple vessels. Most reports indicated that the *Gwendoline Steers* left New York bound for Northport "light" thus indicating that she had no barges in tow during her east-bound trip. The plan was to return to New York with barges that she would have taken in tow had she reached port.

into the harbor. The second boat, bound for Northport remained off Lloyd Point all the time he watched it. He said he last spotted the inbound tug at about 3:15." (*LI*, 17JAN1963)[162]

In an attempt to learn more about the *Gwendoline Steers'* seaworthiness, two former crewmen of the tug boat, who had been on board the tug when she had run aground on the 22nd of December, also testified. "John Whelan, a mate on the tug testified that "the accident [grounding] was his fault and did not result from malfunction of the boat." (*LI*, 17JAN1963) One of the engineers from that same incident was also questioned. "Owen McKay stated that the ship's engines and steering gear were functioning properly when he was aboard her." (*LI*, 17JAN1963)[163]

Despite the testimony provided, Chief Warrant Officer Bannan discounted much of the testimony. He stated that he "couldn't say whether or not witnesses could have seen what they claimed to have seen." But he had serious reservations just the same. According to an interview in the *Long Islander*, Chief Warrant Officer Bannan stated that it "would have been impossible to observe the tug from the Station. He said that there were 'two different vantage points' involved, and that if the tug be seen from the bluffs it would not necessarily be visible from the station." (*LI*, 10JAN1963)

While the Coast Guard and the Suffolk County Marine Patrol and Police Department continued their investigation, the Steers Sand and Gravel Company also continued to support the search efforts for their missing flagship and crewmen.[164] "The Steers Sand and Gravel Company of Northport is painstakingly

---

[162] Interestingly none of the reports I have been able to locate indicate the identity of the first tug boat. The testimony that could have been ascertained by that tug boat's crew would have provided an interesting view of the situation.

[163] Testifying the previous week, Archibald Niven had told Capt. Arzt that "engineers for Steers had made numerous studies of the tug's stability. Capt Arzt ordered Niven to present the results to him. Results have not yet been revealed." (*LI*, 10JAN1963) Most likely these stability reports are contained in the official Coast Guard Investigation notes.

[164] The Steers Sand and Gravel Company had faced a similar situation in January 1958 when their diesel tug, *Jim Steers*, disappeared "between Kings Point and City Island, near Stepping Stones

173

surveying and charting Huntington Bay in an all-out effort to find the missing tugboat," the newspaper article highlighted. (*LI*, 17JAN1963) "A spokesmen from the firm's New York office said yesterday (*LI*, 16JAN1963) surveyors and chart experts are working hand in hand to pinpoint the location of the tugboat," and that "all sightings of the boat have been recorded on a chart. These sightings are then cross-checked and areas for search determined." (*LI*, 17JAN1963) An airplane, in addition to aircraft launched by the United States Coast Guard, searched the area in addition to "crews on land an in boats." (*LI*, 17JAN1963)

Interestingly, the spokesman stated that "no attempt has been made to comb the bottom outside the immediate area of Huntington Bay," even though the "bodies of two crewmembers were found two weeks ago in Smithtown Bay." The spokesman confirmed that it was "believed the ship is still in one piece…as there were no boilers on the boat that could blow up." (*LI*, 17JAN1963) The efforts of the Steers Sand and Gravel Company would continue. On January 23, 1963, a spokesman from the company stated that "the firm is sending craft out to search every day that weather permits…there's nothing new to report." (*LI*, 24JAN1963)

On January 31, 1963, the *Long Islander* reminded its readers that the "Tug Was Lost One Month" prior. Though three men had been found and various flotsam recovered, the following weeks had provided little headway into the investigation. The Steers Sand and Gravel Company informed the newspaper that their search efforts were continuing and were equally as frustrated. The wait for answers continued. Two weeks later, Captain Frederick Arzt officially closed the investigation into the disappearance of the tugboat. He stated that he would write the "report from the testimony" collected during his investigation. (*LI*, 14FEB1963) The *Gwendoline Steers* and six members of the crew remained missing. Captain Arzt declined to "reveal the contents of his report" prior to its formal completion. (*LI*, 14FEB1963)

Light." (Rattray, 153) See *Appendix C* for a short history of the disappearance and recovery of the *Jim Steers*.

Patrolmen J. McCrickert, Thomas Giarratano and Detective J. Harrington identify a life preserver found in the waters near the Coast Guard Station.
Drawing based on photograph. January 10, 1963.

Left: Captain Arzt (center) speaks to Det. Harrington (left) while a diver (foreground) repairs his gear.

Right: Steers Sand & Gravel supervisor speaks with Capt. Arzt.

Bottom Left: Tugboat *Judith Steers* with a Coast Guard 44' on the dive site.
(Drawings based on photographs.18APR63)

A little less than a month after Captain Arzt closed his investigation into the disappearance to the *Gwendoline Steers*, more information surfaced. On April 11, 1963, a body was found in the waters at the entrance to Centerport Harbor. The body, which was discovered by a fisherman, was later identified utilizing papers found in the pockets of his clothes. It was Robert Nolan, the mate of the *Gwendoline Steers*. "Two hours later on the shore of nearby Smithtown Bay," another body was discovered. (*NYT*, 12APR1963) three months after the tragedy, five of the nine crewmen had finally been found. The search for the tugboat continued.

During the same time frame, a deckhand on board the tugboat *Judith Steers* "spotted a hawser floating in the water." (*LI*, 18APR1963) The crew of the *Judith Steers* hauled in the line and was later "identified by the manufacturer as the one made for the *Gwendoline*." (*LI*, 18APR1963) A spokesman from the Steers Sand and Gravel Company stated that "the line had an identifying piece of yarn woven into it" and that "a piece of aluminum mast, similar to the one mounted on the *Gwendoline*, was found attached to the hawser." (*LI*, 18APR1963) Upon the discovery of the hawser line and mast, the crew of the *Judith Steers* marked the area with a buoy. A diving team of three men was brought to the scene to begin an underwater investigation of the area. After waiting a few days due to inclement weather, the divers began their on the bottom search for any other clues.

On April 13, 1963, the divers descended into the spring waters of the Long Island Sound to investigate the tugboat's remains. The *Gwendoline Steers* was finally located, one hundred yards from where the crew of the *Judith Steers* had found the hawser line.[165] "Lying in about forty feet of water," the tugboat was sitting upright in the mud, her superstructure only twenty-feet below the surface. (*NYT*, 15APR1963) The three divers performed an inspection of the hull during their time on the tugboat. They did not see any reason why the tugboat

---

[165] Captain Arzt noted that the *Gwendoline Steers* "had gone down with five degrees of the point where eye-witnesses on Eaton's Neck last saw her on Dec. 30." (*LI*, 18APR1963)

went to the bottom. She was found in the waters off of Huntington Harbor and according to a brief newspaper article, salvage operations began on the 16th in an effort to determine what sent the tugboat and her crew to the bottom of the Long Island Sound. "Soon divers were dispatched, but after inspecting the hull they found no bodies. They also searched accessible areas inside the tug, but found no bodies." (Carr, 38)[166] Though she had been located, determination of why she went to the bottom taking with her, all of her crew with the exception of Hugh Reid who had managed to get into a lifeboat, would remain illusive.

By April 18, 1963, preparations were being made to dynamite the wreck. According to the owners of the tug, "the purpose of finding the boat was to locate bodies, not the hull." (*LI*, 18APR1963)[167] President of the Steers Sand and Gravel Company, J. Rich Steers stated that "we've already written off the value of the hull." (*LI*, 18APR1963)[168] The divers "combed the interior of the sip despite the thick mud which entombs her hold...[they] found no one aboard her." (*LI*, 18APR1963) Because the tugboat was in the channel and posed a possible danger to other vessels navigating the area, something had to be done with the tugboat.

While the United States Army Corps of Engineers conducted their inspection of the wreck for the proposed demolition, a private marine salvage firm, "filed for salvage rights" and that "salvages rights [were] being negotiated."

---

[166] The reference to her hull being inspected is vague. Because she was sitting on her keel in the mud, a thorough inspection of the hull would have been unattainable.

[167] Members of the community, including Albert R. Mead, questioned the failure to raise the tugboat from the bottom of the Long Island Sound. In a letter to the editor of the *Long Islander*, published in the May 9, 1963 edition, he stated that "the frogman type of inspection is good to a point, but if any structural damage caused the tug to sink it probably could not be determined if the break was inaccessible." He further commented that "some consideration should be given to raising this tug and properly inspecting the bottom, since structural failures are by no means scarce in ship construction particularly if improper materials and improper welding techniques were inadvertently used." After providing examples of other larger vessels that were also victims of brittle fracture, he concluded that he thought that "we owe the families of the men who lost their lives and other seamen a more thorough investigation." (*LI*, 9MAY1963) Interestingly, even though the paper had been covering the story for over four months, the spelling of the tugboat's name appeared as *Gwendolyn Steers*.

[168] It was later reported that the Steers Sand and Gravel Company had privately abandoned the tugboat on February 7th, 1963, even though it had not yet been located by their search efforts or government inspectors.

(*LI*, 9MAY1963) The U.S. Army Corps of Engineers stated that either way, the *Gwendoline Steers* "would have to be removed from the federal channel" even if no funds for the job were available from the federal government or if the private firm interested in the salvage of the vessel reneged on their proposal. (*LI*, 9MAY1963)

As divers and officials of the United States Army Corps of Engineers continued to attempt to determine the final fate of the tugboat, another body was found. On Friday May 3, 1963, Howard Riggs found an unidentified body at "Crescent Beach." It was believed that the body was one of the crewmen of the *Gwendoline Steers*. The body was clothed in a pair of "dungarees, a woolen sweater and a lined jacket." (*LI*, 9MAY1963) From May 3 until May 20, Rasmus Nordvick, Claude Markell and John Iverson were recovered in the waters of the Long Island Sound or on the beaches of the north shore. Only one member of the crew remained unaccounted for.

In light of the discovery of the tugboat, Captain Arzt had re-opened his investigation into the *Gwendoline Steers* loss. He reported that he had some "1,200 pages of testimony…[he had] made several recommendations and that he drawn certain conclusions concerning the vessel's sinking." (*LI*, 9MAY,1963) He would not publicly comment however as to the conclusions he had developed until he had the opportunity to complete the report and the report had been reviewed by the Commandant of the Coast Guard. Family members, the Steers Sand and Gravel Company, and the public continued to wait to find out why the tugboat had vanished beneath the waves.

On May 26, 1963, the last body believed to be one of the crewmen from the *Gwendoline Steers* was found in the waters of the Long Island Sound. The unidentified body "was found floating 300 feet north of Race Point at the eastern tip of Long Island." (*LI*, 30MAY1963) The police eventually identified the body as Roy L. Burnett, a deckhand on board the tugboat. All of the crew had finally been recovered. The *Gwendoline Steers* remained on the bottom.[169]

Prior to any determination by the United States Coast Guard investigation, Mrs. Mae Dickman, widow of Capt. Herbert Dickman filed an eight million dollar lawsuit against the Steers Sand and Gravel Company in Manhattan Federal Court.[170] Harry Lipsig, Mrs. Dickman's attorney explained that the case was based on the fact that the defendant, Steers Sand and Gravel Company was "negligent in sending out a vessel that was improperly overhauled," and as a result of their negligence, Captain Dickman "sustained grievous personal injuries resulting in his eventual death when the defendant's tugboat sank with all aboard." (*NYT*, 11JUN1963)[171]

Two weeks after Mrs. Dickman's pending lawsuit was reported, the United States Army Corps of Engineers announced that the *Gwendoline Steers* would remain beneath the waves.[172] "In an official statement...a spokesman for the technical liaison division of the engineers said that the *Gwendoline* is now resting 20 feet below the surface at mean low tide. He said ships that ply waters at the mouth of Huntington Bay will not be endangered by the downed craft." (*LI*, 27JUN1963) This was a change from U.S. Army Corps of Engineers' initial announcement that indicated that "engineers felt the tug constituted a menace to navigation [and that] it would have to be removed from the federal channel." (*LI*, 27JUN1963) Coast Guardsmen from the Eaton's Neck station were ordered to remove the temporary flashing buoy from the site in accordance with the corps'

---

[169] As of May 29, 1963, Captain Arzt had reportedly concluded his report, but had not yet signed off on it. This information was provided by Commander David Brock, who replaced Captain Arzt. Commander Brock did not provide any comment regarding the report. (*LI*, 30MAY1963)

[170] The newspaper report from April 12 and June 11, 1963 both utilize the *Gwendolyn* spelling of the vessel's name. Several histories and websites list the vessel's name in this fashion; however a close examination on an undated photograph clearly identifies the spelling as *Gwendoline Steers*.

[171] A final determination regarding Mrs. Dickman's lawsuit was not found during the author's research.

[172] Why the private marine salvage company determined to not pursue the salvage of the *Gwendoline Steers* could not be determined.

determination. The *Gwendoline Steers* was, as the newspaper article outlined, "Left to Sea and Salvagers." (*LI*, 27JUN1963)

During the first week of October 1963, the investigation into the *Gwendoline Steers* was finally published. The 1,200 page report took nine months to complete, provided three possible "reasons for the tug's disappearance but that none of them could be confirmed." (*LI*, 10OCT1963)[173] In addition, the report did not note any evidence of negligence or violation of navigational regulations in connection with the incident." On the bottom of the Long Island Sound, the *Gwendoline Steers* ended her days along with eight of her nine men. One man, the engineer Hugh Reid had survived long enough to escape the sinking tugboat but froze before he could tell any other soul, what exactly had happened during the final moments of the *Gwendoline Steers*. It will, as indicated in most newspaper reports of the era, "was, is, and probably always will be, a mystery."

Since its loss at the very end of 1962, the *Gwendoline Steers* has attracted many divers and fishermen. "Visibility is generally poor, varying from 2 to 10+ feet. All of the portholes, gauges and other usually sought after souvenirs" were removed during subsequent underwater visits to the wreckage. (Bachand, 46) Scuba diver Harold Acker stated that "the last time I dove the *Gwendoline Steers* was August 2nd 1992. Around that time, due to the affordability of Loran equipment, the site became a popular dive location for local divers and dive shops. The tugboat faces south and is in a straight up-right position. The vessel has been picked clean by divers over the years. On my last dive I was pulling myself along the starboard side toward the bow and a chock pin came off into my hand. (My only souvenir) The wheel house is clean and due

---

[173] The 1,200 page report has also become a bit of a mystery. Multiple attempts were made by the author to locate a copy of the report for the preparation of this chapter. Neither the United States Coast Guard nor the National Archives have been able to locate the report. As of the publication of the first edition of this research, attempts continue to be made to locate the report. If successful in locating the report, subsequent editions will include any pertinent information gathered from the document.

to its height it has the best visibility. The hull has settled into the mud and unless you're lucky, it is difficult to see. The skeleton of the wreck is very much intact. Visibility overall is one of the biggest issues on this wreck. For locals and because of the *Life* magazine photo, which brought the harsh realities of the incident to light, it is a must dive."

The January 11, 1963 issue of *Life* magazine featured the famous photograph of the only crewman of the *Gwendoline Steers* to escape the sinking vessel. How he was able to launch the lifeboat remains one of the unanswered questions. Author's collection.

Though she has been visited, observed and many of her artifacts retrieved by divers, what caused the tugboat to sink beneath the waves on that blistery cold and savage day in late 1962 remains a mystery. The tugboat sits upright on the bottom. Therefore her current position limits examination of her hull. A close inspection of the hull would either validate or dismiss the theory that the repairs made to the damaged area from her previous grounding were completed negligently. If the previously damaged hull was not the cause of the sinking, a buildup of ice was the probable culprit. Unless a terrible storm, similar to the one that sent her to the bottom dislodges the *Gwendoline Steers* from her muddy entombment and places her on her side, the cause will remain a mystery and the crewmen's terrible last moments, an unimaginable memory.

The proceeding histories are just a few of the myriad wrecks in our local waters. To go deeper into the history and beneath the surface, one must be willing to take a proverbial plunge into the past as there are many ways for those wishing to learn more to explore our maritime history. For those who wish to reach down and touch history with their own hands, I would recommend becoming a certified diver. This certification and training allows an individual to begin to descend into the depths so that he or she can visit many of the wrecks that litter our local waters. If one is more relegated and comfortable with the confines of shore, ways abound to learn more... without getting their feet wet.

Becoming a certified diver is a great way to learn more about the nautical world. First gaining popularity after the introduction of the Aqualung and television programs such as *Sea Hunt* and documentaries by Captain Jacques Yves-Cousteau and his crew aboard the *Calypso*, scuba diving is a continually growing hobby and vocation. Once you have decided to take the plunge, your first step is to contact a local dive shop to get trained and certified. Divers learn the fundamentals of diving in the safe environs of a pool and are usually tested during open water dives in relatively shallow waters of either the north or south shores of Long Island or in one of the many quarries in Pennsylvania. By getting certified, divers can then continue with more advanced diving classes and qualifications, travel throughout the world and slip beneath the waves to learn more about the creatures and shipwrecks of the deep. Divers can also join diving clubs and organizations which provide new divers with a band of brothers and sisters who enjoy the depths and can assist in getting over any remaining reservations related to diving.

Landlubbers can also enjoy the wonders of our nautical history by diving into the wealth of work pertaining to the undersea world. Many local libraries have multiple volumes that tell the rich tales of men, their ships and the sea. On-line communities that focus in on ships and shipwrecks stream throughout the internet world and are accessible at the click of a mouse. Historical societies, some based within communities and others, such as the Underwater Historical Research Society and Wrecksploration provide a host of information to those interested in learning more. They also are a welcoming home to those who want to learn more about local history both above and below the waves.

Throughout the tri-state area there is a wealth of museums that house the rich treasures of our history. Some, such as the Long Island Maritime Museum and the Merchant Marine Museum at King's Point focus on nautical history. Others, such as the Suffolk County Vanderbilt Mansion, Planetarium and Museum highlight various aspects of local history. The museums collectively are more than just a refuge for the past, with their glass cases, photographs, and artifacts. They provide both a portal into a by-gone era and also a door to the future of historical reflection and research for the entire family or group of friends.

Ultimately, there are multiple ways for those interested in learning more about the world beneath the waves. By diving beneath the waves literally or by delving into the history books, the world of undersea history is at your fin or fingertips. Enjoy going deeper into the past!

My research into the shipwrecks covered in *Claimed by the Sea* is, like the tides, an ongoing process. As more dives are completed on these wrecks and others and as researchers dig deeper into the archives, more and more information will come to light regarding the amazing maritime history of our local waters. This introduction into the history of local shipwrecks will have hopefully wet the reader's intellectual palette to pursue more reading and research on their own. The readers who would like to learn more will soon realize that there is a wealth of sources available to dive not only into the archives, but also the water to explore, hands on, the history of some of our local shipwrecks.

Author on the bottom of the Long Island Sound conducting research.

Several historical organizations, such as the *Underwater Historical Research Society* and *Wreckslporation* both actively conduct research in the waters off of Long Island, New York. Both organizations open the world of underwater research to those interested in learning more. Whether your interest is in the library, archive or on the internet or on board the dive boat suiting up to take a dip into the shadows below, both organizations are a great way of getting involved. Local dive shops are a great way of getting connected into the world of scuba diving. Once certified as open-water scuba divers, these divers can begin to explore the depths of both local and far away shipwrecks. Added training will provide the diver with additional experience and knowledge of scuba diving which will in turn provide the ability to dive deeper into the depths to visit other wrecks, remains, etc.

When I think back to my initial "immersion" into underwater and maritime historical research, I realize that I started the exact same way. I found myself wanting to know more about the water around me, the wrecks that lie on the bottom, and the animals that made the sea their home. After training, diving, researching, making mistakes, learning from my mistakes and time on task, I have found that I have, figuratively speaking, been claimed by the sea. I have found myself on a dive boat before most people wake up and have their first cup of coffee. I have found myself reading and researching in dusty libraries looking for clues or reference to a long forgotten vessel or military action in the middle of the night. I have found myself looking out to sea and wondering what is below the surface. It is this amazement of the sea that leaves me mesmerized, captured, and claimed.

Robert Frost, one of my favorite poets remarked on the awe of the sea in his poem *Neither Out Far Nor In Deep*.

> *The people along the sand*
> *All turn and look one way.*
> *They turn their back on the land.*
> *They look at the sea all day.*
>
> *As long as it takes to pass*
> *A ship keeps raising its hull;*
> *The wetter ground like glass*
> *Reflects a standing gull.*
>
> *The land may vary more;*
> *But wherever the truth may be –*
> *The water comes ashore,*
> *And the people look at the sea.*
>
> *They cannot look out far.*
> *They cannot look in deep.*
> *But when was that ever a bar*
> *To any watch they keep?*

When I reflect upon this poem, I realize that by being an underwater historical researcher, I can look deeper. I can attempt to find answers and clues. I can descend through the water to a wreck and explore. I can look for information and determine the final moments of the ship. As I ascend from the depths, I can think about what I have seen. Upon my return to the surface I can then reflect upon my experiences, record my findings and begin to tell others. It is a great adventure that starts with one step, or in this case, one leap off of the boat, fin first. It is, in my opinion, certainly a step or leap worth taking on a pathway of lifelong adventure.

In Philippe Diole's book, *The Undersea Adventure*, he explains his never-ending fascination with the deep:

> *"But what am I to say, a sea-explorer whose objective is never reached, and who has never seen the end of those marine vaults, one minute black with shadows, the next hacked with swords of light? Here and there I have managed to snatch the fragments of knowledge, I have tried to use my eyes and understand the meaning of what was before me, and to fit together where I could the pieces of the vague jig-saw of the sea."*(Lewis, 2)

Diole's words resonate with every explorer of the deep and of history that I have ever met or read. These are words that drive me to dive deeper not only to explore and learn more about the rich nautical history of our world, but also to learn more about myself. I hope you have enjoyed this dip into the maritime history of Long Island Waters. I hope that you too find yourself immersed in the abyss of local history and exploring the vast mysterious marine vaults of our local waters!

The idea of writing a volume that focused in on a selected number of shipwrecks had always swayed by an anchor in my mind. Bound by other projects and responsibilities however, I let the idea lay in ordinary. It was not until I was approached to assist with a museum exhibit being sponsored by the Society for the Preservation of Long Island Antiquities did I finally haul in the proverbial anchor line and set out for sea and into the past. While researching for *Claimed by the Sea* I quickly learned that two historians had provided a wealth of information for historians and other researchers. Their work and previous research acted throughout my researching for this book, as a beacon on the sometimes stormy waves between reason, history and legend. The more I dove into the historical record, read old newspapers articles and scanned through various texts, did I realize that two of the historians had spent a huge part of their lives recording the stories of ships, shipwrecks and our local waters.

Both men had spent a large part of their lives researching and writing about various aspects of nautical history. I also learned that both men resided on Long Island, one very close to my own home town. I hoped that I would be able to contact them both for insight and additional information. As I began drafting up letters to both individuals, I quickly learned that I was too late. First, I was saddened while reading the *Gold Coast Gazette* on December 20, 2007. I learned that Mr. Frank Braynard had passed away just ten days prior. While attempting to contact the other hugely influential historian, Mr. Van R. Field, I learned that he too had passed, just two days after Mr. Braynard.

Though I was saddened by the loss of both historians, I realized that they would live on through their various writings, books, artwork and articles. Mr. Braynard left behind a legacy of over forty books and Mr. Field left a voluminous amount of articles and books with one being published posthumously.[174] They had lived amazing lives full of adventure and both had enriched the lives of those who had the opportunity to meet them, read their work and listen to them both spin yarns about the sea which they clearly loved so much.

Saddened yes, but disappointed no. I realized that both men had left to a new generation of researchers, a compass bearing to steer by into the future of historical research. They had provided a solid foundation of maritime and nautical history that I and other researchers could utilize in our efforts to further explore and document the rich legacy of our waters. Both men, having crossed the bar, leave us behind with their work, their accomplishments and their memory. This book is dedicated to the passengers, crews and vessels that were claimed by the sea, but it is also in memory of Mr. Frank Braynard and Mr. Van R. Field. *To the two gentlemen sailor-scholars who crossed the bar in December of 2007 - Thank you for all of the great stories of ships, shipwrecks and the sea.*

---

[174] *Mayday! Shipwrecks and Sea Tales Off Long Island's Eastern Shore* was published in March of 2008 by The History Press.

Notes

Chapter 1 - *S.S. Savannah*

Baughman, James P. *S.S. Savannah: The Elegant Steam Ship - The Journal of Southern History*, Vol. 30, No. 1. (Feb., 1964), pp. 108-109.

Bloomster, Edgar L. *Sailing and Small Craft Down the Ages*. U.S. Naval Institute. Annapolis, Maryland. Originally published in 1940. Second edition published in November 1957.

Braynard, Frank O. *S.S. Savannah: The Elegant Steam Ship*. University of Georgia Press. Athens, Georgia. 1963.

Cavanaugh, Cam, Hoskins, Barbara, & Pingeon, Frances, D. *At Speedwell in the Nineteenth Century*. Speedwell Village. 1981. Available online at www.parks.morris.nj.us/sss/sss.html.

Cussler, Clive & Dirgo, Craig. *The Sea Hunters – True Adventures with Famous Shipwrecks*. Pocket Star Books, Inc. New York, New York. 2003 edition. Originally published in hard cover by Simon & Schuster, Inc. 1996

Ellis, C. Hamilton. *Ships, A Pictorial History from Noah's Ark to the U.S.S. United States*. Peeble Press International Inc., New York, New York. 1974. Originally published by Hulton Press, Ltd., London, England as *A Picture History of Ships*.

Freuchen, Peter. *Peter Freuchen's Book of the Seven Seas*. Jullian Messner, Inc. New York, New York. 1957.

Haws, Duncan. *Ships and the Sea, A Chronological Review*. Chancellor Press. 2nd edition. 1985. Originally published by Hart, Davis, MacGibbon, Ltd. 1976.

Langer, William L. *An Encyclopedia of World History*. Revised edition (3rd). 1952. Houghton Mifflin Company, Boston, Massachusetts. The Riverside Press, Cambridge, Massachusetts.

Marx, Robert F. *Shipwrecks in the Americas*. Dover Publications, Inc. New York. 1987 Edition. Originally published in 1971.

McKenna, Richard. *The Dictionary of Nautical Literacy*. International Marine/McGraw-Hill, N.Y., N.Y. 2003 edition.

National Park Service. *Submerged Resources Center, Projects Listing, Fire Island National Seashore*. Report available online at http://home.nps.gov/applications/submerged

National Underwater and Marine Agency (NUMA). *Expeditions Listing. Savannah*. Available online at www.numa.net/expeditions/savannah.html.

New York Mirror. Newspaper. *Try Again to Find Steamer*. By Harry L. Ober. 14MAY1959.

Rattray, Jeanette Edwards. *Ship Ashore! A Record of Maritime Disasters off Montauk and Eastern Long Island, 1640-1955*. Coward –McCann, Inc. Yankee Peddler Book Company, Southampton, New York Edition. 1955.

Smith, Raymond K. *Patchogue Bay's Part in Delving for the S.S. Savannah. The Ensign*. Official Publication of the U.S. Power Squadron. February 1959.

The Long Island Forum. Amityville, New York.
        Sept. 1957 – page. 176 – *Search for the Savannah*.
        June 1962 – Cover – *Original Drawing of the Savannah* – F. Braynard
        June 1962 – page 121 – *The Two Savannahs*. by Henry. C. Joralemon

The Patchogue Advance. Newspaper. Patchogue, New York.
        May 21, 1959 – *Has 'Savannah' Been Found?*
        July 19, 1960 – *Start Sea Hunt For Savannah, Sunken Ships*
        Aug. 11, 1960 – *Search for Ships*. (Photograph & caption)

Villiers, Alan. Captain. *Men Ships and the Sea. (The Story of Man Library)* National Geographic Society. Washington, DC. First edition, 1962. Second Edition, 1973.

Williams, Guy R. *The World of Model Ships and Boats*. G.P. Putnam's Sons, New York, New York. 1971.

Chapter 2 – *Lexington*

A Full and Particular Account of All the Circumstances Attending The Loss of the Steamboat LEXINGTON, in Long-Island Sound, On the Night of January 13, 1840. H.H. Brown and A.H. Stillwell. Providence, Rhode Island. 1840.

Berman, Bruce D. *Encyclopedia of American Shipwrecks*. The Mariners Press Incorporated. Boston, Massachusetts. 1972.

Cussler, Clive & Dirgo, Craig. *The Sea Hunters – True Adventures with Famous Shipwrecks.* Pocket Star Books, Inc. New York, New York. 2003 edition. Originally published in hard cover by Simon & Schuster, Inc. 1996

Field, Van R. *Wrecks and Rescues on Long Island – The Story of the U.S. Lifesaving Service.* Searles Graphics, Inc. East Patchogue, NY. 1997.

Gentile, Gary. *Shipwrecks of New York.* Gary Gentile Productions, Philadelphia, PA. First Edition. 1996.

Long Island Genealogy website. Article: *Lexington* available online at www.longislandgeneology.com/shipwrecks.

Peters, Harry T. *Currier & Ives – Printmakers to the American People.* Doubleday, Doran & Co., Inc. Garden City, New York. 1942.

Rattray, Jeanette Edwards. *Ship Ashore! A Record of Maritime Disasters off Montauk and Eastern Long Island, 1640-1955.* Coward –McCann, Inc. Yankee Peddler Book Company, Southampton, New York Edition. 1955.

The Long Islander Newspaper. Huntington, New York.*
        August 12, 1842 – page 3
        June 2, 1843 – page 2
        Courtesy of the Suffolk County Historical Society.

Chapter 3 – *Circassian*

Anderson, Bern. *By Sea and by River – The Naval History of the Civil War.* Da Capo Press, Inc., New York, NY. Reprinted in 1989. Originally published by Alfred A. Knopf, Inc. 1962.

Bloomster, Edgar L. *Sailing and Small Craft Down the Ages.* U.S. Naval Institute Press, Annapolis, Maryland. 2nd edition. 1957. Originally published in 1940.

Chapman, Charles F. *Piloting, Seamanship and Small Boat Handling.* The Hearst Corporation, New York, NY. 1964. Motor Boating Vol. 5 – Motor Boating's Ideal Series. (44th edition of the text.) 1965-66 Edition.

Field, Van R. *Wrecks and Rescues on Long Island – The Story of the U.S. Lifesaving Service.* Searles Graphics, Inc. East Patchogue, NY. 1997.

Gentile, Gary. *Shipwrecks of New York.* Gary Gentile Productions, Philadelphia, PA. First Edition. 1996.

Marhoefer, Barbara. *Witches, Whales, Petticoats & Sails – Adventures and Misadventures from Three Centuries of Long Island History*. Ira J. Friedman Division of Kennikat Press. Port Washington, N.Y. 1971.

McKenna, Robert. *The Dictionary of Nautical Literacy*. International Marine-McGraw Hill, U.S.A. 2nd Edition, 2003. First edition published by the same in 2001.

Rattray, Jeanette Edwards. *Ship Ashore! A Record of Maritime Disasters off Montauk and Eastern Long Island, 1640-1955.* Coward –McCann, Inc. Yankee Peddler Book Company, Southampton, New York Edition. 1955.

The New York Times. On-line archives for the following articles:
   Feb. 3, 1857 – *Marine Items*
   Mar. 23, 1857 – *Non-Arrival of the Circassian*
   Mar. 23, 1857 – *News of the Day*
   Mar. 24, 1857 – *Non-Arrival of the Circassian*
   Apr. 7, 1857 – *Arrival of the Circassian at Halifax*
   Apr. 11, 1857 – *Ocean Steamers*
   Apr. 18, 1857 – *Departure of the Circassian*
   Apr. 22, 1857 – *The Steamers Circassian and Khersonese*
   June 1, 1857 – *News of the Day*
   May 23, 1862 – *Our Cruisers in the Gulf*
   June 24, 1862 – *The Prize Steamer Circassian – A Falsehood Nailed*
   July 1, 1862 – *Arrival of the Prize Steamship Circassian of London*
   Aug. 6, 1862 – *General City News*
   Oct. 24, 1862 – *Sale of the Cargo of the Prize Steamer Circassian*
   Feb. 3, 1865 – *Prize Laws – Case of the Circassian*
   Oct. 21, 1865 – *A Passenger Steamship Ashore – No Lives Lost*
   Oct. 25, 1865 – *Negro Insurrection at Jamaica –*
                  The Circassian's Passengers
   Feb. 8, 1872 – *Burned at Sea*
   May 7, 1874 – *Loss of the Steam-ship Linda*
   Dec. 15, 1876 – *Ill-fated Vessels*
   Dec. 31, 1876 – *History of the Circassian*
   Dec. 31, 1876 – *Loss of the Circassian*
   Dec. 31, 1876 – *Statement of a Custom-House Inspector –*
                  Appalling Scenes at the Wreck.
   Jan. 1, 1877 – *The Circassian Wreck*
   Jan. 2, 1877 – *The Wreck of the Circassian*
   Jan. 3, 1877 – *The Pilot Commissioner*
   Jan. 3, 1877 – *The Wrecked Ship Circassian*
   Jan. 8, 1877 – *The Circassian Victims*
   Jan. 11, 1877 – *A Mistaken Policy*

Jan. 19, 1877 – *The Loss of the Circassian*
Jan. 30, 1884 – *The Circassian Disabled*
May 3, 1888 – *The Circassian Disabled*

Chapter 4 - *Seawanhaka*

Schaer, Sidney C. *Centennial of a Shipwreck, Remembering a tragedy for Island commuters*. *Newsday*. June 28, 1980. Long Island, New York.

The New York Times. On-line archives for the following articles:
June 29, 1880 – *A Steam-Boat in Flames*
June 29, 1880 – *Mr. V. Lopez's Story*
June 29, 1880 – *The Burned Steam-Boat*
July 1, 1880 – *The Seawanhaka Disaster*
July 1, 1880 – *The Seawanhaka Victims*
July 2, 1880 – *More Bodies Discovered*
July 3, 1880 – *Ten More Bodies Found*
July 4, 1880 – *Searching for the Dead*
July 5, 1880 – *Burial of Joseph I. Stein*
July 6, 1880 – *The Ill-Fated Seawanhaka*
July 7, 1880 – *Hunting For Seawanhaka Relics*
July 8, 1880 – *Derelict Steam-Boat Owners*
July 13, 1880 – *Examining the Seawanhaka's Crew*
July 25, 1880 – *Her Boilers Burst First*
July 30, 1880 – *Loss of the Seawanhaka*
July 31, 1880 – *How the Fire Occurred*
Aug. 3, 1880 – *The Seawanhaka Tube*
Aug. 8, 1880 – *City and Suburban News*
Aug. 11, 1880 – *The Seawanhaka Indictments*
Aug. 12, 1880 – *The Seawanhaka Disaster*
Oct. 23, 1880 – *Brave Boys Rewarded*
Oct. 28, 1880 – *City and Suburban News*
Nov. 24, 1880 – *The Seawanhaka Disaster*
Dec. 1, 1880 – *City and Suburban News*
Feb. 15, 1881 – *The Seawanhaka Disaster*
Mar. 24, 1881 – *The Seawanhaka Disaster*
Mar. 29, 1881 – *For Neglect of Solemn Duty*
Apr. 10, 1881 – *They Might Have Agreed*
Apr. 11, 1881 – *The Seawanhaka Case*
July 25, 1881 – *Capt. Charles P. Smith Dead*
July 27, 1881 – *The Obsequies of a Hero*
Aug. 15, 1881 – *A Brave and Gallant Man*

Chapter 5 - *U.S.S. Ohio*

Berg, Daniel. *Long Island Shore Diver*. Aqua Explorers, Inc. 3rd Edition. 2001.

Bloomster, Edgar L. *Sailing and Small Craft Down the Ages*. U.S. Naval Institute. Annapolis, Maryland. Originally published in 1940. Second edition published in November 1957.

Gentile, Gary. *Shipwrecks of New York*. Gary Gentile Productions, Philadelphia, PA. First Edition. 1996.

Naval History Division, Office of the Chief of Naval Operations, U.S. Navy Department. *Dictionary of American Naval Fighting Ships*. Available on-line at http://www.history.navy.mil/danfs/index.html

Naval History Division, Office of the Chief of Naval Operations, U.S. Navy Department. *Dictionary of American Naval Fighting Ships. Appendix IV of Volume IV, Ships-of-the-Line.* Available on-line at http://www.hazegray.org/danfs/line/sotl.htm (Note - this is referenced within the chapter as DANFS, Appendix IV)

Smithsonian Institution Research Information System (SIRIS), Smithsonian American Art Museum. *Art Inventories Catalog*. Available on-line at http://siris-artinventories.si.edu/ipac20/ipac.jsp?uri=full=3100001~!344454!0

The Long Island Forum. Amityville, New York.
>   Sept. 1950 – pages 167, 171-172 – *The Story of a Figurehead* by Dr. Clarence A. Wood.
>   Oct. 1951 – pages 190-191 – *Hercules a Domestic Carving**
>   Dec. 1951 – pages 228-230 – *More About Hercules**
>   July 1952 – page. 129 – *Sidney Jennings*
>   Nov. 1952 – cover photograph – *U.S.S. Ohio*
>   Nov. 1952 – page 202 – *The Battleship Ohio**
>   *indicate a letter to the journal's editor, subsequently published.*

The New York Times. On-line archives of the following article:
>   November 24, 1895 – *Two Queer Figureheads*

Chapter 6 – *Oregon*

Field, Van R. *Wrecks and Rescues on Long Island – The Story of the U.S. Lifesaving Service*. Searles Graphics, Inc. East Patchogue, NY. 1997.

Gentile, Gary. *Shipwrecks of New York*. Gary Gentile Productions, Philadelphia, PA. First Edition. 1996.

The Long Island Forum. Amityville, New York.
      May 1963 – pages 101-102, 117-118 – *Underwater Research* – by Charles D. Dunn.

The New York Times. On-line archives for the following articles:
      May 21, 1884 – *The Steam-Ship Oregon Sold*
      February 2, 1886 – *New Cunard Line Arrangements*
      March 15, 1886 – *The Oregon Run Down*
      March 15, 1886 – *Landed at Fire Island*
      March 15, 1886 – *The Oregon's History*
      March 15, 1886 – *Capt. Cottier's Story*
      March 16, 1886 – *Over Three Million Lost*
      March 17, 1886 – *Two Masts Above Water*
      March 19, 1886 - *Around the Sunken Steamer*
      March 22, 1886 – *No Clue in the Life Preserver*

Rattray, Jeanette Edwards. *Ship Ashore! A Record of Maritime Disasters off Montauk and Eastern Long Island, 1640-1955.* Coward –McCann, Inc. Yankee Peddler Book Company, Southampton, New York Edition. 1955.

Chapter 7 – *Louis V. Place*

Bailey, Paul. *Historic Long Island in Pictures, Prose and Poetry*. Long Island Forum Publications. Amityville, New York. 1956.

Field, Van R. *Wrecks and Rescues on Long Island – The Story of the U.S. Lifesaving Service*. Searles Graphics, Inc. East Patchogue, NY. 1997.

Gonzalez, Ellice B. *Storms, Ships & Surfmen – The Lifesavers of Fire Island*. Eastern National. 2nd Edition. 2000. Originally published 1982.

Rattray, Jeanette Edwards. *Ship Ashore! A Record of Maritime Disasters off Montauk and Eastern Long Island, 1640-1955.* Coward –McCann, Inc. Yankee Peddler Book Company, Southampton, New York Edition. 1955.

The *Brooklyn Daily Eagle.* On-line archives for the following articles:
      Feb. 11, 1895 – *Cut Down the Icy Corpses*
      Feb. 12, 1895 – *The Mate's Body Found*
      Feb. 15, 1895 – *Latest Long Island News*
      Feb. 17, 1895 – *Frozen in the Rigging*
      Feb. 23, 1895 – *Latest Long Island News*

Feb. 25, 1895 – *Money for Mrs. Captain Squires*
Feb. 27, 1895 – *Another Body from the Wreck*
Mar. 1, 1895 – *Latest Long Island News*
Mar. 11, 1895 – *A Danish Sailor Buried*
Mar. 12, 1895 – *Captain Squires' Letter*
Mar. 24, 1895 – *A Hero of Five Wrecks*
Mar. 28, 1895 – *Captain Squires' Widow*

The New York Times. On-line archives for the following articles:
Feb. 8, 1895 – *Three Bodies Encased in Ice*
Feb. 10, 1895 – *About Zero Through New-England*
Feb. 10, 1895 – *Disasters in the Sound*
Feb. 11, 1895 – *Rescued by Life Savers*
Feb. 12, 1895 – *The Place's Cargo was Insured*
Feb. 14, 1895 – *Rode Out the Storm*
Feb. 24, 1895 – *Capt. Squires' Body Comes Ashore*

United States Life-Saving Service. *Annual Report of the Operations of the United States Life-Saving Service for the Fiscal Year Ending June 30, 1895*. Government Printing Office. Washington, DC. 1896.

Chapter 8 – *General Slocum*

Gentile, Gary. *Shipwrecks of New York*. Gary Gentile Productions, Philadelphia, PA. First Edition. 1996.

McKenna, Richard. *The Dictionary of Nautical Literacy*. International Marine/McGraw-Hill, N.Y., N.Y. 2003 edition.

National Underwater and Marine Agency (NUMA). *Expeditions Listing:* General Slocum. Available online at www.numa.net/expeditions/general_slocum.html.

Oppel, Frank. *Tales of Gaslight New York*. Castle Books, Edison, NJ. Originally published 1985. 2nd Edition published in 2000.

Randall, J.G. & Donald, David. *The Civil War and Reconstruction*. D.C. Heath and Company. Boston, Massachusetts. 2nd edition. 1961.

The New York Times. On-line archives for the following articles:
April 19, 1891 – *The General Slocum Launched*
July 30, 1894 – *Excitement on the Gen. Slocum*
August 16, 1894 – *The Slocum on a bar in the Storm*
August 17, 1894 – *Slocum Floated on Evening Tide*
September 2, 1894 – *A Tug Disables the Slocum*

August 18, 1901 – *Riot on Excursion Boat*
June 16, 1902 – *Rockaway Steamboat Fast on a Sandbar*
June 16, 1904 – *The Skipper's Story*
June 16, 1904 – *1,000 Lives May Be Lost in Burning of the Excursion Boat Gen. Slocum*
June 16, 1904 – *The General Slocum an Unlucky Craft*
June 16, 1904 – *This Girl Missed the Boat*
June 16, 1904 – *Disasters Similar to Slocum Horror*
June 18, 1904 – *Bodies Unrecovered; Companies Wrangle*
June 19, 1904 – *Says Men in Boats Robbed the Dying*
June 24, 1904 – *Slocum Wreck Raised; Towed to Flushing Bay*
January 28, 1906 – *Slocum Captain Guilty: Gets 10-Year Sentence*
October 3, 1907 – *No Longer the General Slocum*
December 6, 1911 – *The General Slocum Gone*

Weber, Harvey. *The Great Slocum Disaster*. *Newsday*. June 10, 1979. Long Island, New York.

Wilbanks, Ralph L. *Search for the General Slocum*. National Underwater and Marine Agency. Available online at www.numa.net/articles/search_for_the-general_slocum.html.

Chapter 9 – *U.S.S. San Diego*

Albert, Captain George J. *The U.S.S. San Diego and the California Naval Militia*. Article available online at www.militarymuseum.org/USSSanDiego.html.

Berg, Daniel. *The U.S.S. San Diego Shipwreck*. Available online at www.aquaexplorers.com/SanDiego.htm.

Berlitz, Charles. *The Bermuda Triangle*. Doubleday and Company, Inc. Garden City, N.Y. 1974.

Gentile, Gary. *U.S.S. San Diego – the Last Armored Cruiser*. Gary Gentile Productions. Philadelphia, PA. 1989.

Hagan, Kenneth J. *The People's Navy – The Making of American Sea Power*. The Free Press, A Division of Macmillan, Inc. New York, N.Y. 1991.

Hutchinson, Robert. *Jane's Submarines – War Beneath the Waves from 1776 to the Present Day*. Harper Collins Publishers. New York, N.Y. U.S. Edition, 2001.

Massie, Robert K. *Castles of Steel – Britain, Germany, and the Winning of the Great War at Sea*. Ballantine Books. New York, N.Y. 2003

Naval History Division, Office of the Chief of Naval Operations, U.S. Navy Department. *Dictionary of American Naval Fighting Ships*. Available on-line at http://www.history.navy.mil/danfs/index.html

Pitt, Barrie. *The Battle of the Atlantic*. WWII - Time-Life Books. Alexandria, Virginia. 1977.

Rattray, Jeanette Edwards. *Ship Ashore! A Record of Maritime Disasters off Montauk and Eastern Long Island, 1640-1955*. Coward –McCann, Inc. Yankee Peddler Book Company, Southampton, New York Edition. 1955.

Rattray, Jeanette Edwards. *The Perils of the Port of New York – Maritime Disasters from Sandy Hook to Execution Rocks*. Dodd, Mead & Company. New York, N.Y. 1973.

Sweetman, Jack. *American Naval History – An Illustrated Chronology of the U.S. Navy and Marine Corps, 1775-Present*. Naval Institute Press. Annapolis, Maryland. 2nd edition. 1991.

The Long Island Forum. Amityville, New York.
  May 1963 – pages 101-102, 117-118 – *Underwater Research* – by Charles D. Dunn.

The New York Times. On-line archives for the following articles:
  Jan. 23, 1915 – *Explosion Kills Five on Cruiser*
  Jan. 26, 1915 – *Sixth Death on San Diego*
  Mar. 21, 1915 – *Commends Brave Seamen*
  July 20, 1918 – *Sank After Explosion*
  July 20, 1918 – *100 Survivors Here*
  July 20, 1918 – *San Diego Once California*
  July 21, 1918 – *San Diego's Crew Differ As To Sinking*
  July 21, 1918 – *San Diego's Loss Still Unexplained; 1,183 Reach Port*
  July 21, 1918 – *The Sinking of the San Diego*
  July 21, 1918 – *Mine Sinks San Diego, Sec'y Daniels Thinks*
  July 23, 1918 – *Think Mine Sank San Diego*
  July 24, 1918 – *Only 8 San Diego Men Missing*
  July 25, 1918 – *Six Lost on the San Diego*
  Aug. 5, 1918 – *U-Boats Sink Three American Schooners; Germans Say Mine Sank Cruiser San Diego*
  Aug. 6, 1918 – *Decide Mine Sank Cruiser San Diego*
  Dec. 9, 1918 – *Daniels Reports on Navy's War Work*
  Jan. 14, 1919 – *Lost Bonds of the San Diego's Men*
  July 17, 1919 – *To Reissue Bonds Lost on San Diego*

Uboat.net – online archive of information. Available at www.uboat.net

Van Deurs, Rear Admiral G. *And the Navy Got Its Wings*. Article. *American Heritage*. October edition. American Heritage Publishing Company. New York, NY. 1956.

Chapter 10 – *Andrea Doria*

Bright, David. *Prototype Car of the Future on the Andrea Doria – Norseman*. Blog Entry. www.shipwreck.blogs.com.

Cousteau, Jacques-Yves and Dugan, James. *Captain Cousteau's Underwater Treasury*. Harper & Row, Publisher. New York, NY. 1959. *Exploration of the Sunken Liner Andrea Doria*, by Ramsey Parks. Pages 305-309.

Gentile, Gary. *Andrea Doria – Dive to an Era*. Gary Gentile Productions. Philadelphia, P.A. 1989.

Graves, William. *Treasure Hunting: The Professionals*. Chapter 4 of *Undersea Treasures*. Breeden, Robert L. (Editor) The National Geographic Society. National Geographic Society. Washington, D.C. 1974.

Hoffer, William. *Saved! The Story of the Andrea Doria – the Greatest Sea Rescue in History*. Summit Books. New York, N.Y. 1979.

Imperial Club. *The Story of Ghia & Chrysler*. Article. www.imperialclub.com

Keatts, Henry. *New England's Legacy of Shipwrecks*. American Merchant Marine Press. Kings Point, N.Y. 1988.

Kearney, Joseph F. *Andrea Doria Replica*. Available online at www.andreadoriareplica.com

Life Magazine. New York, N.Y.
   Aug. 6, 1956 – Lord, Walter. *An Epic Sea Rescue*.
   Sept. 17, 1956 – MacLeish, Kenneth. *Divers Explore the Sunken Doria*.

McKenna, Richard. *The Dictionary of Nautical Literacy*. International Marine/McGraw-Hill, N.Y., N.Y. 2003 edition.

Pathé Pictures, Inc. *Down to the Andrea Doria*. Newsreel. (6 minutes in length) 1956.

Roy, Rex. *Ten Concepts Detroit Should Have Built*. Article. Available online at www.thecarconnection.com

Chapter 11 – *Gwendoline Steers*

Bachand, Robert G. *Scuba Northeast, Shipwrecks, Dive Sites & Dive Activities Rhode Island to New Jersey. Volume II*. Sea Sports Publications. Norwalk, CT. 1986. Pages 46-47.

Carr, Edward A.T. *Faded Laurels – The History of Eaton's Neck and Asharoken*. Heart of the Lakes Publishing. Interlaken, N.Y. 1994. Second edition. Originally published in 1994.

Coleman, Tim & Soares, Charley. *Fishable Wrecks & Rockpiles*. MT Publications. Mystic, CT. 1989. Pages 66-67.

Glick, Les. *Diver's Guide to Long Island Waters*. Amphibian Enterprises. Manorville, NY. First Edition, 1990. 2nd Edition, 1992. Page 46.

Life Magazine. New York, N.Y.
> Jan.11, 1963 – *A Cruel Storm Stamps Its Silent Seal of Ice...*

The Long Islander Newspaper. Huntington, New York.*
> Jan. 3, 1963 – *Search In Icy Waters for Tug and Crew*
> Jan. 10, 1963 – *Mystery Deepens In Disappearance of Steer's Tug, And Its Crew.*
> Jan. 10, 1963 – *Editorial – Tragic Tribute*
> Jan. 17, 1963 – *Witnesses Shed No Light on Tug's Fate*
> Jan. 17, 1963 – *Bay Charted In Effort To Locate Tug*
> Jan. 24, 1963 – *Tug Search Continues*
> Jan. 31, 1963 – *Tug Was Lost One Month Ago*
> Apr. 18, 1963 – *May Dynamite Abandoned Tug*
> May 9, 1963 – *No Decision Reached on Gwendoline's Fate*
> May 9, 1963 – *Letter to Editor – Gwendolyn Steers Hull May Yield Cause of Sinking.*
> May 16, 1963 – *Believe Body that of Tug Crewmember*
> May 23, 1963 – *Believe Body that of Eighth Crewmember*
> May 30, 1963 – *Find Last Gut Crewman, Boat Still on Bottom*
> June 27, 1963 – *Ill-Fated Tug Left to Sea and Salvagers*
> Oct. 10, 1963 – *Tug Tragedy Here Remains a Mystery*

The New York Times. On-line archives for the following articles:
> Feb. 13, 1936 – *R. Steers is Dead.*
> Apr. 12, 1963 – *2 Bodies from Lost Tug Washed Into L.I. Waters*

Apr. 15, 1963 – *Sunken Tug Found Off L.I.*
June 11, 1963 – *8 Million Dollar Suit Filed by Widow of Tug Captain*

Chapter 12 – Going Deeper

Chapter 13 - Conclusions

Lewis, Jon E., Editor. *The Mammoth Book of the Deep – True Stories of Danger and Adventure Under the Sea.* Carroll & Graff Publishers, New York, N.Y. 2007. Excerpt from *The Undersea Adventure* by Philippe Diole. Originally published in 1951.

Solley, George C. & Steinbauth, Eric. *Moods of the Sea, Masterworks of Sea Poetry.* United States Naval Institute. Annapolis, Maryland. 1981.

Post Script - In Memory

Gold Coast Gazette. Newspaper. Glen Cove, New York.
    December 20, 2007 – *Community Mourns Braynard.* Page 1

Long Island Boating World. Magazine. Copiague, New York.
    February 2008 – *Van R. Field Passes On.* Page 33

Appendix A   Salvagers of the Sea

Floherty, John J. *Men Without Fear.* J.B. Lippincott Company. New York, N.Y. 1940.

Mystic Seaport. Coll. 1 & Coll. 2, Manuscripts Collection, G. W. Blunt White Library, Mystic Seaport Museum, Inc.

Quinn, William P. *Shipwrecks Around New England (Illustrated) – A Chronology of Marine Accidents from Grand Manan to Sandy Hook.* The Lower Cape Publishing Company. Orleans, Massachusetts. 1979.

Rattray, Jeanette Edwards. *The Perils of the Port of New York – Maritime Disasters from Sandy Hook to Execution Rocks.* Dodd, Mead & Company. New York, N.Y. 1973.

The New York Times. On-line archives for the following articles:
    Apr. 22, 1858 – *Marine Intelligence*
    May 29, 1878 – *Trouble Among the Wreckers*
    Dec. 15, 1911 – *Capt. I.J. Merritt Dead*

Time Magazine. *Hauling down the Horse Flag?* Friday, March 10, 1967. Available on-line at www.time.com.

Wikipedia. The Free Encyclopedia. (I have to offer a special thanks to the various authors and contributors of the Merritt-Chapman & Scott listing. It provided an excellent overview of the corporation and I would be remiss not to thank those who have worked and continue to work on the information contained within.)

Appendix B   Saviors of the Sea

Hamilton, Alexander. *Federalist Papers*. Federalist No. 12, The Utility of the Union In Respect to Revenue. Available on-line at http://www.foundingfathers.info/federalistpapers/fedindex.htm

Krietemeyer, George E., *The Coast Guardsman's Manual*. Naval Institute Press. Annapolis, Maryland. 2000. 9th Edition.

Ross, Worth G. *Our Coast Guard, A Brief History of the United States Revenue Marine Service*. Originally published in Harper's New Monthly Magazine, Volume 73, Issue 438, November 1886. Available on-line at: http://www.uscg.mil/history/regulations/USRM_HistoryHarpers.pdf

United States Coast Guard Historian's Office. *U.S. Coast Guard – A Historical Overview*. Available on-line at: http://www.uscg.mil/history/h_USCGhistory.html

Appendix C   Without a Trace

Ancestry.com Website. Web-pages dedicated to the ancestry of Reichert Family Name. (No original source provided and dates only indicate that the articles were published after January 19, 1958. Further research necessary to determine the date and source of the various articles, however, reference to other contemporary newspaper articles provide a chronological outline.) On-line archives of the following articles:
> *Sunk Tug Found in L.I. Sound*
> *Two Local Men Missing in Tug May be Found*
> *Divers Set to Search Sunken Tug*
> *Sunken Tug Is Raised, One Body Recovered*
> *Body May Be Steers Crewman*

Rattray, Jeanette Edwards. *The Perils of the Port of New York – Maritime Disasters from Sandy Hook to Execution Rocks*. Dodd, Mead & Company. New York, N.Y. 1973.

The New York Times. On-line archives for the following articles:

Jan. 20, 1958 – *3 Missing on Tugboat*
Jan. 21, 1958 – *Search of Sound Fails to Find Tug*
Jan. 22, 1958 – *Lost Tug Feared Collision Victim*
Jan. 23, 1958 – *Objects from Tug Washed Up in L.I.*
Jan. 24, 1958 – *Minesweeper Joins Search for Tugboat*
Jan. 25, 1958 – *Divers in L.I. Sound Fail to Locate Tug*
Feb. 18, 1958 – *Shipping News and Notes*
Feb. 28, 1958 – *Missing Tugboat Believed Found*
Mar. 2, 1958 – *Sunken Tugboat is Raised in Sound*
Mar. 3, 1958 – *Recovered Tug in Yard*
Mar. 11, 1958 – *Shipping Events: F.B.I. Called In*
Apr. 23, 1958 – *2d Tugboat Victim Found*
May 17, 1958 – *Body May Be Tug's Captain*
May 18, 1958 – *Lost Tug's Captain Identified*
Jan. 13, 1961 – *Coast Guard Counsel Made Captain*
May 30, 1964 – *Coast Guard Captain is Appointed by S.L.A.*

Appendix D   Wreck Locations

Bachand, Robert G. *Scuba Northeast, Shipwrecks, Dive Sites & Dive Activities Rhode Island to New Jersey.* Volume II. Sea Sports Publications. Norwalk, CT. 1986. Pages 46-47.

Coleman, Tim & Soares, Charley. *Fishable Wrecks & Rockpiles.* MT Publications. Mystic, CT. 1989. Pages 66-67.

Field, Van R. *Wrecks and Rescues on Long Island – The Story of the U.S. Lifesaving Service.* Searles Graphics, Inc. East Patchogue, NY. 1997.

Gentile, Gary. *Shipwrecks of New York.* Gary Gentile Productions, Philadelphia, PA. First Edition. 1996.

Glick, Les. *Diver's Guide to Long Island Waters.* Amphibian Enterprises. Manorville, NY. First Edition, 1990. 2nd Edition, 1992. Page 46.

Keatts, Henry. *New England's Legacy of Shipwrecks.* American Merchant Marine Press. Kings Point, N.Y. 1988.

Wreckhunter.net Website. Available online at www.wreckhunter.net.

Appendix E   Nautical and Diving Terminology

Chapman, Charles F. *Piloting, Seamanship and Small Boat Handling*. The Hearst Corporation. New York, N.Y. Motor Boating – Volume V – Motor Boating's Ideal Series. 1965-66 Edition. 1st Edition published in 1922.

Field, Van R. *Wrecks and Rescues on Long Island – The Story of the U.S. Lifesaving Service*. Searles Graphics, Inc. East Patchogue, NY. 1997.

Grimwood, V.R. *American Ship Models*. Bonanza Books. New York, N.Y. 1942.

Lords Commissioners of the Admiralty. *A Seaman's Pocket-Book*. MJF Books, Fine Communications. New York, N.Y. 2006. Originally published in June 1943 by His Majesty's Stationary Office, London, England.

McKenna, Robert. *The Dictionary of Nautical Literacy*. International Marine/McGraw-Hill, N.Y., N.Y. 2003 edition.

PADI. *The Encyclopedia of Recreational Diving*. Hornsby, Al. Editor-In-Chief. PADI International. Santa Ana, California. 1988/1989 edition.

Since the first ship "wrecked" there have been those who have braved the shallows and the depths to repair the wrecked vessel, retrieve the cargo, or salvage the remains. One of the most prolific salvage companies that existed in the New York area from before the American Civil War and remained in operation until the late 1960's early 1970's was the Merritt-Chapman & Scott Corporation. The following is a brief account of the company's formation, history, the myriad maritime operations conducted, and a look at a Merritt-Chapman & Scott hard hat diver on the job.

Salvagers of the Seas

A Brief History of the Merritt-Chapman & Scott Corporation

Company History

"In the spring of 1860 the Board of Marine Underwriters of New York City undertook to solve the problems presented by mounting losses from shipwrecks and the intolerable state of salvage along the Atlantic seaboard." (Mystic) Their action in that year set forth a chain of events that formed what would eventually become known as the Coast Wrecking Company. To lead the company, the Board of Marine Underwriters chose seasoned sea captain and salvager Israel J. Merritt.[175] The consistent losses at sea, in harbors and along the beaches of the

---

[175] Capt. Merritt had been involved in marine salvage for a large part of his career at sea. According to Jeanette Rattray, Merritt "had been in the salvage business since 1935" and had "received a gold medal from the Life Saving Benevolent Association in 1856 for the mid winter rescue of an entire ship's crew on Barnegat shoals" and in 1859 had been "awarded $500 in gold for saving the sixty-five-man crew of the *Black Warrior* off Rockaway, NY." (Rattray, 82) Merritt is also mentioned as an "underwriter agent" in an April 22, 1858 article in the *New York Times*. The article briefly explains that the *"Narcissa,* from Gloucester with fish…was got off by Capt. Merritt." (*NYT*, 22APR1858)

East Coast, proved to be a financially rewarding vocation, and over the next one hundred years, the humble beginnings of the small salvage company expanded well beyond the horizon of the Board of Marine Underwriters' original vision. Due to Merritt's hard work and commitment, the Coast Wrecking Company gained momentum and a solid financial foundation. "Within a score of years after the establishment of the Coast Wrecking Company, Merritt was in a position to buy the business and reorganize it as Merritt's Wrecking Organization." (Mystic) The company, which would evolve into myriad versions, mirrored the eventual diversification of the company's projects, subdivisions, and scope. Eventually the company, which had started out in the waters of New York, found its fleet working on various operations throughout the United States and its waters, all of its ships flying their house flag – a black horse on a stark white background.[176] Similar to the English Union Jack, the sun rarely set on the salvage house's flag.

Merritt however was not the sole *game in town* during the early years of his business. His major competitors in the New York and Long Island waters were the Chapman Derrick & Wrecking Company of Brooklyn, N.Y., owned and operated by William E. Chapman and later the T.A. Scott Company of New London, Connecticut. Merritt's wreckers had often been met by the wreckers of the Chapman Company. Over the course of "some twenty years of routine chores around New York Harbor," the companies butted their proverbial heads on various salvage operations and contracts. (Rattray, 82) This rivalry came to a head with legal proceedings regarding the salvage of the American Liner *St. Paul*. (Rattray, 82) "The insurance people decided the salvage job should be shared between the two contenders." (Rattray, 82) A year later in 1897, the two

---

[176] "Merritt selected for his flag a galloping black horse on a field of white as a tribute to the agents in isolated areas who raced on horseback to the nearest telegraph station to notify the Coast Wrecking Company of vessels in distress. These agents have been referred to as the 'Pony Express of the Beaches." (Mystic)

companies merged to form the Merritt-Chapman Derrick & Wrecking Company.[177]

In 1922, Merritt-Chapman merged with the T.A. Scott Company, forming the Merritt-Chapman & Scott Corporation. The company, would over the course of the next forty-plus years, adapt to changes in the slave and maritime world. Eventually, the corporation was "taken over in 1951 by Louis E. Wolfson...perhaps the U.S.'s most renowned corporation raider." (*Time*)[178] The last business records indicated the corporation's existence ending sometime in 1970-71. The house flag, the black horse in gallop, is no longer flown at sea. However the legacy and stories of the Merritt-Chapman & Scott Corporation will remain as an integral part of the Nation's maritime history.

Vessel's Assisted

The following is a list of just some of the vessels and incidents of which the company was involved. A volume in and unto itself would be necessary to list the host of maritime operations completed by the Merritt-Chapman & Scott Corporation or its earlier variations.

1860's - *Bohemian* (S), various sunken hulks removed from North River, *James Crosby* (B), *Rangoon, Comanche, Santiago de Cuba, Oceanus* (ST), *Heiress* (ST), *Morning Star.*

1870's - *R.W. Griffith* (B), *Mary Graham*, $30,000 of sliver ore from a sunken barge, *Granite State* (ST), *Henry Chauncey* (ST), Un-named coal barge, *Cuba* (ST), *Calvin P. Harris* (S), *H.T. Hedges* (S), *Atlantic, Curacoa* (B), *Idaho, Alexander Levallev, Vulcan* (ST), *J. Leighton* (BR), *Mohawk, Nellie C. Cook* (S), *Rjukan, L'Amerique, Rusland, Massachusetts, Georgia, Vindicator, Italia* (B), *Cuba* (S), Unknown three masted schooner, *C.B. Payne, Cutelin do l'Orso* (B), *Mary Chilton* (S).

---

[177] Prior to the merger of the Merritt-Chapman companies, another smaller company was merged into the Coast Wrecking Company in 1874. The Atlantic Coast Wrecking and Submarine Company which had been founded as an "investment concern," with hopes of its original investors, the same underwriting company, as "an auxiliary to that business" and to "diminish their losses and not to yield profits" was merged with the payment made to the original investors being stock in the Coast Wrecking Company. (*NYT*, 29MAY1878)

[178] "Since he became the principal share holder Wolfson has been stung with a dozen suits by angry investors, last fall [1966] was indicted by a federal grand jury on charges of fraudulent dealings in Merritt-Chapman stock." In addition under his leadership the corporation began to fall on hard economic times. In 1966, "there was a loss of $740,000 and no dividend at all." (TIME)

The *Dromore Castle* – Pre-1942 – Brooklyn, N.Y. Author's collection[179]

1880's - *Castilla* (B), *Emma C. Babcock* (S), *Augustina, light-boat, Sarah Ellen* (B), *Narragansett* (ST), *City of New York* (ST) *Tsernogora, Dupay de Lome* (ST), *Oregon* (ST), *Empire State* (ST), *Scotia, Scythia, Scotland* (B), *Mars* (ST).

1890's - *Yale* (S), *Ashburne* (ST), *Windermere, San Pedro* (ST), *Cepheus* (ST), *Central Railroad of N.J. Barge No. 6, Emily T. Whitney, Andes* (ST), *Persian Monarch* (ST), *Lamington* (ST), *Otranto, Badsworth* (ST), *U.S.S. Maine* (WS).

1900-1940's - *Mola* (S), *College Point*, Unknown Steamship, *Remedius Pasqual, George P. Hudson* (S), *H.M. Whitney* (ST), *Clan Galbraith* (B), *Dustin G. Cressy* (S), *Robert E. Lee* (ST), *U.S.S. Moody* (WS) (Intentionally sunk for a Hollywood film – *Hell Below*.), *Northern Sword* (F), *King Philip* (EV), *William T. Rossell, New Bedford, S.S. Normandie.*

Key   S – Schooner   ST – Steamer   WS – Warship   EV – Excursion Vessel
         B – Bark   F – Freighter

---

[179] The *Dromore Castle* was constructed by Harland & Wolff at Greenlock at a length of 412 feet, 6 inches, a beam of 54 feet, 4 inches and 5242 gross tonnage. (Harland & Wolff also constructed a more famous vessel...*Titanic*) She was originally launched as the *War Poplar* but completed as the *Dromore Castle* as a "modified 'B' type standard ship with extra derrick posts." She served as a merchant vessel but at the outset of the Second World War she was "deployed carrying war materials across the Atlantic." On December 12, 1942, while in a convoy, she was mined and sunk "20 miles south-east of the River Humber without any loss of life." (www.wrecksite.edu) The photograph indicates that at some point the *Dromore Castle*, which transited into New York waters during her merchant career on a regular basis, underwent repairs of some type, possibly associated with the Merritt-Chapman & Scott Corporation. No further information regarding her association with the company could be determined.

Other Projects

The following is a sampling of some of the projects of which the Merritt-Chapman & Scott Corporation or its earlier variations were associated with during its one hundred-plus years of existence. Many of the early construction projects assisted in the corporation's ability to weather the financial difficulties of the Great Depression.

Projects

Waldo-Hancock Bridge - Marquette Ore Docks - Mt. Vernon Memorial Highway - Hunting Creek Bridge - Escanaba Ore Docks - Washburn Tunnel - Delaware Memorial Bridge - John Greenleaf - Whittier Bridge - Tasman Mill - Kingston-Rhinecliff Bridge - Walt Whitman Bridge - Mackinac Bridge - Throgs Neck Bridge - Glen Canyon Dam - Tallmadge Bridge - Chesapeake Bay Bridge-Tunnel - New Jersey Turnpike

An illustration of a diver and his gear from the 1880's. Author's collection.

The following is a list of vessels operated by the corporation during its history. It is by no means a comprehensive listing, but it is provided here as an illustration of the scope of the company and its maritime operations.

Salvage Tug *Relief* – Pre-WWI. Courtesy of the U.S. Navy.

Vessel Name	Type	Year	Note
Townley	steam tug	1865	
Relief	steamer	1865	
Phillip	steam tug	1866	
Winans	steamer	1869	
John Fuller	steamer	1871	
Resolute	steamer	1871	
Perit	steamer	1873	Chartered for use.
Lackawanna	steamer	1873	
Meteor	schooner	1876	
Cyclops		1876	
Burke	tug	1876	
Sallie Merritt	schooner	1877	
Meta	schooner	1877	
Johnson	schooner	1879	
J.D. Jones	steamer	1889	
Rescue	tug	1899	Largest wrecking tug in the world
Lochinvar			
William E. Chapman			
I.J. Merritt			
Willet	tug		

Hard hat divers of the Merritt-Chapman & Scott Corporation. Courtesy Lostlabor.com.[180]

Throughout the company's history thousands of newspaper articles or briefs referred to and recounted their operations. Some listings were just a few words while others echoed in detailed description, the trials and tribulations of their salvage efforts, legal proceedings or project updates. Many of these reports include accounts of the various underwater operations of the divers and wreckers of the Merritt-Chapman & Scott Corporation on some well known and many unknown wrecks and construction projects. One of the more intimate reviews of the hard hat divers of the company was highlighted in John J. Floherty's 1940 publication, *Men Without Fear*. The chapter titled *Deep Down Under* provides an insightful and respectful accounting of the types of dangers that faced the deep sea divers during their eventful hours below the surface as they negotiated contaminated water, the lifeless bodies of those lost on the wreck, jagged steel and underwater creatures, among the usual dangers associated with hard hat surface-supplied diving equipment. The men who braved the depths under the Black Horse Fleet truly were men befitting Floherty's book as they were without fear.

In addition to telling several interesting stories about deep sea divers in both commercial and military work environments, author John J. Floherty eloquently describes the offices and the diver with whom he visited with to write the chapter. The chapter and his accurate and respectful reflection of the diver's

---

[180] This photograph originally appeared in *Merritt-Chapman & Scott Corporation – Black Horse of the Sea* by Robert D. MacMillen in 1929.

responsibilities provide a very interesting look at the mission and history of the Merritt-Chapman & Scott Corporation.[181]

Floherty describing the offices…

A drawing of the President's office circa 1930. Author's collection.

"In a luxurious suite of offices overlooking the harbor in downtown New York, I sat with an officer of a great salvage corporation. The walls of his spacious office were covered with photographs. Each was the story of a drama in which the eternal triangle, man, a ship and the sea were the actors. Some showed ships hopelessly enmeshed among waves-swept rocks or stranded high on lonely beaches. Others showed helpless hulks battered and broken by the onslaughts of a mad ocean, being towed to port after being raised from the bottom. Here was a warship impotent as a dead mackerel. Elsewhere were barges, scows and vessels of all kinds, victims of the sea but saved to sail again through the miracle-work of divers and their attendant salvage crews." (Floherty, 115)

---

[181] The chapter titled *Deep Down Under* does not specifically refer to the Merritt-Chapman & Scott Corporation. However, a thorough review of the book's acknowledgement section, author John J. Floherty thanks, among many other commercial and private companies, the Merritt, Chapman & Scott Corporation…"for the access they gave me to places that few are permitted to enter."

Floherty describing the salvage diver…

> "A man in his late thirties leaned against the deck house of the scow. He had the steel-blue eyes and searching look of men who follow the sea. Under his blue sweater were the contours of a powerful torso. The knitted skull-cap he wore emphasized a well shaped head. His strong face was furrowed with tell-tale lines etched by anxious periods spent far below the surface. He was as typical a diver as one would find along the coast from Maine to Miami." (Floherty, 116)

Conclusion

When researching shipwrecks including - maritime repairs, lightening, rescue, recovery, salvage and construction - one will surely find reference to a marine salvage company. The Merritt-Chapman & Scott Corporation was one of the largest and most encompassing of these companies. It was a mainstay in the dangerous - on the water and under the water - businesses. Countless lives, vessels, property and fortunes were salvaged as a result of the Merritt-Chapman & Scott Corporation's operations and efforts. Their legacy is not only as a significant and integral player in the histories of many of the post-Civil War shipwrecks of our nation's waters, but in the day to day activities of millions of Americans due to their extensive infrastructural projects. The horse flag is flown no longer, but the foundation of a large part of our maritime history and infrastructure remains as a solid and silent reminder of the salvagers of the seas.

Answering the call of distress since 1790, the United States Coast Guard continues its long standing tradition of providing assistance to mariners in peril. The United States Coast Guard is an amalgamation of several services and agencies that collectively continue to meet various missions as set forth by the United States government. Researching shipwrecks and marine disasters highlights the heroics, triumphs and close calls of the guardians of the seas. This rich history acts to inspire today's Coast Guardsmen to live up to the core values of Honor, Respect and Devotion to Duty. The following is a brief review of the service's history and formation. For more information regarding the United States Coast Guard, its history, or how to get involved in either the active, reserve or auxiliary components, please refer to the Getting Involved listing.

Saviors of the Seas

A Brief History of the United States Coast Guard

During the early days of the formation of the United States, one of the major obstacles facing the new nation was the collection of revenues. Without a strong financial base, the government would be limited in its ability to address the needs of the country and its citizens. Prior to the ratification of the United States Constitution, Alexander Hamilton outlined the need for a service to collect revenues at sea, in the *Federalist Papers*, No. 12 titled, *The Utility of the Union In Respect to Revenue*. "A few armed vessels, judiciously stationed at the entrances of our ports, might at a small expense be made useful sentinels of the laws. And the government having the same interest to provide against violations everywhere, the co-operation of its measures in each State would have a powerful tendency to render them effectual," Hamilton stated. His vision, coupled his research into the matter regarding the collection of customs eventually led to the formal establishment of the Revenue Marine Service in 1790. With ten armed cutters built at an expense not to exceed $1,000 each, the Revenue Marine Service was authorized. In effect, one of the earliest foundations of the modern Coast Guard had been formed.

As the nation grew in size and scope, the need for additional government action regarding maritime and revenue concerns also expanded. "An act of Congress in 1799 gave authority to the President to maintain as many revenue cutters as should be necessary," so that the United States government could "provide for the proper collection of import and tonnage duties." (Ross, 4) In addition to the expanded ability to collect revenues, which then provided for the costs of the government and its responsibilities, the nation also began to expand its borders. As the United States expanded westward, additional services were necessary over navigable waterways. All aspects of the society, including agricultural and manufacturing production, increased immigration, and advances in maritime commerce and ship building also increased the need for governmental regulation and assistance. Earlier established services, such as the Lighthouse Service, which had been established and run at the colony-level from 1716, continued to expand in its scope and responsibilities under the auspices of the Treasury Department.

Increased maritime traffic also posed a significant problem for the United States. With travel being relegated to overland and underway options, the number of those placed at the mercy of the sea was staggering. Equally staggering was the number of vessels that were lost at sea, run aground in storms, or lost in the fog of mystery. In 1848, ten years after the establishment of a service to assist in the regulation and inspection of steamboats, the United States government established the Life-Saving Service. This service then provided an organized form of assistance, within their area of responsibilities, to those who were imperiled by nature, disaster, or other calamity. A lone surfman would walk along the beach at night, lantern in hand, keeping a sharp watch along the shore line for vessels in distress. If he happened along a shipwreck or grounded vessel, he would return to his station, alert the crew and a rescue would be attempted. Also established in 1848 was the Bureau of Navigation.

In 1915, the Life-Saving Service and Revenue Cutter Service were joined by an act of Congress. From that point forward, the other services which naturally fell under the umbrella of responsibilities were added, shaping the missions of and responsibilities of the service.

To recount or attempt to summarize the thousands of examples of the heroic efforts of the men and women associated with the individual services and agencies, would be an exercise in futility. As outlined throughout the individual chapters of this text, the bravery and determination to help those in need is clearly illustrated. Volumes upon volumes have been written that identify the circumstances of those in peril and those willing to go out in the midst of the storm to execute their safe return to shore. Nonetheless, the importance of the services and agencies that eventually formed the modern United States Coast Guard should and will continue to be, examples of the dedication to the principles of the service – Honor, Respect and Devotion to Duty.

Services that formed the United States Coast Guard

The following services formed the United States Coast Guard in 1915 when the Revenue Cutter Service and the Life-Saving Service merged. Separately, the Lighthouse Service joined the Steamboat Inspection Service in 1903. Then the Steamboat Inspection Service and the Bureau of Navigation were combined into the Bureau of Navigation and Steamboat Inspection Service in 1932, joining the United States Coast Guard in 1942. During the Second World War this service served under control of the U.S. Navy, as did the U.S. Coast Guard. Each service brought a specialized set of skills and responsibilities that over time became the foundations for the missions of today's modern United States Coast Guard.

The U.S. Coast Guard fell under the Treasury Department, with the exception of periods during World War I and World War II when it served under the U.S. Navy. In 1967, the U.S. Coast Guard became part of the Department of Transportation. In 2003, the U.S. Coast Guard transitioned into a main segment of the Department of Homeland Security.

Military Involvement of the United States Coast Guard

The United States Coast Guard and its predecessor services have been in the thick of battle from the Quasi War of 1798-1801 to present. Throughout the first one hundred years of the nation under the United States Constitution, the Revenue Marine Service was actively involved in military insurrections and operations including the Quasi-War of 1798-1801, the War of 1812 and the Mexico War. Military operations would be the cornerstone of the service and since its formation, the Revenue Marine Service and its modern-day equivalent, the United States Coast Guard, has served in every war or conflict that our country has been involved. In addition to the wars that they have been involved with, the United States Coast Guard has had additional responsibilities on two other wars, including the Rum War during the era of Prohibition and the War on Drugs which is ongoing to this day.

The following is a listing of the military conflicts/actions/wars that the U.S. Coast Guard has served.

Quasi-War of 1798-1801 - War of 1812 - Mexican War - Civil War –
Spanish/American War - World War I - World War II - Korean War - Vietnam
Desert Shield/Desert Storm - War on Terror - Iraq War

Missions of the United States Coast Guard

Forged from multiple services, the U.S. Coast Guard continues many aspects of their predecessor services. The following is a listing of the missions performed on a *daily* basis. This information is provided by the United States Coast Guard.

Safety

-Saves 14 lives.
-Assists 98 people in distress.
-Conducts 74 search and rescue cases.
-Completes 31 Port State Control safety and environmental exams on foreign vessels.
-Performs 18 safety examinations on commercial fishing vessels.
-Conducts 24 marine casualty investigations.
-Issues 102 Certificates of Inspections to U.S. commercial vessels.

Security

-Interdicts 17 illegal migrants at sea.
-Seizes or removes over 1,000 pounds of illegal drugs. ($12.9M value)
-Administers 25 International Ship and Port Facility Security (ISPS) Code vessel exams.
-Escorts over 20 larger passenger vessels, military outload vessel, High Interest Vessels (HIVs) or vessels carrying especially hazardous cargo.
-Boards 193 ships and boats.

Stewardship

-Services 135 aids-to-navigation and corrects 23 aids-to-navigation discrepancies.
-Boards 17 vessels at sea to enforce domestic fisheries and marine protected species regulations.
-Facilitates safe and efficient marine transportation on the Nation's 15,000 miles of inland waterways.
-Inspects 53 HAZMAT containers.
-Responds to 12 Oil Pollution/Hazardous Chemical Material spills.

Conclusion

The United States Coast Guard, now over two hundred years old, continues to forge through the fog of uncertainty as it completes its missions. Whether the crew of a forty-seven foot motor life boat is charging through the surf to effect a rescue of those in need, or if a port security small boat is guarding a maritime asset, the missions of the United States Coast Guard have certainly evolved, but in the same way, changed little since its inception. As the nation enters into unknown waters of homeland security issues, advances in technology, and new threats to our security and safety, the men and women of the United States Coast Guard will adapt to meet the needs of its citizens, its government and the world. The history of the service, highlighted by individual and team accomplishments in the face of grave danger, will continue to augment the day in and day out actions of those men and women who live by the motto of the service...Semper Paratus.

The Steers Sand and Gravel Company of Northport, New York faced the loss of two of its tugboats and twelve of her men as a result of two shipwrecks between January 19, 1958 and December 30, 1962. The Gwendoline Steers remains on the bottom of the Long Island Sound but a smaller sister tug Jim Steers was also lost in the waters of the Long Island Sound. The following is a brief history of the tragic loss of the Jim Steers.

Without a Trace - The Loss of the Tugboat *Jim Steers*

The *Jim Steers* after recovery. Author's collection.[182]

On January 19, 1958, Captain Albert Reichert, his son Albert Jr., and Herbert Johnson were all aboard the *Jim Steers*. The 37-foot diesel powered steel tugboat was heading east in the Long Island Sound for its homeport in Northport, New York. The tug and her crew had delivered a "loaded sand barge to Hunt's Point in the Bronx," and the tugboat was without a barge or light on her return

---

[182] The drawing by the author is based on a photograph which was published on March 2, 1958. (*NYT, 2MAR1958*)

219

trip. (*NYT*, 21JAN1958) The *George Steers*, her companion tugboat making the same trip, was within sight and in radio communication.

On board her companion tugboat was Captain Ernest Gildersleeve and his single crewman, Joseph Thompson. They later reported that they were experiencing choppy waters and "northwest winds of twenty-five to thirty-five miles an hour" at midnight. (*NYT*, 21JAN1958) At 12:15 in the morning, "off the Throgs Neck in the Bronx," the *George Steers* saw the *Jim Steers* for the last time. (*NYT*, 21JAN1958) Moments later, the tugboat *Jim Steers* and her three man crew disappeared into the blackness of the night without a trace.

The United States Coast Guard searched for six hours on the 19th of January and resumed a "dawn-to-dusk search of the Long Island Sound by Coast Guard air and surface units" on the following day, but "failed to turn up any trace of the tugboat." (*NYT*, 21JAN1958) On January 22, 1958, a few clues surfaced for investigators and searchers. A 1956 log book from the tugboat, a life ring with "Jim Steers Northport, N.Y." emblazoned on it, and a "four-foot ladder made of wood and painted red…unmarked but…similar to the type used on tugs," were recovered "about one and one-half miles east of Stepping Stones Light." (*NYT*, 23JAN1958) In addition to the flotsam recovered, information from another skipper on the waters that night provided some insight into the *Jim Steers* disappearance.

Captain Anthony Hines, "Master of the tug *Chaplain*," explained that he had seen "two small vessels going east in the Sound Sunday" and that the tank barge he was towing, "struck an unidentified object between 12:30 and 1 A.M., shortly after passing the two vessels." (*NYT*, 23JAN1958) Captain Hines however was not completely notified of all of the details regarding the striking the barge until he arrived at Pier 9 in Staten Island upon the completion of his trip. Captain Trond Osthus "informed him that the barge a struck a submerged object about 1 A.M." (*NYT*, 23JAN1958) Osthus explained that at about "12:45 A.M. he heard a noise and that the barge bounced." (*NYT*, 23JAN1958) He continued to explain that "the first bump was felt on the forward part of the barge and then along the bottom of the barge." (*NYT*, 23JAN1958) After he signaled with a light to Captain Hines aboard the *Chaplain*, "he [Osthus] ran on deck from his cabin aft...looking from the stern he saw bubbles and then a black object, about fifty feet astern, which he took to be a buoy." (*NYT*, 23JAN1958)[183]

Hines noted the incident in his logbook and recollected later that the only lights he saw on the water that night while transiting the area was the green light from the lighthouse. Commander Frederick Arzt, the lead Coast Guard investigator in the case, posed to Captain Hines a question regarding the possibility that the object that the barge in tow had struck was the *Jim Steers*?[184] Captain Hines responded that "unless the tugboat was already submerged it would have been impossible for it [the tug] to get under the barge's tow ropes and strike the front of the barge." (*NYT*, 23JAN1958) The investigation into the disappearance continued.

On January 24, 1958, as the Coast Guard continued to search for the tug and investigate the disappearance, two divers began searching "two of the six areas marked for investigation in a search...by the Navy minesweeper *Redwing*," which had "employed sonar underwater detection gear," the day before. (*NYT*, 25JAN1958) The divers, under the direction and employ of the Steers Sand and Gravel Corporation did not find any trace of the *Jim Steers*. Deteriorating weather hindered the underwater search, but diving operations were later resumed with the same negative results. But the Steers Sand and Gravel directed divers continued their search for the *Jim Steers* and finally on February 27, 1958, diver Anthony Opalka located what he believed was the missing tugboat. He stated that he had found a tugboat in "seventy feet of water 500 feet northeast of

---

[183] Capt. Osthus of the tank barge, *Hygrade 18*, stated that "the object" he saw behind the barge "was not lit," nor did he hear any "cries for help." (*NYT*, 23JAN1958)

[184] Commander Frederick Arzt, senior investigating officer for the Coast Guard's N.Y. Marine Inspection Office would attain the rank of Captain in May of 1961, lead the investigation into the disappearance of the *Gwendoline Steers* in 1963 and would retire in 1964. Upon his retirement after 35 years of civil service, he was appointed as the Deputy Commissioner of the State Liquor Authority. (*NYT*, 12JAN1961 and 30MAY1964)

Stepping Stone Light." (*NYT*, 28FEB1958) A definitive answer was able to be made by the diver according to Frank Clancy, the Steers Sand and Gravel Corporation's vice president because "it was too dark and the tide too strong for [the diver] to make positive identification." (*NYT*, 28FEB1958) According to the diver, the vessel he discovered and believed was the *Jim Steers* was on the bottom, snarled in grapnel lines.[185]

On March 1, 1958, the identity of the mystery vessel was verified when she was "raised by a floating derrick." (*NYT*, 2MAR1958) In the engine room of the *Jim Steers*, the salvage crew found the body of Albert Reichert Jr. The salvage vessel towed the *Jim Steers* to the Sound Shipbuilding Corporation at College Point in Queens so that the United States Coast Guard investigators could examine the tugboat.[186]

Upon closer examination of the tugboat by the Coast Guard, Commander Arzt explained that a "nylon-type substance" had been found "in some screw heads on the *Jim Steers*." (*NYT*, 11MAR1958)[187] The substance was sent to the Federal Bureau of Investigation for testing because there was the possibility that the nylon substance was from a "nylon towline" which the *Chaplain* may have been using to tow the tank barge *Hygrade 18*. (*NYT*, 11MAR1958) While the investigation into the cause of the *Jim Steers'* untimely demise, another discovery was made in the waters of the Long Island Sound.

"A mile off the American Yacht Club" in Rye, New York, a body was found in the water by the "crew of the tanker *Ellen Bushey II*." (*NYT*, 23APR1958) The body was later identified as the *Jim Steers'* engineer, Herbert

---

[185] On February 18 it was reported that Commander Arzt was reviewing the findings of paint scrapings that had been taken from the hull of the tanker *Hygrade 18*. The result of this aspect of the investigation were ever reported to media outlets. (*NYT*, 18FEB1958)

[186] According to an unverified source, "thousands of spectators lined the Kings Point shore as salvage workers, using a huge floating crane and a number of pontoons, brought the tug to the surface."

[187] According to a Steers Sand and Gravel Corporation spokesman, the *Jim Steers* was going to be surveyed "with a view to" put her back "into service." (*NYT*, 3MAR1958) The tugboat was two years old and valued at $58,000 at the time of her initial loss. No further record of the vessel's use could be determined.

Johnson. A second body was discovered on the evening of May 16, 1958. An inspection by police officers found "paper's bearing the captain's name," but waited until a family member could identify the body to release their findings. (*NYT*, 17MAY1958) The following day, Edward Reichert positively identified the body as his brother, Captain Albert Reichert. (*NYT*, 18MAY1958) The three men and the tugboat *Jim Steers* had been found and recovered. It marked a tragic end for the three men and their families. Unfortunately a similar tragedy would be eerily replayed a few years later when another tugboat of the Steers Sand and Gravel Company's fleet, the *Gwendoline Steers*, also disappeared without a trace.[188]

---

[188] According to an unverified source, Captain Albert Reichert Sr. was the father of 10 and his wife Anne, "gave birth to their ninth child, her fifth son, twelve days after the *Jim Steers* sank." His son Albert Jr., was married and had one child.

The following is a listing of coordinates for the wrecks covered in this text. The latitude and longitude coordinates have been collected from a variety of sources. The accuracy of this information is intended to be utilized as a guide only. The author takes no responsibility for the accuracy of this information.

<u>Vessel</u>	<u>Location</u>	<u>Lat/Long.</u>		<u>Loran</u>
Savannah	Fire Island, N.Y.	Unknown		N/A
Lexington	L.I. Sound, N.Y. N/A	N/A		26652.1 43962.8 (WH) 26652.1(2) 43962.8 (RB)
Circassian	Bridgehampton, N.Y.	N/A		N/A
Seawanhaka	New York, N.Y.	Scrapped		N/A
U.S.S. Ohio	Greenport, N.Y.	N/A		Off Fanning Pt.
Oregon	Off Long Island, NY *(Off Moriches, N.Y.)*	N/A	(Stern) (Mid) (Bow)	26452.7(9) 43676.3 (RB) 26453.0(2) 43676.2 26453.0(2) 43676.5(6)
Louis V. Place	Sayville, N.Y.	N/A		N/A
General Slocum Aka barge *Maryland*	Corson's Inlet, NJ	N/A		N/A
U.S.S. San Diego	Off Fire Island, NY	40'33.256 073'01.306 (DB)		26542.(2-9) 43692.9(3.3-8)
Andrea Doria	Off Nantucket, RI (50 miles off)	40'29.30 69'50.36 (WH) 40'29.4 69'50.5 (HK)		25147.7 43480.7 (WH)
Gwendoline Steers	Off Huntington, NY	N/A		26798.7 43951.3 (WH) 26798.6 43951.4 (RB)

Key to Source Listings:

N/A	Not applicable	WH	Wreckhunter.net website	RB	Robert Bachand
DB	Captain Dan Berg	HK	Henry Keatts		

The following terms and definitions are compiled and included to assist the reader with the sometimes confusing and very specific "language" of nautical and diving circles. The definitions are based on various sources which are listed alphabetically in the Sources chapter.

Admiralty Law – set of rules, regulations, treaties that govern vessels, cargo, and transportation on the high seas and inland waters as directed. Also known as *Maritime Law*.

Aft – any movement towards or reference to the stern or back of a boat or vessel.

Aloft - any area above the deck.

Amidships – the center point or close to the center point of a boat or vessel.

Beam – the widest part of a ship from starboard to port, expressed in a length of measurement.

Binnacle – a box or stand that houses a ship's compass.

Bitter end – the working end of a line.

Boatswain's Mate – originates from the "keeper of the boat." Provides maintenance and handling of boats or vessels. Knowledgeable in the "deck" operations of a boat or vessel. Shortened to Bosun or BM in most nautical circles.

Bosun – a shortened version of Boatswain's Mate.

Bosun's Chair – a rig, usually consisting of line and a plank for sitting, used primarily by deckhands or boatswain's mate to lower themselves or others over the side of a ship to paint, clean, etc.

Bottom Time – the amount of available time on the "bottom" for SCUBA or Surface Supplied Divers. Failure to adhere to this specific time could result in not enough air to safely complete the dive.

Bow – the forward section of a boat or vessel.

Bowsprit – the spar projecting forward from the bow of a ship or vessel.

Breaches Buoy – a rig, usually consisting of line and a canvas seat that is suspended under a life preserver. It is attached to the vessel and land or another vessel to transport personnel, one at a time.

Breakers- the type of waves that break on shore.

Breakwater – a man made structure, like a wall, or rock pile that is used to provide shelter and protection from heavy seas or waves.

Brig – (Location) Part of a vessel or onboard a shore installation that is used to contain offenders of rules and regulations, particularly sailors, marines and Coast Guard personnel. (Vessel type) A two masted square rigged sailing vessel, shortened for Brigantine.

Bulkhead – the wall on board a vessel or ship. Vertical partitions between compartments.

Buoyancy Compensator – a vest or jacket worn by SCUBA divers or skin divers to provide "buoyancy" on and below the surface. Variations exist, but all can be manually or orally inflated utilizing various devices. Standard equipment for all SCUBA diving operations.

Caboose – an older term for a ship's galley or cooking area.

Capstan - machine on deck that is used to heave or hoist.

Carronade – a short-barreled cannon.

Chart – a representation of a nautical environment and coastal areas. Includes latitude and longitude lines, sometimes LORAN, and charted water depths. Sometimes incorrectly referred to by novices as "maps."

Chief – Military rank for senior enlisted personnel in naval services. Three separate levels are recognized: Chief, Senior Chief, and Master Chief.

Clipper – a sailing ship with three or more masts, square rigged.

Collier - vessel utilized to carry coal.

Cutter – type of sailing vessel, more modern use indicates a Coast Guard vessel over 65 feet in length.

Cross-trees - crosspieces at the top of a ship's mast that spread apart the upper lines that support the masts.

Dead Reckoning – a type of navigation that is based on known information such as course, speed and distance traveled.

Decompression – any dives that require a safety stop or decompression stop, to allow for "off gassing" of nitrogen from the human body. Recreational diving utilizes set decompression stops based on depth of dives. A Safety stop at fifteen feet is a standard stop to act as an added safety measure for most divers. Also can be used in Decompression Sickness or commonly referred to as the "bends" or "Caisson's Disease."

Dive Flag – International – the nautical flag, Alpha is recognized world wide for diving operations, used internationally for most commercial diving operations.

Dive Flag – United States – the "Diver Down" flag, red with horizontal white stripe, is primarily used in the United States and Caribbean for recreational diving.

Divemaster – First level of professional diving, recognized internationally for a higher level of understanding and education in the laws and aspects of SCUBA diving. Responsible for maintaining safe diving conditions for newer or novice divers.

Dive Tables – charts that are utilized by divers that provide safety margins for any dives below the surface of the water. Various tables exist but most popular are those based on the Haldanian theory. After World War II, most recreational divers utilized U.S. Navy tables.

Eddy - circular motion of water caused by two opposite currents meeting.

Fathom – a length of six feet, specifically used in providing nautical depths. Example, six fathoms would be thirty six feet.

Fins – used for SCUBA and skin divers to assist their movements while in the water. Various styles exist. Also referred to by non-divers as "flippers."

First Stage – a pressure reducing valve that is sealed to the diving tank. (Usually reduces pressure from 300 to 10 BAR.) The first stage is attached to the second stage or regulator.

Flotsam – floating wreckage or debris from a vessel.

Forward - any movement towards or reference to the bow or front section of a boat or vessel.

Galleon – a type of vessel. Square rigged ship of various types. Popular from the 1600-1800's.

Gate Valve – type of valve used when a straight line flow of fluid and minimum restriction is desired.

Gunwale - upper rail of vessel.

Hail - to call at to another vessel or crew on a different part of the vessel.

Halyards - lines used for lowering yards, sails, etc.

Hawser – a large line utilized for towing, mooring and for passing to another vessel.

Helm – wheel or controls that control the rudder of a vessel.

Hermaphrodite Brig – a type of brigantine sailing vessel. Two masted rig with the foremast of a brigantine and a mainmast of a schooner.

House flag – a personalized flag for a company used to distinguish their vessels at sea.

Jetsam – cargo or parts of a vessel that are jettisoned overboard to lighten the vessel when it is in distress.

Kapok – a type of material utilized in life preservers. An older term for life-jackets.

Keel – the backbone of a boat or vessel.

Keel-haul – a punishment for sailors underway. The offender is lashed to a line and then is passed under the keel of the boat from one side of the ship to the other.

Knot – one nautical mile an hour. Two or more lines tied together form a knot.

Latitude – a distance north and south utilizing the equator as its base line.

Lead Line – a line with specific markings on it utilized to determine the depth of water.

Lee – the side of a vessel that is protected from the wind. (the opposite term would be windward.)

Lighter – a boat or barge utilized to offload or lighten cargo from a larger ship or vessel.

Line – a rope in use.

Loran – acronym for a long-range navigation system developed during the Second World War. Various transmissions could determine a fix or position, approximate. GPS or global positioning systems quickly surpassed the efficiency and effectiveness of the Loran system. Many older captains utilize Loran coordinates for wreck sites.

Longitude – a distance east and west utilizing the prime meridian as its base line.

Lyle Gun – a cannon utilized to project a line to a ship in distress.

Mast – a long spar utilized to support the sails, rigging or equipment of a sailing ship.

Mate – a deck officer on a vessel that answers to the captain or skipper.

Mizzen-mast – mast located aft (or behind) a vessel's main mast.

Navigate – to travel over land, water, or through the air. The skills utilized to safely travel from one location to another.

Navigation Rules – Rules of the Road. Established international and in-land water way rules to provide for safe operation and navigation of all types of military and civilian small craft and vessels. Published by the United States Coast Guard.

Nitrogen Narcosis – a dangerous aspect of SCUBA diving, as nitrogen is not able to "off gas" as a diver ascends from a dive below sea level. A euphoric dangerous situation, originally coined "rapture of the deep" by SCUBA pioneer, Jacques Cousteau and colleagues.

P.A.D.I. - Professional Association of Diving Instructors. Provides training and certification for SCUBA Divers worldwide.

Petty Officer – Military rank for junior officers in naval services. Three separate levels are recognized: Third Class, Second Class, and First Class (First Class being the highest Petty Officer rank before Chief.)

Pilot – a person who steers or navigates a vessel. Pilots are utilized when a vessel is entering a port. They are transported to the larger vessel by a pilot boat.

Port – the left side of a boat or vessel.

Power Inflator – a push bottom device on a BCD or Buoyancy compensator that allows the diver to inflate the BCD with air from their tank.

Prime Meridian – meridian of zero degrees. Basis for longitudinal distance around the world. Located in Greenwich, England.

Radar – "radio detection and ranging" device that sends out radio waves to determine distance to other objects. The device allows for a determination of range and direction relative to the device.

Ratlines – cross lines that are attached to the shrouds of a mast. They form steps which allow sailors to go aloft.

Regulator – device used by SCUBA divers to breath underwater. The regulator is attached to the tank allowing a demand flow of air to the diver. Various types exist including on demand or free flow. (On demand is the most popular.)

Rigging – lines of a ship's masts. Can also refer to the set-up of lines on a specific vessel. Also can be used to describe the specific set-up of equipment for a diver, self-contained or surface-supplied.

Rope – strands which are bound together to form a strong woven cable of sorts.

Schooner – a sailing ship fore and aft rigged with a minimum of two masts.

Scope – refers to a length of measurement used to describe the amount of anchor line utilized. Example, a large or longer scope is used in heavy seas.

S.C.U.B.A. – Acronym for Self Contained Underwater Breathing Apparatus, open-circuit diving equipment. Made famous by Jacques Cousteau and his "Aqualung" after World War II. Utilizes a regulator, either single or double hose type to provide air to the diver using either a free-flow or on-demand regulator.

Second Stage – technical term for a regulator.

Ship – a larger ocean traveling vessel. (A boat can fit on a ship, but a ship cannot fit on a boat.)

Skipper – person in charge of a boat or vessel, usually the captain of the boat or vessel.

Sloop – a sailing vessel fore and aft rigged with one mast and one jib.

Sonar – acronym for "sound navigation and ranging." A device that sends out sound waves to identify objects below the surface. (British version was originally referred to as ASDIC)

Spanker – the mast closest to the stern of a fore and aft rigged sailing vessel.

Starboard – the right side of a boat or vessel.

Steerage – type of passenger that pays the least amount to travel on board a ship. They were usually kept towards to the rear of a vessel, thus the term.

Stern – the back section of a boat or vessel.

Surface Interval – the amount of necessary time on the "surface" between multiple dives, either surface supplied or SCUBA. Failure to adhere to specific times established could result in nitrogen build up in the body which could lead to decompression sickness, etc.

Surface Supplied – Any type of diving that requires the diver to be attached to an air hose. Various types of surface supplied "rigs" are available, including "hookah" or free-flow diving helmets, like the Navy Mark V helmet or hard hat diving set up.

Tank – contains the "air" for SCUBA divers. Various sizes exist depending on the type of dive being completed. (Various types are constructed of steel or aluminum, ponies or small emergency back up tank.) Tanks can hold a variety of mixtures such as nitrox.

Top Gallant Mast - the third mast above the deck.

Topmast - second mast above the deck.

Weather – to go through a vicious storm. The type of atmospheric conditions.

Windward – the side of a ship where the wind is blowing. (The opposite term would be leeward.)

Yacht – a type of sailing or motor vessel that is primarily used for pleasure.

Yawl – a fore and aft rigged vessel with two masts, with her mizzen-mast aft of the rudder.

Suggested Reading

A Night to Remember by Walter Lord

Capt. Cousteau's Underwater Treasury by J.Y. Cousteau and James Dugan

Long Island Shore Diver by Daniel Berg

Lost Voyages – Two Centuries of Shipwrecks in the Approaches to N.Y. – Bradley Sheard

Men, Ships and the Sea by Captain Alan Villiers

On the Bottom by Commander Edward Ellsberg

Perils of the Port of New York by Jeanette Edwards Rattray

Peter Freuchen's Book of the Seven Seas by Peter Freuchen

Scuba Diving the Wrecks and Shores of Long Island, NY by David Rosenthal

Shadow Divers by Robert Korson

Ship Ablaze – The Tragedy of the Steamboat General Slocum – Edward T. O'Donnell

Ship Ashore! A Record of Maritime Disasters off Montauk and Eastern Long Island, 1640-1955 by Jeanette Edwards Rattray

Shipwrecks in the Americas by Robert F. Marx

Shipwrecks of New York and *U.S.S. San Diego – The Last Armored Cruiser* by Gary Gentile

S.S. Savannah – The Elegant Steamship by Frank O. Braynard

The Bermuda Triangle by Charles Berlitz

The Dictionary of Nautical Literacy by Richard McKenna

The Mammoth Book of the Deep by Jon E. Lewis

The Sea Hunters (Volume 1 & 2) by Clive Cussler

The Silent World by Captain Jacques-Yves Cousteau

Wrecks and Rescues on Long Island – The Story of the U.S. Lifesaving Service by Van R. Field.

Getting Involved!

Underwater Historical Research Society – The UHRS is dedicated to the history of our local maritime history. The society conducts several outreach programs, speaking engagements, and publishes a quarterly journal, in addition to their published research projects. For more information see the next page and visit www.uhrs.org

Wrecksploration – "Shipwrecks + Exploration = Wrecksploration. This organization is a non-profit organization dedicated to the exploration of our local waters in search of undiscovered and unidentified shipwrecks. For more information visit www.wrecksploration.org

Long Island Divers Association – LIDA is a not-for-profit regional organization that consists of more than thirty member dive clubs. LIDA organizes numerous dives, seminars, meetings, social events and an annual film festival. www.lidaonline.com

Maritime & Underwater Historical Research

Aqua Quest Publications – www.aquaquest.com
Hunting New England Shipwrecks – www.wreckhunter.net
Naval Historical Center - www.history.navy.mil
New Jersey Scuba – www.njscuba.net
Northeast Dive News Magazine – www.nedivenews.com
Underwater Historical Research Society - www.uhrs.org
United States Coast Guard Historian's Office - www.uscg.mil/history
Wrecksploration – www.wrecksploration.org

Diving and Military

National Association of Underwater Instructors – NAUI – www.naui.org
Professional Association of Diving Instructors – PADI – www.padi.com
Scuba Schools International – SSI – www.divessi.com
United States Coast Guard – www.uscg.mil
United States Navy – www.navy.mil
United States Marine Corps – www.usmc.mil

Ship Models

The *Andrea Doria* Replica – www.andreadoriareplica.com
Bluejacket Ship Crafters – www.bluejacketinc.com

Index

The following index is provided for reference. Due to the specific listing of vessels in chapter order, a sub-heading has been indicated if the entry is part of an introduction or if it is a detailed history of the entry. *Example* Vessel Name, Detailed History, 32 would indicate several pages regarding that vessel starting on page 32.

M

MacLeish, Kenneth, 145
Malden, 127
Malle, Louis, 159
Manchester, Captain Stephen, 22
Maryland
  Detailed History, 106
Maxter Metals Corporation, 137
Meeker, Captain, 25
Merchant, 25
Merchant Marine Museum, 183
Merritt, Israel J., 205
Merritt's Wrecking Organization, 206
Monroe, President John, 15
Montauk Light, 46
Moran Towing and Transportation
  Company, 18
Mother, 160

N

Nantucket
  Lightship, 153
National Party Boat Owners Alliance, 137
National Underwater and Marine Agency,
  20
naval blimps, 19
Naval Historical Center, 143
New England Archeological Museum, 20
New Jersey Steam Navigation Company, 23
Nordenson, Captain Gunnar, 153
Norseman
  Concept Automobile, 149
North Brother Island, 113
North German Line, 76
NUMA. *See* National Underwater and
  Marine Agency

O

Oceanic Historical Research Society, 79
Oregon
  Detailed History, 71
  Introduction, 9

P

Palmer, Rear Admiral Leigh C., 129
Pearson, Zachariah C., 36
Perry, Commodore Matthew C., 64
Pfeiffer, Bill, 144
Phantom, 75

Port Royal, 36
Prettyman, Lee, 20
Pvt. William H. Thompson, 155

R

R.M.S. Titanic
  In Reference to, 9
R.T. Sayre, 109
Rescue, 42, 78, 199, 210
Rhode Island, 26
Riker's Island, 117
Robert E. Hopkins, 155
Rogers, Captain Moses, 13
Rogers, Stevens, 16
Roosevelt, Franklin D.
  Asst. Sec. of the U.S. Navy, 136
Roosevelt, President Theodore, 121
Rosenthal, David, 143
Roslyn Cemetery, 61

S

S.S. Savannah
  Detailed History, 13
  Introduction, 9
Saliger Ship Salvage Corporation, 136
Sand City, 166
Savannah Steamship Company, 14
Scythia, 73
Sea Cliff Tabernacle, 60
Sea Hunt, 182
Sea Hunter III, 80
Seawanhaka
  Detailed History, 49
  Introduction, 9
Shinnecock Canal, 70
Shinnecock Indians, 44
ship-of-the-line
  Definition of, 63
Silverstein, Mark
  Diving on the *Andrea Doria*, 161
  Diving on *U.S.S. San Diego*, 139
  Diving the *Oregon*, 79
Sing Sing prison, 118
Sirius, 18
Smith, Captain Charles P., 49
Society for the Preservation of Long Island
  Antiquities, 187
Speedwell Iron Works, 15
Squires, Captain William, 90
Steers Sand and Gravel Company
  Regarding *Gwendoline Steers*, 166

236

Underwater Historical Research Society

The Underwater Historical Research Society was co-founded in the winter of 2004 by Adam M. Grohman and Andy Campbell. The main purpose of the society is to research and document underwater wrecks and sites. The Society's membership is open to the general public. The UHRS Dive team is comprised of a select group of divers but based on upcoming projects, additional divers may be needed. Proceeds from the sale of books, films, and assorted paraphernalia fund upcoming projects. To become a supporting member of the society, visit http://www.uhrs.org. The Society publishes a journal of activities quarterly. The journal is a gift to all current members of the society. Your support allows historical research to continue. Join today!

UHRS Publications

Dive GTMO – Scuba Diving in Guantanamo Bay, Cuba
Non Liquet – The Bayville Submarine Mystery
Runner Aground – A History of the Schooner William T. Bell
Mask, Fins & Knife - A History of the U.S. Navy UDT & SEAL Diving Equipment from World War II to Present
In Depth – Journal - Official Publication of the UHRS – published quarterly.

UHRS - Ships of the Seas – SOS Series

Ugly Duckling – Liberty Ship - *S.S. C.W. Post*
Beneath the Blue & Grey Waves – Sub-Marine Warfare of the American Civil War.

UHRS – Future Projects & Titles

Presidential Plunge - A History of President Theodore Roosevelt's submarine adventure onboard the *U.S.S. Plunger* and his U.S. Navy Legacy.
Sunken Heroes – The UHRS research and diving search for two WWII-era aircraft and two WWI-era submarine chasers in the Long Island Sound, New York.

About the Author

Adam Matthew Grohman was born and raised in Pomona, New Jersey. He received his Associate in Science and Associate in Arts from Atlantic Cape Community College and then went to Long Island University at C.W. Post and completed his Bachelor in Fine Arts degree in Film. He is a boatswain's mate in the United States Coast Guard Reserve and has served in Cape May, New Jersey, San Diego, California, Guantanamo Bay, Cuba as a member of a USCG Port Security Unit Detachment, and most recently, Jones Beach, New York. Adam is a PADI Dive Master and plunges into the water for much of his research. Adam writes a monthly column, *In Our Waters*, for *Long Island Boating World* and researches many aspects of maritime and nautical history. Adam, Kendall, and their two sons Aidan and Liam live in Long Island, New York.

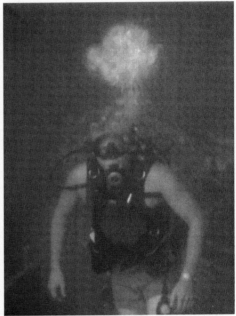

Also by Adam M. Grohman

UHRS Journal
In *Depth*

Fiction

Non-Fiction

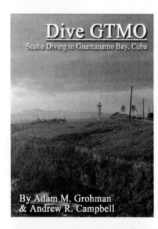

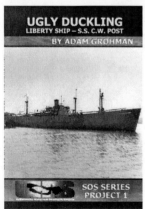

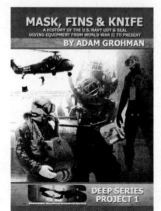